T0320515

Global Virtual Enterprises in Cloud Computing Environments

N. Raghavendra Rao
FINAIT Consultancy Services, India

A volume in the Advances
in Computer and Electrical
Engineering (ACEE) Book Series

Published in the United States of America by
    IGI Global
    Engineering Science Reference (an imprint of IGI Global)
    701 E. Chocolate Avenue
    Hershey PA, USA 17033
    Tel: 717-533-8845
    Fax: 717-533-8661
    E-mail: cust@igi-global.com
    Web site: http://www.igi-global.com

Library of Congress Cataloging-in-Publication Data

Names: Rao, N. Raghavendra, 1939- editor.
Title: Global virtual enterprises in cloud computing environments / N.
   Raghavendra Rao, editor.
Description: Hershey, PA : Engineering Science Reference, [2019] | Includes
   bibliographical references.
Identifiers: LCCN 2018051347| ISBN 9781522531821 (hardcover) | ISBN
   9781522531838 (ebook)
Subjects: LCSH: Virtual corporations--Computer networks. | Cloud computing. |
   Business networks--Communication systems. | International business
   enterprises--Data processing. | Electronic commerce.
Classification: LCC HD30.37 .G578 2019 | DDC 658/.056782--dc23 LC record available at https://
lccn.loc.gov/2018051347

This book is published in the IGI Global book series Advances in Computer and Electrical Engineering (ACEE) (ISSN: 2327-039X; eISSN: 2327-0403)

British Cataloguing in Publication Data
A Cataloguing in Publication record for this book is available from the British Library.

All work contributed to this book is new, previously-unpublished material.
The views expressed in this book are those of the authors, but not necessarily of the publisher.

For electronic access to this publication, please contact: eresources@igi-global.com.

Advances in Computer and Electrical Engineering (ACEE) Book Series

ISSN:2327-039X
EISSN:2327-0403

Editor-in-Chief: Srikanta Patnaik, SOA University, India

MISSION

The fields of computer engineering and electrical engineering encompass a broad range of interdisciplinary topics allowing for expansive research developments across multiple fields. Research in these areas continues to develop and become increasingly important as computer and electrical systems have become an integral part of everyday life.

The **Advances in Computer and Electrical Engineering (ACEE) Book Series** aims to publish research on diverse topics pertaining to computer engineering and electrical engineering. **ACEE** encourages scholarly discourse on the latest applications, tools, and methodologies being implemented in the field for the design and development of computer and electrical systems.

COVERAGE

- Computer Hardware
- VLSI Design
- Optical Electronics
- VLSI Fabrication
- Analog Electronics
- Qualitative Methods
- Programming
- Electrical Power Conversion
- Sensor Technologies
- Circuit Analysis

IGI Global is currently accepting manuscripts for publication within this series. To submit a proposal for a volume in this series, please contact our Acquisition Editors at Acquisitions@igi-global.com or visit: http://www.igi-global.com/publish/.

Titles in this Series

For a list of additional titles in this series, please visit:
https://www.igi-global.com/book-series/advances-computer-electrical-engineering/73675

New Perspectives on Information Systems Modeling and Design
António Miguel Rosado da Cruz (Polytechnic Institute of Viana do Castelo, Portugal) and
Maria Estrela Ferreira da Cruz (Polytechnic Institute of Viana do Castelo,Portugal)
Engineering Science Reference ● ©2019 ● 332pp ● H/C (ISBN: 9781522572718) ● US $235.00

Advanced Methodologies and Technologies in Network Architecture, Mobile Computing...
Mehdi Khosrow-Pour, D.B.A. (Information Resources Management Association, USA)
Engineering Science Reference ● ©2019 ● 1857pp ● H/C (ISBN: 9781522575986) ● US $595.00

Emerging Innovations in Microwave and Antenna Engineering
Jamal Zbitou (University of Hassan 1st, Morocco) and Ahmed Errkik (University of Hassan
1st, Morocco)
Engineering Science Reference ● ©2019 ● 437pp ● H/C (ISBN: 9781522575399) ● US $245.00

Advanced Methodologies and Technologies in Artificial Intelligence, Computer Simulation,
and Human-Computer Interaction
Mehdi Khosrow-Pour, D.B.A. (Information Resources Management Association, USA)
Engineering Science Reference ● ©2019 ● 1221pp ● H/C (ISBN: 9781522573685) ● US $545.00

Optimal Power Flow Using Evolutionary Algorithms
Provas Kumar Roy (Kalyani Government Engineering College, India) and Susanta Dutta
(Dr. B. C. Roy Engineering College, India)
Engineering Science Reference ● ©2019 ● 323pp ● H/C (ISBN: 9781522569718) ● US $195.00

Advanced Condition Monitoring and Fault Diagnosis of Electric Machines
Muhammad Irfan (Najran University, Saudi Arabia)
Engineering Science Reference ● ©2019 ● 307pp ● H/C (ISBN: 9781522569893) ● US $225.00

For an entire list of titles in this series, please visit:
https://www.igi-global.com/book-series/advances-computer-electrical-engineering/73675

701 East Chocolate Avenue, Hershey, PA 17033, USA
Tel: 717-533-8845 x100 ● Fax: 717-533-8661
E-Mail: cust@igi-global.com ● www.igi-global.com

Table of Contents

Detailed Table of Contents

Section 1
Business Intelligence and Digital Economy in the Cloud Computing Environment

Chapter 1

> *Venkatesh Rajagopalan, VIT University, India*
> *Sudarsan Jayasingh, SSN School of Management, India*

Organizations need to make quick and quality decisions to survive in today's competitive environment. The business intelligence (BI) market has moved away from IT-centric solutions to user-driven solutions. Business intelligence and cloud computing are two important technologies that have been widely adopted in business organizations in recent years. Interestingly, the two technologies have merged together to deliver superior benefits for businesses. Business enterprises are moving their business applications to cloud platforms to become more agile and accessible. The key benefit of cloud-based business intelligence applications is the ability to access on multiple devices like laptops and mobile phones from different locations. In this chapter, the authors outline the benefits, challenges, and trends involved in deploying business intelligence technology through cloud computing platforms. They discuss how the consolidation of these two emerging technologies can enhance the businesses to improve decision-making processes. They also address the challenges cloud-based BI faces.

Chapter 2

Abbas Strømmen-Bakhtiar, Nord University, Norway

From the invention of writing to the steam engine and to computers, human history has been one of technological inventions and change. In our relatively recent past we have witnessed several technological revolutions which rapidly replaced one set of technologies by another, and in the process created what Schumpeter called the creative destruction. Today, we are witnessing a technological revolution that is changing the way we live, work, and communicate. We call this the digital revolution which brings with it new technologies, methods, and business models. This chapter discusses the digital revolution and the platform business model. This business model is used by many "sharing economy" businesses such as Airbnb and Uber. The success of this business model is dependent on the rapid expansion of its user-base. This business model requires infrastructure and applications that can cope with this rapid expansion. Cloud computing has been providing these services.

Section 2
Requirements of Virtual Enterprises

Chapter 3

José Carlos Martins Delgado, Universidade de Lisboa, Portugal

A key characteristic of a virtual enterprise (VE) is the heterogeneity of the applications that compose its enterprise information systems (EIS), since it builds on the EIS of the individual enterprises that are part of the collaborative network of that VE. This raises an application integration problem, which is even more serious than within any given EIS because a VE has a temporary nature, and therefore, integration requirements can change frequently. Current integration technologies, such as Web Services and RESTful APIs, solve the interoperability problem but usually entail more coupling than needed, since they require sharing data schemas between interacting applications, even if not all values of those schemas are actually used. The fundamental problem of application integration is therefore how to provide at most the minimum coupling possible while ensuring at least the minimum interoperability requirements. This chapter proposes compliance and conformance as the concepts to achieve this goal.

Chapter 4

R. Todd Stephens, AT&T Corporation, USA

In the context of cloud computing, the service catalog is a critical component of the cloud computing architecture. Most cloud computing projects will invariably begin with a discussion of what IT services an enterprise needs. Even when end users have a cloud environment, the business still wants to know which cloud services we need and how much does it costs. Information Technology Infrastructure Library (ITIL) service design defines a service catalog as a list of technology-enabled services that an organization provides, often to its employees or customers. More specifically, the service catalog is an expression of the operational capability of a service provider or enterprise within the context of an end customer, a market space, or an internal business unit stakeholder. Unfortunately, most service catalogs are built by technologists for technologists. This design methodology is fine assuming the user of the catalog is an information technology professional.

Section 3
Business Models in the Cloud Computing Environment

Chapter 5

N. Raghavendra Rao, FINAIT Consultancy Services, India

Multidisciplinary experts are required to develop a model for resource management in a country. Various concepts in information and communication technology are required to be applied in designing and developing a model for the management of natural resources. The concepts such as cloud computing along with social media play an important role. Case illustrations are discussed in this chapter stressing the role of cloud computing along with the concepts of collaborative technology in developing models for the benefit of citizens in a country.

Chapter 6

N. Raghavendra Rao, FINAIT Consultancy Services, India

The concept of cloud computing provides a good scope for making use of information for knowledge updating among the medical fraternity. Large data are generated and available for analysis. One should know how well the data can be used for analysis and taking care of the patients. Medical fraternity needs to update with the latest knowledge to provide good healthcare services to patients. Software tools along with the concepts of collaborative technology are required to make use of the data and information stored in the cloud computing environment by the healthcare service institutions. Medical research group and software professionals can form a team to develop business models useful to the healthcare sector. This chapter explains with case illustrations designing and developing business models under the cloud computing environment with the concepts of collaborative technology.

The basic functions such as production, marketing, and finance continue to be the same from an agricultural economy to an industrial economy. Business processes, procedures, methods, strategy, management thinking, and approach related to basic functions have been changed due to global market competition. Consequent to global competition, business activities have become more complex. Due to this complexity, the type and quantum of information required by the business enterprises are increasing. It is interesting to note that information and communication technology is providing many new concepts to handle and manage the complex information to remain competitive in the global market. The concepts such as big data and cloud computing along with other collaborative technology facilitate creating conceptual business models for facing realities in the global market. This chapter mainly explains with two case illustrations of the importance of the above concepts for developing business models for textile and retail sectors.

Section 4
Service Models in the Manufacturing Sector

Cloud-based manufacturing is a computing and service-oriented model developed from existing advanced manufacturing models and enterprise technologies with the support of cloud computing, IOT, and virtualization. In this chapter, various definitions of cloud manufacturing are discussed. New service models other than the existing cloud computing service models are being discussed elaborately. Cloud-based design manufacturing is also being discussed. A comparison of cloud manufacturing and cloud-based design manufacturing is elaborately discussed. Key technologies and challenges in cloud manufacturing are highlighted.

Preface

INTRODUCTION

Globalization coupled with the technical revolution has created many opportunities in the various fields of business activities. Consequent to this the boundaries of the business are not clear. Expansions are taking place in the multiple new areas simultaneously. These expansions are also leading to uncertainty in business. Uncertainty in business is due to the threats from the most unexpected quarters and new competition. Further, these threats and new competition have made the business activities more complex. The type of quantum of information required by business enterprises is increasing.

Many technologies tend to be applicable only in a specific industry or defined areas of operations in business. In the case of information and communication technology is different. The potential of information and communication technology in any sphere of activity in a business or any discipline is more useful. Information and communication technology is a driving force in providing a good scope of the creative new concepts in this discipline. The concept of cloud computing is one among them. This concept has proved to be significant in the todays pervasive world.

The concept of cloud computing is facilitating in establishing of virtual organizations across the globe. The present business environment is also forcing many enterprises to conduct their business differently. Further, the need for interdisciplinary approach is gaining importance in the present pervasive business world. It has now become a necessity for business enterprises to evaluate the core competence in relation to their products and services. The elements in the external competency are patents, brands, monopoly, and trade secrets. The elements in the internal competency consist of process technology, distribution channels, advantages costs and size of plants. Assessment of these core competencies will help business enterprises will help them to know their competitive advantage in the global market.

A plethora of opportunities is making business enterprises realize the importance of global virtual enterprises. The concepts such as open innovation, knowledge management, knowledge harvesting, and business intelligence are some of the important concepts that facilitate business enterprises in creating business models. It is possible in developing business models with the above concepts by global virtual enterprises in the cloud computing environment.

The word "Harvesting" is generally applicable in the field of agriculture. It refers to the practice of increasing the yield from the cultivable land. In the same way the organizational databases can be considered as an equivalent to the cultivable land. Employees's wisdom related to their business can be considered to be the 'manure'. Employees wisdom helps themselves to convert the data into useful business information. Knowledge harvesting is an integrated set of processes that captures the often hidden insight of human expertise in business. Knowledge is more than book learning. But knowledge solely in a specific discipline is insufficient to bring an idea to the market place. In the present business scenario knowledge from many disciplines will be required. One need not be a master of all things. Global virtual teams need to be aware of the knowledge associated with purposeful with their business. It would be easy for global virtual teams to create knowledge harvesting system for their global virtual organizations in the cloud computing environment.

The concept of virtual reality helps to unlock the innovative thinking in enterprises for carrying out incremental and radical innovation in their enterprises. The essential element of virtual reality is that interactive simulation with navigation between widely scattered heterogeneous databases. The cloud computing facilitates to have an access to heterogeneous databases in its environment. The concept of virtual reality is very useful, especially in the global virtual enterprise scenario for developing business models to face the ground reality in the global market. These business models facilitate an enterprise to design new types of products and production facilities for their business.

There are many more concepts in the disciplines of management and information and communication technology can be made use of developing business models. Designing any business model in the global virtual environment huge data and information are needed. The cloud computing environment facilitates enterprises to store huge data and information for business purposes and developing business models. Global virtual teams play an important role in making use of the heterogeneous database for creating business models in an innovative for their business activities.

The cloud computing environment eliminates geographic distance and permits global real-time execution for business. Collective intelligence is the need of the hour. Great accomplishments, mostly occur in the collaborative environment.

FOCUS OF THE BOOK

This book highlights the importance of inter discipline concepts in the cloud computing environment. It also indicates the advantages in applying this approach by global virtual enterprises.

BENEFITS OF THIS BOOK

Global virtual team's participation in the virtual enterprises in the cloud computing environment facilitates collaborative thinking in managing business issues in the globalization scenario. Knowledge management, skills of the qualified people, and open innovation approach by enterprises are very important in the present global economy.

TARGET AUDIENCE

The book will be useful for corporate executives, research scholars, software professionals, and students pursuing the courses in the areas of management, and information and communication technology disciplines.

GIST OF THE CHAPTERS

In the introductory chapter N Raghavendra Rao explains the importance of the concept of cloud computing in the global virtual enterprise scenario. The collective intelligence of the global virtual teams can face many challenges in the present globalization scenario. The author stresses the need for making use of the interdisciplinary concepts for designing business models.

In today's knowledge-rich environment, global virtual enterprises can leverage internal and external sources of ideas for adopting an innovative approach in their business activities. The author explains the importance of capital budgeting method is required to be applied by the service providers on the investment of their infrastructure.

Sudarsan Jayasingh and Venkatesh R in their chapter "Business Intelligence and Cloud Computing: Benefits, Challenges, and Trends" talk about the importance of cloud based business intelligence for business organizations. The authors are of the opinion that data visualization feature in business intelligence facilitates for taking better decision by the executives in an organization. They also observe that mobile business intelligence helps to get an access to intelligent tools. These tools guide the users to create insights on the mobile device itself. While talking about the benefits of cloud business intelligence, the authors have considered the cost efficiency, flexibility, fast deployment and accessibility as important elements in the cloud business intelligence. In respect of challenges the authors stressed it is essential to understand the elements such as data integration, data quality, data security, and user proficiency in the cloud computing environment for business intelligence.

Abbas Strommen-Bakhtiar observes in the chapter titled "Digital Economy, Business Models, and Cloud Computing" that many advancements are taking place in information and communication technology. Earlier these advancements are known as technical revolution. In the present era it is termed as digital revolution. The digital economy is the result of the digital revolution. The digital economy is considered to be a knowledge based economy. The digital economy is effective in the virtual business world. The author observes that the concept of cloud computing is the backbone of the digital economy. The author explains the general purpose technology. Further the author observes that the quantum computing is likely to create many advancements in the various activities.

Jose C Delgado in the chapter titled "Cloud-Based Application Integration in Virtual Enterprises" says that many enterprises prefer to become more agile and efficient The author talks about the evolution of enterprise information systems. The author explains a few selected enterprise scenarios. They are the traditional enterprise, the changing enterprise, the agile enterprise, the optimizing enterprise, the resilient enterprise, the cloud oriented enterprise, and the virtual enterprise. Further, the author discusses about compliance and conformance as a means to reduce application coupling.

Todd Stephens in the chapter titled "A Requirement Approach for Building an Enterprise Cloud Service Catalog" gives an overview of cloud computing, usability and design standards and traditional services of a cloud registry. The author explains business oriented cloud service catalog and business layer of this service. Further, the author discusses the usability criteria for the application systems.

Raghavendra Rao N in his chapter titled "Cloud Computing for E-Governance" mainly talks about the importance cloud computing in managing natural resources in a country. The author explains the need for maintaining a centralized database in the private cloud environment by a government in providing a good governance to their citizens. The discussions and views expressed by the citizens of a country in their social media channels need the attention of the government while framing polices. The author also suggests the ways of making use of the data and information in the cloud computing environment.

Raghavendra Rao N in his chapter titled "Providing Healthcare Information in the Virtual Environment" talks about the participation of medical students in the virtual knowledge sharing teams. The author explains the case-based learning by the medical students with the concept of virtual reality. Social workers have been guided by medical doctors for educating health care tips to the people living in rural areas. The importance of the private cloud for hospitals is emphasized.

Hariharanath K in his chapter "Big Data: An Enabler in Developing Business Models in Cloud Computing Environments" explains about the importance big data in the cloud environment for the benefit of business enterprises with case illustrations. The author also talks about the various tools in the context of big data. The author indicates that big data and virtualization provide a good scope for adopting innovative approach in developing business models for the benefit of business enterprises.

Umashankar and Sudarsan in their chapter "Cloud-Based Design and Manufacturing" compared the various definitions related to manufacturing. While talking about cloud based manufacturing model, they have expressed that this model will help to reduce the product life cycle costs and to allow for optimal resource allocation in a manufacturing setup. They have explained the integration of multiple sensor data within the cloud computing infrastructure. They have also explained cloud based design in manufacturing. They have observed that one of the main key characteristics of cloud based design and manufacturing model is the ubiquitous access to the distributed large data sets

IMPACT OF THIS BOOK

Cloud computing is one among a number of other concepts emerging from the discipline of information and communication technology. Cloud computing is providing a good scope for radical changes in business processes in global virtual organizations. The concept of cloud computing is considered to be the backbone for the creation of global virtual organizations. This book mainly talks from the perspective of virtual enterprises in the cloud computing environment.

N. Raghavendra Rao
FINAIT Consultancy Services, India

Acknowledgment

At the outset, I would like to offer my special thanks to IGI Global for giving me the opportunity to edit the publication. The editorial guidance provided by Colleen Moore is excellent. Finally, I thank my wife Meera for her continuous encouragement and support in my scholastic pursuits.

N. Raghavendra Rao
FINAIT Consultancy Services, India

Introduction

BACKGROUND

The present business scenario is witnessing many changes in the business environment. Mainly two factors are contributing to the changes in the present business scenario. One is globalization policy followed by many countries across the globe. Another factor is many new concepts are emerging in the Information and communication technology discipline. Enterprises are forced to adapt to these changes for either to remain competitive in their business or to take advantage of the opportunities available in the globalization scenario (Choudhary Prashant, 2012). The concept of cloud computing facilitates enterprises to create virtual enterprises for facing the above challenges in the global business scenario. The advancements in information and communication technology has led to the ubiquity of cloud computing. The concept of cloud computing provides support for virtual teams in virtual enterprises (Chaka,2013). Virtual collaboration cannot take place without the support of cloud computing and the emerging concepts in information and communication technology. Global virtual teams are those that spare time zones and geographic boundaries. Information and communication technology eliminates geographic distance and permits global real time execution.

Business and industry have started realizing and accepting the fact that they cannot thrive in their business activities, if they continue to follow the same old business methods and procedures(Mamta Vysas, 2014). Innovation also cannot be carried out only in the four walls of their research and development department. This has become true. It is because of business becoming highly competitive and dominated by a set of aggressive marketing oriented players completely different from matured players. Theory and practice are generally divergent. Developing an effective business model has become challenging (Hameed, Counsell, & Swift, 2012). Globalization offers the best chance to participate in the present economy of this century (Semolic & Baisya, 2013).

NEED OF THE HOUR

Integrating business the knowledge of the experts and the various concepts in interdisciplinary are the basic elements of a proactive approach in the present scenario. Collective intelligence is needed to face the business scenario. Business assets such as the Intellectual and information of an enterprise can play a determinative role in its success. Great accomplishments are most likely to occur in the collaborative environments. The concept of Cloud computing along with the collaborative technology concepts can be used more effectively in managing uncertainty and complex situations in business. All the above concepts can be considered as a medium for transmitting or exchanging information. Many business enterprises are under enormous pressure to respond quickly to changes in the global market. Business enterprises need to be clear in identifying the concepts that will help them in making logical decisions.

NEED FOR CLOUD COMPUTING

In the early days of computing, many enterprises shared a single computer system that was located in a remote data center. The system personnel would allocate and manage resources for each user's application. Users could request for more or less computing time by adjusting the amount of time they utilize for sharing the resources. Similarly cloud computing offers various components from deployment models and mix and match for the solutions that are sought. One can make use of a component such as a storage service from one service provider. Database as a service can be made use of the other service provider (Hoffer, Ramesh, & Tudi, 2013). Services from a third service provider can be obtained for a complete application development and deployment of platform also. It is to be remembered that cloud computing facilitates the use of different cloud computing deployment models over the internet.

USE OF CLOUD COMPUTING

The main use of cloud computing is the storage of data. Data is stored in multiple servers rather than in the dedicated severs used in network data storage (Janikiram Dharanipragada, 2016). A user sees it as a virtual server. It is just a pseudo name used to refer virtual space carved out in the cloud. In reality the user's data could stored in any one or more systems used to create the cloud. The collaborative platforms along with the communications network services and hardware provides the pipeline to enable the flow of knowledge, its context and the medium for conservations.

DATA INTENSIVE APPLICATIONS

Cloud computing is more useful for data intensive applications in the scientific and business domains. Research scholars require a mechanism to transfer, publish, replicate, discover, share, and analyze data across the globe. Similarly, business applications in the domains such as finance, products, marketing, and engineering need to maintain database consistency, regionally, or worldwide. Further, these applications have to manage data replication for facilitating data discovery and responding dynamically to changes in the volume of data in databases.

INTEGRATION OF COMPONENTS IN CLOUD COMPUTING

There are four components need to be integrated under cloud computing environment for the development of business models for virtual enterprises.(Esposito & Evangalista, 2014). They are business processes, application software, system software, and infrastructure such as servers, network, and databases. Adding intelligence to the process of developing new models or existing models and their management makes lots of sense because some business models need considerable expertise.

VIRTUALIZATION IN THE DATA STORAGE

There are many advantages of virtualization. Some of the advantages are given below.

Space and Power

Virtualization facilitates to consider infrastructure, thereby reducing the space and power requirements.

Utilization

Virtualization helps in increasing utilization, thereby resulting in the decrease of capital investment

Cost Containment

Virtualization concentrates on increasing utilization and consolidation of hardware, thereby reducing the operational costs in cabling and maintenance costs in hardware and software.

Business Continuity

Virtualization allows business processes to run independent of the hardware, thereby enabling to move the process to other systems at runtime.

Data Recovery

The data may be replicated in multiple storage servers, thereby enabling recovery of the data rapidly with a minimum loss of time. Virtualization sometimes is also seen as a low cost alternative to disaster recovery.

Management

Virtualization helps the system group to use the system with fewer problems.

Virtual Enterprises

In the earlier days managing a business means renting an office space, arranging for phone line connection and other utilities, hiring staff and the other related activities. The executives of a business enterprise would commute to the office in the morning and stay till the evening. The executives of the business enterprise would attend all the activities of the business enterprise during the office hours only. They would leave the work at the office and clear the pending work on the next working day. Now the scenario has changed by the internet and cloud computing. Web based applications have also created the new scenario for the virtual office environment. Expensive office space is no longer needed. One can work for an enterprise from the comfort of one's home over the internet. A notebook computer the access over the internet wherever wifi connection is available.

The real power of cloud computing is that it lets anyone run one's enterprise operations from anywhere. Web based applications support all the business activities that would take place in the physical office environment. The cloud computing lets even the smallest business organization operate like a like a large organization over the web. It is the age of the virtual enterprise. One should know taking advantage of all that cloud computing offers.

VIRTUAL ENTERPRISES AND FACILITIES

Virtual enterprises need to organize the following facilities for their business.

1. Creation of virtual task forces or groups to solve the specific problems or issues related to their organization.
2. Managing the dynamic collection of resources from the heterogeneous providers based on users' needs and the different levels of handling the issues.
3. Deciding the formation of a secured governance model and common management model for all the resources related to the virtual organization.
4. Management of resources, including utilization and allocation to meet a budget and other economic criteria.

CLOUD COMPUTING

Many new concepts are emerging in the information and communication technology discipline. Close analysis of these concepts indicates many of these concepts are the extension of the existing concepts. Every new concept has an advantage over the previous concept. Sometimes, two or more concepts or technology are combined to evolve a new concept. Cloud computing is one among them. It is said that cloud computing has contributed to the success of globalization policy followed by many countries across the globe. One more interesting aspect of the cloud computing is the emergence of global virtual enterprises. Further, these enterprises are changing the business landscape across the borders of the countries.

DATA IN THE VIRTUAL ORGANIZATIONS SCENARIO

In the present business environment data is generated at a rate never seen before in the history. Data pours from multiple systems, channels, and regions around the clock. A new type of large and realtime data are virtually created in the current digitization scenario across a broad range of industries. The challenge is making use of these data for an enterprise's purpose (Schulz, 2012). Data by itself is not useful. One needs to know the extracting value from it. Before one can harness the power of information, one needs to understand the data insights for one's business purposes.

INTERDISCIPLINARY CONCEPTS

In the present globalization scenario, interdisciplinary concepts are required for developing business models. The concepts in management along with the concepts in information and communication technology with the data in the cloud computing environment can be made use of developing business models for enterprises. The concepts such as business intelligence, innovation, open innovation, and simulation facilitate enterprises in developing business models.

Innovation

Till recently the standard process in carrying out innovation in enterprises has been a linear method of research through design, development and then manufacturing. Now many of these processes are carried out concurrently and collaborating with the concepts in information and communication technology in the cloud computing environment (Mathur, Singh, & Mohan, 2013).

Open Innovation

In today's knowledge rich environment, enterprises can no longer afford to rely entirely on their ideas for improving their own business. They cannot also restrict their innovation to a single path to market. As a result the traditional model for innovation which has been largely internally focused or a "closed one" has become obsolete. Emerging in its place is a new paradigm "Open Innovation". This strategically leverages internal and external sources of ideas and takes them to market through multiple paths.

Global virtual enterprises can take advantage of unique knowledge and resources wherever they are located (Clutter Buck, 2012). Information and communication technology has increased virtualization in business activities and ways of working.

RESEARCH COLLABORATION

Research oriented organizations and universities are involved in the advanced research in the specialized areas of their interest (Jainarain Sharma, 2011). Global virtual research organizations can involve themselves in their collaborative research activities. They need a tremendous amount of storage space for the volumes of data for their research purpose. In addition to this thousands of computing processors are also needed for their activities. The concept of cloud computing provides mechanisms for sharing of the resources by them. These organizations are constituted to resolve scientific research problems with a wide range of participants from the different parts of the world.

BUSINESS INTELLIGENCE

The word "Intelligence" means the application of information, skills, experiences and reasoning to solve business issues. Data and information acquired from a wide variety of sources facilitate analysts utilizing them in depth for business purposes. Further, analysts can add an additional dimension to business intelligence in designing business models and solution methods.

SIMULATION

Modeling is a key element in a business intelligence system. There are many classes of models and there are also many specialized techniques for solving business issues. Simulation is a common modeling approach followed by many business enterprises. The data in the cloud computing environment facilitates business enterprises to simulate various types of models for taking decisions.

VIRTUAL REALITY

Before any major change has to be made in a business enterprise in the area of product development or adding new features in the existing product or changing a business process, the enterprise would like to visualize before it is implemented. Visualization of the above activities is possible through simulation. This time of simulation can be termed as virtual reality. The concept of virtual reality facilitates in visualizing the new ideas for business purposes. Business enterprises have choices to evaluate their new ideas by making use of the concept of virtual reality. Global virtual enterprises can hire the services of the domain experts in the required area of specialization from any part of the world(. The domain experts and their team members can operate from their respective countries. The required infrastructure such as hardware and software can be provided to them by the enterprises who have hired them. This is possible under the cloud computing environment.

KNOWLEDGE HARVESTING SYSTEM

Knowledge and wisdom are the important elements in a knowledge harvesting system. One of the inputs for knowledge harvesting system is a codification of human centered assets in a business enterprise. This is required to be stored in an information system relating to knowledge in a business enterprise. This creates value to business enterprises and it belongs to them. Further, it can be used for guidance and decision making. All critical decisions recorded in this system will help to create meta knowledge for adapting changes in business. The importance of reuse of knowledge in this knowledge harvesting system is possible only when leveraging the expertise of others who are not in the current team in an enterprise.

The concept of knowledge harvesting is useful for global virtual enterprises. Global virtual teams who are working at the different locations of the enterprise across the globe will get benefited for their professional work. Knowledge harvesting system will create an open innovation environment for global virtual teams. Involvement of the global virtual teams in an open innovation environment makes them to take professional pride. They also get a feeling that they are the backbone of their organization. The concept of cloud computing provides a scope for creating a knowledge harvesting system for the benefit of their global business activities.

INVESTMENT FINANCIAL SECTOR

The International financial mainly comprises the corporate securities, foreign exchange, metals, and commodity segments. Investment decisions and rendering advice by the financial consultants need vast information pertaining to the various financial markets across the globe. Information pertaining to the corporate sector, natural resources such as metals, commodities is required at a each segment for every country level for analysis by financial analysts. The types of databases which can hold higher volume of data and information are required for designing and developing various business models. Sophisticated software tools are also needed for analyzing the data and information from the above databases

One of the most interesting aspect in sophisticated software tools is the availability of dynamic nature of the technological capabilities in every segment in the financial sector. The technology provides a vast amount of usable information. Financial analysts must know to make use of the analytical tools for creating a relevant context with the usable information in the above databases. The relevancy and context that would come out of the analysis will help the financial analysts to advise and guide their clients.

Analytical tools will provide insights to investment analysts to explore the incredible amount of data about financial instruments, markets, and other related aspects of the international financial markets. These tools help them also to analyze the different market segments, price movements, economic forecasts, and news events. They can react to the above information with their professional experience. They can also determine the patterns from their observations.

The above type of analysis is possible because of the cloud computing and virtual enterprises. Financial experts who are familiar with the various aspects of the financial markets across the globe can work as a global virtual team to extend their professional services under the cloud computing environment

VIRTUAL ORGANIZATION FOR WEATHER PREDICTIONS

This type of virtual organization requires resources such as weather prediction software applications to perform mandatory environmental simulations associated with predicting weather. Special hardware resources to run the respective software, as well as high speed data storage facilities are required to maintain the data generated from performing the simulation.

Cloud computing architecture is capable of providing the facilities that required for the above scenario. The following resources are needed for the above scenario.

1. Dynamic discovery of computing resources based on their capabilities and functions
2. Immediate allocation and provisioning of these resources based on their availability and the user demands or requirements
3. Provisioning of secure access methods to the resources and building with the local security mechanisms
4. Provisioning of multiple automatic features for the resources that can mainly take care of self-configuring and self-management

TOOLS ACROSS TECHNOLOGY AND DOMAINS

Generally, the following tools are used depending on the type of requirement in the cloud computing environment for different applications:

- **Search Engines**: New algorithms to analyze large unstructured data can be used. The algorithms will be based on working in parallel multiple resources to process huge amount of data.

- **Business Intelligence Tools**: These analytical tools will be able to provide new and creative visualizations to intuitively depict the meaning of the data.
- **Storage Management Tools:** Cloud storage systems can provide facilities to store huge amount of data.
- **Analytical Tools**: Many analytical tools can be applied with ease in the cloud computing environment.

EVALUATION OF INVESTMENT IN INFRASTRUCTURE IN CLOUD COMPUTING ENVIRONMENT

There are two types of players in the cloud computing environment. One is a service provider. Another one is making use of the services provided by a service provider. A service provider owns the various types of hardware and software. Here software consists of system and business application software. The amount spent by a service provider for acquiring hardware and software is considered as capital expenditure or investment. A service provider applies the capital budgeting method to evaluate the investments of the above assets before taking a decision on the investment.

It is general practice in business enterprises to estimate the anticipated return on the amount to be spent as a capital investment in their proposed business projects. Projected cash flows and profit and loss statements are prepared to assess the worthiness of the project before a business venture starts. In the case of service provider in the cloud computing environment, the service provider needs to acquire hardware, system and business application software. Capital investment in networking is to be made by a service provider. There are concepts such as capital budgeting, opportunity cost, cost benefit analysis, and activity based costing are applied depending on the type of cost incurred by an enterprise (Bhabatosi Banerjee, 2010). The above concepts are briefly explained below.

CAPITAL BUDGETING

Capital budgeting method is applied to determine whether an enterprise's long term investment in new hardware, replacement of existing hardware, purchase of system and application software from software vendors. Investment in designing and developing system and business application software at the service provider's office for their own purpose and client requirements can be considered as a capital investment. This approach indicates whether the investment in the above infrastructure is worth funding cash or not.

Time value of money is an important in capital budgeting decision. It allows a business enterprise to adjust cash flows for the passage of time. This process is known as discounting to the present value and allows for the preference of dollars received today over the dollars to be received at a later date.

Cost of capital is another important element in capital budgeting method. It stresses the minimum rate of return an enterprise must earn from its capital investments in order to satisfy the expectations of investors who provide the funds to enterprises. It is always measured as the weighted arithmetic average of the cost of various of finance received from different sources by an enterprise. Generally three rules are applied while following using the discounted cash flow method. They are 1-net present value, 2-internal rate of return, and 3-profitability index. In the case of the present value, the rule says acceptance of net present value is greater than zero. Internal rate of return suggests acceptance of internal rate of return is greater than the cost of capital. In the case of profitability index, profitability index is greater than one.

Cost benefit analysis is one more method applied in the evaluation of capital investments. In this method all the costs and expenditure in a proposed venture are taken into account. The benefit that is likely to be derived from a business venture will be evaluated for taking investment decisions.

Activity based costing is a costing methodology that identifies the activities in an enterprise and assigns the cost to each activity with resources to all products and services according to the actual consumption of material and service. Apportioning of a cost or incurring cost in a particular activity later it is related to each activity cost to outputs.

Opportunity cost talks about a benefit, profit or value of something is given up to acquire or achieve something else. Resources such as land, money, time, and other assets can be put to alternative use. Every action, choice or decision is forgone to achieve something else has an associated opportunity cost.

All the above methods can be made use by a service provider depending upon the type of requirement in their organization. Cost benefit analysis and activity based costing methods are relevant to the enterprises who make use of the services provided by the service provider.

EVALUATION OF OPTIONS

Many business enterprises are establishing virtual enterprises across the globe for the various needs of their business activities. Service providers have understood the requirements of the global virtual enterprises in the cloud computing environment. The requirement of the global virtual enterprises varies according to the specific functions of their organizations. The requirements of these virtual enterprises are

1-Latest software tools, 2-Business application software with as many features as possible, and 3-Sophisticated hardware infrastructure.

Investment on the latest software tools and business application software falls under the four categories. They are 1-Developing their own software tool/business application software, 2-Enhancing the existing software tool/business application software, 3-Acquiring a new software tool/the latest business application software from the market, and 4-Engaging the services of a software company who has a special skill in developing a sophisticated software tool/business application software with many latest features.

Developing Own Software Tool/Business Application Software

This type of venture is only possible in any service provider organization where the organization has qualified software professionals with practical experience. Generally software professionals are not familiar with the business functions and practices. So the services of functional specialists are required to guide them in the development of software tool/business application software. The various stages of the software development life cycle, such as system requirement study, the finalization of specifications, design, coding, testing, and implementation have to be meticulously assessed. Person month efforts in respect of the above activities need to be worked out.

Enhancing the Existing Software Tool/ Business Application Software

Some service providers have already their own software tool/business application software available on the same platform or in different platforms without integration. It will be required to assess the efforts to be put for integrating them. Minor and major changes for carrying out this exercise can be ascertained from this assessment.

Acquiring a New Software Tool/Business Application Software

However, much a readymade package has all the features required by a service provider organization, some amount of customization are needed for using the package effectively. If the package is of international repute, business process re-engineering exercise is required to be carried out. This exercise is essential because these ready-made packages are developed keeping in view the business practices followed in their countries. Naturally the business practices followed in some countries do not match with these packages. The cost of customization is to be obtained from the vendors.

Engaging the Services of a Software Company

It should be ascertained whether the profiles of the professionals are going to be associated with the development of software tool/business application software to suit the requirement of the clients of the service provider. Some software companies may have software developed for one of their clients. In some cases this software tool/business application software with changes or without changes.

The above-mentioned parameters are only guidelines. They are not exhaustive. Areas which attention can be identified by the respective service providers in consultation with their clients.

GLOBAL VIRTUAL TEAMS

The members of global virtual teams who work at different locations in the globe need to share their professional knowledge. The constant interaction among themselves is required to accomplish the task assigned to them. Cloud computing environment facilitates them to achieve their professional goal. Three main components such as stakeholders in various geographical locations, business environments, and the collaborative technology are the backbone for effective teamwork among the members of the global virtual teams. Shared understanding among themselves is a collective way of collaborating in designing and developing business models. The business environment plays an important role in the innovation process for them.

A successful innovator taps into the business to come up with an idea that would drive a change. An innovator must be in constant touch with the business environment to understand the changing business landscape, recognize parallel trends and tune into competitive forces and shape the innovation cycle. In other words the global virtual team can successfully integrate ideas and business environment towards the achievement of developing an effective business model. Virtualization overcomes time and distance. Virtualization facilitates for generating business opportunities.

Business opportunities lead to innovation. Innovation converts knowledge into new products, services, business processes (Knot, 2017). Collaborative business networks are another source of innovation and economic development.

CONCLUSION

One of the key challenges for today's executives in business enterprises is the formulation and execution of a strategy. That strategy must be capable of adapting to the many complexities in the global market environment. New ideas, new technologies and the emerging concepts in information and communication technology are required to be understood clearly by business enterprises. The concept of cloud computing in the global virtual enterprises makes the business enterprises more competitive in the international market.

N. Raghavendra Rao
FINAIT Consultancy Services, India

REFERENCES

Banerjee, B. (2010). *Fundamental of Financial Management*. New Delhi: PHI Learning Private Limited.

Chaka. (2013). *Virtualization and Cloud Computing Business Model in the Virual Cloud*. Hershey, PA: IGI Global

Clutter Buck, D. (2012). *The Talent Wave*. London: Kogan Press.

Dharanipragada, J. (2016). *Grid and Cloud Computing. New Delhi: McGraw Hill Education*. India: Private Limited.

Esposito & Evangalista. (2014). Investigating Virtual Enterprises Models. *International Journal of Production Economics*.

Hameed, M. A., Counsell, S., & Swift, S. (2012). A Conceptual Model for the process of IT. *Innovation Adoption in Organizations. Journal of Engineering and Technology Management*.

Hoffer , & Tudi, . (2013). *Modern Database Management*. New Delhi: Pearson.

Knot. (2017). *How Innovation Really Works*. Chennai: McGraw Hill Education (India) Private Limited.

Mathur, H. P., Singh, S. K., & Mohan, A. (2013). Creating Value through Innovation. New Delhi: Shree Publishers & Distributors.

Pandey & Kumar. (2012). *Computer Applications in Business*. New Delhi: Variety Book Publishers and Distribution.

Prashant, C. (2012). *The Unlimited Business Opportunities on the Internet*. Indore: Xcess Infostore Private Limited.

Schulz, G. (2012). *Cloud and Virtual Storage Networking- Your Journey to Efficient & Effective Information Services*. New York: CRC Press.

Semolic & Baisya. (2013). *Globalization and Innovative Models*. New Delhi: Ane Books Private Limited.

Sharma, J. (2011). *Research Methodology-The Discipline and Its Dimensions*. New Delhi: Deep & Deep Publications Private Limited.

Vysas. (2014). *Business Process Transformation*. New Delhi: Regal Publishers.

KEY TERMS AND DEFINITIONS

Analytical Tools: Methods that use mathematical formulas to derive an optional solution directly or to predict a certain result, mainly in solving structured problems.

Business Intelligence: Using analytical methods either manually or automatically to derive relationships from data.

Collaborative Technology: Various interdisciplinary concepts are applied for designing or developing a business model for an enterprise.

Data: Raw facts that are meaningless by themselves.

Innovation: Innovation deals with bringing in new methods and ideas resulting in required changes in an enterprise.

Knowledge Harvesting: Data and information from the knowledge management system are made use of depending on the wisdom of each employee in an enterprise.

Knowledge Management: This involves collecting, categorizing, and disseminating knowledge.

Knowledge-Based Economy: The present global economy is driven by what people and organizations know rather than only by capital and labor.

Open Innovation: Stakeholders who are associated with an enterprise, are prepared to share their knowledge, and exchange knowledge to improve the existing products or services of an enterprise. Generally, these stakeholders are shareholders, employees, vendors, and customers of an enterprise.

Virtual Enterprise: An organization in which people work wherever and whenever it is appropriate. It is also known as a virtual organization.

Section 1

Business Intelligence and Digital Economy in the Cloud Computing Environment

Chapter 1
Business Intelligence and Cloud Computing:
Benefits, Challenges, and Trends

Venkatesh Rajagopalan
VIT University, India

Sudarsan Jayasingh
ⓘD https://orcid.org/0000-0002-3754-1033
SSN School of Management, India

ABSTRACT

Organizations need to make quick and quality decisions to survive in today's competitive environment. The business intelligence (BI) market has moved away from IT-centric solutions to user-driven solutions. Business intelligence and cloud computing are two important technologies that have been widely adopted in business organizations in recent years. Interestingly, the two technologies have merged together to deliver superior benefits for businesses. Business enterprises are moving their business applications to cloud platforms to become more agile and accessible. The key benefit of cloud-based business intelligence applications is the ability to access on multiple devices like laptops and mobile phones from different locations. In this chapter, the authors outline the benefits, challenges, and trends involved in deploying business intelligence technology through cloud computing platforms. They discuss how the consolidation of these two emerging technologies can enhance the businesses to improve decision-making processes. They also address the challenges cloud-based BI faces.

DOI: 10.4018/978-1-5225-3182-1.ch001

INTRODUCTION

Business organizations are moving towards adopting Business Intelligence (BI) to address the challenges of business decisions posed by vast amounts of data (Market Research Future, 2018). Organizations today are moving from traditional reporting to real-time analytical tools that accelerate data preparation and data cleansing. The business intelligence (BI) can be defined as set of technologies, applications and practices for the collecting the raw data, analyzing and presentation meaningful and useful business related information (Evelson and Nicolson, 2008). The BI involves the process of collecting data, cleanse the data, store,, analyze, present and delivery (Zheng, 2017). It has the ability to transform the data collected through business transactions, interactions, social exchanges or other methods into business insights. The main purpose of business intelligence systems is to support management decision-making process using data. Business intelligence provides historical, current and predictive reports of business operations using the data gathered from data warehouse and data marts

The speed of business activities is accelerating and organizations need to react very fast to customer interactions, operational commitments, competitiveness and other time sensitive issues (Russom, Stodder and Halper, 2014). The recently data management technologies can handle real-time data than comes from online sources including machine data, sensors, robots, mobile and social media. Streaming data can come from various sources but special software are required to manage it and it creates new applications for monitoring business, surveillance, customer service, automated responses and so on. Organizations today are moving towards real-time reporting which provides the insight live to the managers. Not only reporting real-time analytic models are widely used to understand customer interactions, fraud detection and situation intelligence.

According to Gartner, the BI market will touch US$22.8 billion by 2020 which includes tradition BI, cloud BI, social BI and mobile BI (Ghosh, 2018). Top management, operations and sales are the key roles driving business intelligence adoption (Columbus, 2018). Dashboard, reporting, end user self service, advanced visualization and data warehousing are the top five technologies and initiatives of BI in 2018. According to Walters (2018) business intelligence market guide report shows that's 50% of BI professionals use BI for operational analytics and to present visualization tools to the business to help strategic decisions making (Walter, 2018). The report also mentions that 8 out of 10 professional plan to use BI for dashboard reporting. Increasing adoption of cloud may act as a major driver in the growth of business intelligence market.

BI can be classified into four types; they are reporting, analysis, monitoring and predictions. Analysis BI can be classified into three types; they are spreadsheet analysis, visualization and ad-hoc query. Dashboard is type of monitoring BI, which shows the insight in form of visual display and arranged on a single screen. The dashboards primarily display the key performance indicators (KPIs). Prediction BI covers data mining tools and predictive modeling. More cost effective BI in form of cloud computing are be widely adopted by organizations. Moving from in-house infrastructures eliminates overheads and reduce the cost of BI to great extent. Self-Service BI helps the users to generate their own customized data reports and analytical queries without intervention of specialized IT people are seen as some of the recent trends in BI.

CLOUD BUSINESS INTELLIGENCE

The cloud is changing the business landscape of business intelligence. It's clear from previous research that cloud based software as a service (SaaS) for BI, analytics, and data warehousing are maturing. It is important getting right information to run business but the main challenge is the data is stuck in the systems where it's difficult to get it. Modern technology like cloud computing and in-memory analysis with business intelligence has lower the risk, cost, fast to implement. The research shows that more organizations are deploying their BI in cloud. The business gets major benefits from the newly introduced cloud BI than traditional BI. The business intelligence tools are useful for company to analyze their data but implementing and managing involves high cost for the company. It becomes challenging for the company to manage effectively and efficiently the increasing size of data. This leads to use of cloud computing. According to BARC research Flexibility, cost and scalability are the three important reasons for implementing cloud BI (Bange and Eckerson, 2017).

The cloud BI offers numerous benefits for businesses that want to use reports and dashboards. The cloud BI needs no software or hardware to buy or need any IT people to manage or produce reports. The BARC research shows that dashboard, ad hoc analysis, reports are three purposes for using cloud BI by majority of the organization in their survey (Bange and Eckerson, 2017). According to Grant Thorntorn (2015) studies the key benefits derived from cloud BI are unified, secure view of real-time data, and ease of implementation, and scalability. The BARC research shows that businesses 25% of customers are fully committed to cloud

Table 1. Difference between traditional BI and cloud BI

Factors	Traditional BI	Cloud BI
Implementation Time	Long	Short
Cost	High Cost	Low Cost
Custamizable	High	Low
Mobility	Low	High
Agile	Low	High
Securtiy	High	Low

BI and 29% are partially committed to cloud (Bange and Eckerson, 2017). BARC research also shows the adoption of cloud BI was 29% and it has rised to 43% in 2016. The survey results finding reveals that most of executives use BI tools on the premises of their jobs (54%) as compared to cloud-based BI tools (20%) or a mix of the two (26%) (Walters, 2018). The BARC research also shows that sentiment mean increased from 2.68 to 3.22 (above the level of "important") between 2017 and 2018, this finds indicates that companies show more importance to Cloud BI compared to last year. The Asia-Pacific region found to show higher importance mean proponents of cloud computing regarding both adjusted mean (4.2 or "very important") and levels of criticality.

The most of businesses continue to struggle to get the desired outcome from their BI investments. The biggest problem most of the business users face is related to their capability to retrieve the data to support a decision using BI applications. The problem they usually face are not availability or inaccessible data, excessive or irrelevant data, unreliable data, unusual long time to generate new reports or using other BI tools that may not be appropriate for the job. Cloud computing and business intelligence are right combinations which helps to provide right information to the right people in real-time. The cloud BI usually expected to be easy to use and also easy to install and maintain. Cloud based BI applications costs less, easy to setup, consumes less time to setup, also got the ability to share with others and easy to maintain. Traditional BI tools usually are on-premise and needs more time to setup the application, design, develop and install. The traditional BI tools need support of expensive hardware, software and experts to install and maintain it. The only biggest advantage the traditional BI got over cloud BI is that the data is under your control so it looks like it's more secured and safe.

BARC Research and Eckerson Group did a joint research study; the finding shows that 78 percent of the businesses plan to adopt cloud for Business Intelligence and Data Management use cases in the next year. To this end, nearly half (46 percent) of those that responded to the study use public cloud for these two use cases compared to less than a third for hybrid cloud, and fewer than 25 percent for private cloud (BARC, 2017).

CLOUD BI VENDORS

When it comes to business intelligence tools Microsoft Power BI and Tableau comes to our mind. Tableau is the market leader in BI tools and data analytics. Tableau is considered more expensive than Power BI therefore it maybe used in larger enterprises. Data visualization is good and clear in Tableau than Power BI. Power BI comes as SaaS model whereas Tableau comes in both on-premises and cloud options. Tableau looks like a better solution for handling large volume of data. Many feels that Tableau is better connected with programming tools like R than Power BI.

Qlik's is a type of Cloud BI has the capability of visualizing the patterns using in-memory engine and producing associative analytics which cannot be produced using SQL. The in-memory feature of Qlik's is scalable and it can be integrated with many types of data sources. It can create a unified dashboard, which exhibits analytics, metrics and key performance indicators (KPIs) of interest. Qlik's BI tool has the ability to choose the features or tools based on the business needs. Tools can be selected based on the sector and the focus of the business as the focus

Table 2. Features of top three BI platforms

Features	Tableau	Qlik Sense	Power BI
Date Introduced	2003	2005	2013
Best Use Case	Ad-hoc Analysis	Self Service	Dashboards
Cost	High	High	Low
Large Datasets	Very Good	Good	Good
Infrastructure	Any	SaaS	SaaS

and requirement changes according the business needs. Some of the factors to be considered for selection of BI cloud vendors are:

- Volume of data
- Number of users
- Budget
- Vendor Stability
- Ease of Use
- Business Needs

Gartner researchers finds shows that there will be increased growth of adoption of BI and it will move towards the cloud. The BI intention to adopt is found to be increasing year after year (Ilieva, 2015). The Gartner survey shows increase in percentage of respondents agreed to implement or planning to implement their Cloud BI in either private, public or hybrid cloud next year (Ilieva, 2015). List of major vendors and their features is explained below. The global business intelligence market is highly competitive and organized with few well-established players leading the market. Some significant players include SAP, Microsoft, SAS, Tableau and Qlik (SelectHub, 2018).

Tableau is an online cloud-based analytics platform. One of the key benefits is to create dashboards and publish the discoveries and insights with others. It does have the capability of inviting the colleagues and customers to explore hidden opportunities with interactive visualizations and accurate data. It does have mobile apps support to access it from anywhere. One of the features of Tableau is the ability to collect the data from different sources such as database, spreadsheet and cloud-based apps like Google Analytics and salesforce.com (Ilieva, 2015). Tableau dashboard is an interactive in nature, which allows slicing and dicing datasets for producing relevant findings, insights and forecasting opportunities. Tableau users can able to analyze data around various regions, territories, demographics etc., and create interactive maps. Tableau feature can do interactive visualization using the story and data analyze which can be shared with other participants.

Power BI is a business analytics tools that deliver insights and discoveries to the organization. It has the ability to get connected to many types of data sources; data preparation is made simple and able to conduct ad-hoc analysis. Power BI is a product of Microsoft and it has the ability to deliver reports, and it can be shared with important stakeholders of your organization on the web and mobile devices. The organizations can able to create customized dashboards, which give a clear 360-degree view of their organization. The dashboard view covers the key performance indicators and scale across the organization and its stakeholders. The third-party cloud service providers like Gibhub, Marketo and Salesforce.com can also access the Power BI self-service access. The most interesting part is Microsoft Power BI is available as a free versions and paid versions for professionals. The free version can create and view but cannot download or print the results and 1GB data only can be analyzed and stored. The professional version cost around $10 per user per day for 10 GB storage and usage.

Sisense is one of the popular business intelligence advanced tools used to manage and support large volume of business data and able to produce analytics, visuals and reporting outputs. Sisense helps to organization to get connected with data from different sources and able to combine them into a single database. The combined data can be arranged into user-required format. This data can be used be manager to view and also conduct slicing, dicing etc. using multiple filters, which in turn helps to do advanced business analytics. Sisense solutions able to develop advanced dashboards and scorecards using the data from various sources like data warehouse and able to extract, transform and load into their database and helps to derive reports based on the queries. The sisense dashboards are presented in various formats like chars, scatter plots, KPIs and maps. Sisense can be installed as an on-premises or it has the option of using it as cloud-based SaaS application.

Qlik Sense is one of business intelligence software which helps to provide insights using the query-based data and it supports wide range of use cases. The Qlik has the ability to collect data from various sources and combine into single database to do advanced analytics. It can be deployed in desktop or cloud and able to develop customized dashboards which is embedded with live query-based analytics. One of the unique features of Qlik is it can be deployed as a self-service visualization app and it can be scalable as per the user requirements. The Qlik sense cloud helps the organization to make correct and quick decisions based on the insights and able to work collaboratively with other stakeholders.

IBM Cognos Analytics is another popular BI tools from IBM, which can collect and analyze data from multiple sources. The data sources can be found quickly using natural language and it has the ability to automate modeling and also verifies the data and data sources. The Cognos able to provide visualizations and reports using the queries entered by the users. The Cognos is also cloud-based and on-premises, which can help, view data from various devices and help many users to view and use from different locations. Cognos comes in three editions they are workgroup, standard and enterprise editions. Cognos make it easier and faster to prepare dashboards and interactive reports.

SAP Lumira is a business intelligence (BI) platform designed for businesses of all sizes. The product can be deployed both on-premise and in the cloud and caters to multiple business roles, such as business analysts, data designers and BI administrators and managers. SAP Lumira features data visualization, which allows users to drill down and explore data in the real-time. They can also create storyboards for data interpretation. SAP Lumira is designed to meet the self-service data visualization and real-time analysis needs of business users, while enabling technical power users to create more sophisticated analytic applications. As a result, it lets everyone execute with greater agility and with greater focus on core business transformation goals

SAS Visual Analytics is a cloud-based Business Intelligence solution designed for businesses of all sizes across various industries. Accounting and CPA firms, advertising agencies, banking institutions, manufacturing companies, government entities, technology companies, and several others can tailor the solution to accommodate their needs. The solution can also be deployed on-premise. SAS Visual Analytics can also be accessed via mobile devices. Support is offered via phone, email and through an online knowledge base. SAS visual analytics helps to create quick and fast interactive dashboards and reports based on the query. SAS can able create visual storyboard using the KPI and KPY, which shows the trend and action to user to understand and take necessary actions.

TIBCO Spotfire is one of the popular BI tools, which are secured, and is AI driven. It can help the user to create AI based dashboards and visualization reports derived from query and KPI. Sportfire can be easily connted with R and other connectors to create live predictive models. It can be hosted in cloud and capabilities of distribution to multiple users and highly scalable as the organization requirements. The data from various sources like simple excel files, relational and non-relational databases and web services. The spotfire can able to in-depth data wrangling for very complex data and it can covert into a simple easily data which can be used for analysis.

MicroStrategy is another popular analytics tool which is can be deployed on-premises and cloud-based platform. This application helps to do data discovery, data visualization and create dashboards. It is highly user friendly and can be used by users with minimum technical skill from their desktop or mobile. The MicroStrategy is an intelligence tool, which can derive the data from various sources and blend it to a centralized single data to conduct data analysis. MicroStrategy has a large library of 300 mathematical, financial and data mining functions, which helps to do advanced statistical analysis. It has the ability to create live dashboards using the live data, which helps real-time monitoring, and take quick actions or decisions. The product is priced on a metered or named-user basis. The mobile version is priced on a named-user and CPU core basis.

Table 3. Review of business intelligence platforms (Source: Gartner, 2017)

Vendors	Overall Rating
Tableau	4.3
Microsoft	4.2
Qlik Sense	4.1
Sisense	4.5
TIBCO Software	4.2
Domo	4.5
MicroStrategy	3.9
SAP	3.8
SAS	4.1
IBM	4.0

Domo is a BI tool which is cloud-based which connects all the users to view and engage real-time data and use it for analyzing and generating reports. The Domo able to get a holistic view of the data by integrating data from 500 data sources. It able to create interactive visualizations using simple drag and drop interface. This feature makes Domo as user-friendly tool, which can handle complex sets of data with simple clicks. The Domo has an interactive chat tool which allows instant access, share, collaborate with users and able to discuss online about the reports. The data analytics can be viewed and done from the mobile devices also and which provides fully interactive mobile experience. It has the ability to scale the data automatically according to users requirements and deliver optimized security for all type of businesses.

FEATURES OF CLOUD BI

Different businesses will require different features, depending on their key areas of service. For example, financial services would benefit greatly from end-user self service programs, but have little need for deep data mining. On the other hand, healthcare companies need more data discovery capabilities, along with in-memory support and data cataloging. Some of the key features required by industry are Ad-hoc query, visualization, personalized dashboards, end-user self-service, production reporting, data integration, data discovery and search interface. Some BI vendors provide auto-charting, which explore the appropriate data and automatically select the best visualization graphs for your data analyze. It has the ability to explore the trending topics in social media and conduct sentiment analysis to provide the positive and negative sentiments to users. If there is negative sentiments are noted then decision makers can initiate immediate remedial actions.

Visual Analytics

Visualization is presenting the data in form of images, charts, graphs, coded maps and other forms so that data can be read and understood better than presenting as statements or numbers. Today we are exposed with more volume of information and research shows that color visuals help to increase the interest to read by 80%. Visualization tools helps to view the data faster and able to get the insights to be communicated easily and shared with others in organization. Good number of visualization technologies is available in markets, which are usually user-friendly and can be used by users with minimum technical skills. Visual analytics is one of the ways to communicate the data, to management and other decision-makers to take effective decisions. The visualization tools can able to show the data change over time, compare, rank, distribution, correlation and geographical information in form of maps. According to the Deloitte survey of financial executives, Cost transparency: Helping finance create business value, nearly two-thirds of the respondents said the most important function of cost information and related business analytics is supporting strategy and strategic decision making. Organizations that embrace complexity and use visual analytics to better understand their data can accelerate performance and gain competitive advantage.

Dashboards

Dashboards display the data in a visual format, usually in form of graphs or maps. It shows the current status of organization performance using the key performance indicators (KPIs) in real-time. These visuals help to evaluate performance of the organization and also allow the users to view the trends and outliers. Dashboards organize all the data and arrange it according to user defined metrics or performance scorecards and it can be viewed on a single screen. The dashboards can be customized to organization requirements and display the metrics they are looking for in a single screen or it can be narrowed down to single department requirements. One of the important feature organization require in a dashboard is ability to customize the interface and view real-time data from different sources. The dashboard needs to be user-friendly and the interface should allow the managers to view and analyze complex data relationships in an easily understandable format. It should also need to provide real-time updates of the performance metrics like income statement or profits and display alerts when it show any negative trends which need immediate actions.

Self-Service BI

Self-service BI is one of the features, which is required by many organizations to make the users to get involved in key decision making processes using the data analytics. It helps to load and blend large volume data, with automatic modeling feature which helps to do easy and quick analysis even in absence of technical skills of users. Gartner defines self-service BI as "as end users designing and deploying their own reports and analyses within an approved and supported architecture and tools portfolio". One of the benefits of self-service BI is that it can do quick data discovery and fast insights. It also empowers the employees to view and use data to make fast decisions. The biggest challenge of self-service is the concern of security as the data are shared with many employees. The self-service BI maybe challenging to implement when the databases are complex and difficult for the common users to process.

Interactive Reporting

Interactive reporting is one of new features organization is looking for in BI reporting solutions which provides employees the access to customize the reports using drilling, slicing of the data, filtering and sorting the data. Today organization is looking for information to be delivered in web and mobile devices which should be real-time and actionable. Actionable information helps the employees to view current data, performance metrics and dynamically change the views based on their requirements.

Ease-of-Use

The organizations look for BI tools with interface available in the online and able to handle ad-hoc query and can be viewed as customized dashboards, which can do live analyzing. The BI tools need to be easy to use by users who don't have any advanced technical skills. The features like click from the list, drag and drop of data, live chat features, online 24/7 technical support, filter data and automated modeling of data from database are required by organization. Gartner 2017 survey report shows that ease-of-use is one of the important features ranked by users and which is ahead the functionality of BI tool. Easy of use is considered as the important selection feature for the first time purchaser of BI tools.

Mobile

Today the BI tools are available on any mobile devices, which give opportunities to share, collaborate and view information and able to derive quick reports using the mobile apps. This new feature available in mobile helps the users to access company information in mobile from any location and in user friendly way. This leads to better insights, and improved and faster decision making due to delivery of real time bi-directional data access. The mobile Business Intelligence (BI) is new technology, which is estimated to grow to 11 billion USD by 2012 from 4.08 billion USD in 2016. The average annual growth rate of 21% is expected for Mobile BI. One of the key features of mobile is to create mobile apps rich in interactive visualization and able to distribute anywhere, which can work in any device or any screen size.

The main features of BI tools of leading vendors are presented above and it shows that complexity of data due to different structure and sources and availability of options for extracting, integrating the data and ease to implement significantly increases companies' competitiveness. Some of the important features expected in cloud BI is to provide information to decision makers quickly, create story around business data with visually stunning analytics, view, analyze and act on data in the cloud or on-premises and create mobile analytical apps with rich, interactive visualizations without writing a single line of code.

Benefits of Cloud BI

The cloud based BI solutions are developed, installed and used by many organizations as it involves lower cost and easier deployment. There are many benefits of Cloud Business Intelligence and the key benefits of are listed below.The biggest benefit of the right BI tool is that it gives you an accurate picture of the current situation across your business.

- **Gain Insight for Growth:** One of the key benefits of cloud based BI is to view business insights like sales opportunities, lead analysis, market demand, customer profile, trends and opportunities. The insights if presented in form of graphs and charts will be easy to understand by the users and take appropriate actions. The key performance indicators like supply and demand, production status and market positions can be view in real-time and inference can be generated and collaborated with others to make right decisions. BARC results shows that 59% of respondents feel there is increased revenues due to use of BI software..

- **Cost Efficiency:** The cloud based BI do not require any investment in hardware or software so it reduces the overhead cost. The companies only pay according to the features they use so generally cloud BI is consider cheaper than traditional BI, which involves costly asset acquisitions and maintenance (Al-Aqrabi, Liu, Hill and Antonopoulos, 2015).
- **Flexibility:** Cloud BI applications main feature is the ability to allow greater flexibility, altered quickly to give technical users access to new data sources, and experimenting with analytical models. The users can access the insights and reports of BI anytime and from anywhere. BI will also make the process very flexible through avoidance of long-term business commitments. The companies will be autonomous in catering to the needs of data usage.
- **Scalability:** Business today needs BI tools, which is easy to scale up when there is sudden need. As the business grows the need to expand the IT infrastructure rises, if the BI is cloud based then it will be easy to add more users, storage, and features to meet their new business needs. Cloud BI systems found to have higher scalability than traditional BI. It helps to the organization decision makers to react faster to the market changes, make it efficient, and also making it easier to upscale or downscale the needed resources. Cloud BI can be scaled quickly to accommodate sudden increase in the number of users in an organization.
- **Fast Deployment:** Since cloud BI does not require to develop any infrastructure so it can help to deploy the software very fast. Cloud computing is very easy and simple to deploy and it also require not additional or heavy hardware or software installations. Cloud based BI usual delivered as pre-configured so it require less time to set-up and use.
- **Accessibility:** Cloud BI can be accessed on web browser or mobile device from any location. This is considered one of the biggest advantages for the organization. If the information is not accessible then the entire business suffers. It is necessary for the information to be easily available to enhance the performance. Cloud BI helps the company to make the information accessible right at employee fingertips.

The main industries that are using the Cloud BI are retailing, food, telecom, oil and fashion. In retail industry BI are used to monitor supply chain and check inventory levels. Food industry key application is optimize the distribution routes, telecom consolidate huge volumes of data from subscriber details, mobile phone usage, billing information etc. The cloud-based BI provides various benefits to organization users in terms of easy of use, access real-time data, fast decisions and huge cost savings.

CHALLENGES OF IMPLEMENTING CLOUD BI

The implementation of BI in the cloud raises the many challenges (Abello and Romero, 2012). The major challenge of BI is the companies to derive large volume of data from multiple sources and analyzing the large data sets. The biggest challenge is security, as it is believed that cloud BI is less secured than traditional BI. Getting information is difficulty today as the data is spread across different systems. In some organization turning the raw data into useful information is difficult, as it requires applying business rules or complicated formulas. Cloud BI may lead to disaster due decreased profits increased sales cycles and frustrated employees. The main barriers to the adoption of BI are cost and complexity. Departmental silos remain one of the principal obstacle along with other factors such as employee resistance to adoption of new technology, lack of CIO participation in decision making, lack of expertise to utilize the technology to its fullest potential. The BARC research study shows that 45% of businesses had not adopted BI yet and 6% are totally against it. Over half of SMEs rated their strategy usage as very low and many still not using the cloud for any of their BI applications (Dudharejia, 2018).

- **Data Integration:** Cloud BI requires collecting data across different systems and geographies. One of challenges companies face are every department within a business have issues in accessing private or sensitive data's like financial or customer data. This may lead to increased wait time to gather specific data which completely kills the purpose of cloud-based BI.
- **Data Quality:** The BI require different data field, so bringing different sources together can take more time to clean data. BI does not generate new data, it draws from other sources and if it is not properly organized then it will be big challenge in cloud also. Inaccurate data leads to misleading or inaccurate reports.
- **Data Security:** Moving data to the cloud can potentially affect the data security and increase systems risk. Security is rated as top issue by businesses, which have implemented cloud, based BI systems (Dudharejia, 2018). Increase the data security involves protecting the data points and secure (especially during transfer), businesses must use cloud providers with network segmentation, strong password requirements, and heavy encryption for maximum protection. One of the biggest risks to an organization's information security is often due to employee's action and not due to technology control environment. It becomes a big threat which self-service BI come into focus where employees are allowed to view and use the data.

- **User Proficiency:** When organization moves to cloud BI the employees need to be properly trained. They should able to gather insights from the application and it should create positive experiences. TDWI research shows that 33% business respondents mention the biggest challenge for cloud computing is related to inadequate staffing and skill (Russom, Stodder and Halper, 2014). Switching to cloud based business intelligence system is a cumbersome process and it require everyone in the company to get involved. Most BI systems fails in this regards as 49% of the employees report that they use very less features due to lack of training (Dudharejia, 2018). If the employees are not trained then it may lead to disaster including longer sales cycles, losses and frustration of employees.

FUTURE TRENDS OF CLOUD BI

Many organizations have realized that the data democratization and usage of self-service analytics tools for better and quicker decisions at all managerial levels. Due to expansions and innovations of self-service analytics tools, data- governance process will undergo significant modifications as well. BARC's research finding shows that cloud BI was not adopted by 45% of businesses with 6% mentions that they will not adopt cloud BI at all in near future. "Date quality, data discovery using visualization and self-service service BI are the three topics BI practitioners' identity as the most important in 2018" (Bi-survey, 2018).

There is notable decline of perpetual on-premises licensing offered by vendors in 2018 compared to 2017 (Columbus, 2018). The number of vendors offering subscription licensing continues to grow for both on-premises and public cloud models. Vanson Bourne survey shows that 83% of the companies agree that the cloud is the best platform to run analytics. It is expected by year 2023 most organization will run all their analytics in the cloud (Teradata, 2018). According Gartner research multi-cloud strategy will be the common strategy adopted by 70 percent of the business in 2019. They use the second host as backup in case of incompetency or failure of the main cloud hosting company. The new way of building modern and smart analytic solution refers to the use of agile software development; preferable Cloud based BI to generate fast and live reports that maybe time consuming to generate using traditional BI. The reports which are generated fast and current will be useful for understanding the business opportunities and take better business decisions.

According to Dresner Advisory Services study, technology, financial services and education are the industry that will adopt Cloud BI (Berman, 2018). The study also shows those dashboards, reporting, end-user self-service BI and visualization important features required by the businesses. Self-service business intelligence is an type of BI which enables employees to view and analyze using advanced statistical formulas even without any knowledge in modeling or acquire the data.

Mobile BI is ability to access intelligence tools and create insights on the mobile devices. Mobile BI provides immediate access to all BI content like analyses, dashboards and multi-touch gestures. This will prove greater interactivity using swipe and touch gestures. Mobile BI is anticipated to witness a positive growth due to increase usage of BYOD. Increasingly, BI will adopt features that are informed, or powered by, machine learning (ML) and artificial intelligence (AI). More companies are moving to apply deep learning or artificial intelligence to BI software. Tableau, Power BI and other vendors plans to add a new machine learning recommendations engine to its platform that will help algorithms surface contextually relevant data.

CONCLUSION

The business has recognized the importance of cloud based business intelligence. The rapid emergence of emerging cloud technology has created opportunity to accelerate the transition to enterprise-wide cloud-based BI. Cloud BI is capable of keeping the businesses competitive by providing many benefits like cost effectiveness, rapid elasticity and easy of management. Data visualization is the most important feature of BI applications that helps the managers to take quick and better decisions. The business users both technical and non-technical able to use BI tool to generate visual insights in form of graphs, charts and interactive dashboards. Advanced visualization like predictive analysis and geographical maps can be derived from the data. According to Gartner Tableau, Power BI and Qlekare the three top prepared vendor for Cloud BI. Each tool has its strengths and weaknesses, so there are many factors to consider before finalizing on a tool or set of tools. Flexibility, scalability, fast deployment, easy to use and use from various locations are some of the benefits of using cloud based BI. Despite some benefits cloud BI also face some challenges like security, data integration and data quality. The cloud BI future trends looks promising as the research shows increase in adoption by companies. The data discovery using visualization and self-service service BI are two features found to be important in future. Many companies are planning to adopt features which include machine learning and artificial intelligence. In the future, BI will be further assisted by web 3.0 technology, making its future even brighter.

REFERENCES

Al-Aqrabi, H., Liu, L., Hill, R., & Antonopoulos, N. (2015). Cloud BI: Future of Business Intelligence in the Cloud. *Journal of Computer and System Sciences, 81*(1), 85–96. doi:10.1016/j.jcss.2014.06.013

Bange, C., & Eckerson, E. (2017). *BI and Data Management in the Cloud: Issues and Trends*. Retrieved April 9, 2018 from https://www.eckerson.com/articles/bi-and-data-management-in-the-cloud-issues-and-trends

BARC. (2017). *BI and Data Management in the Cloud: Issues and Trends*. Retrieved June 23, 2018 from https://s3.amazonaws.com/eckerson/content_assets/assets/000/000/115/original/BARC_Research_Study_BI_and_Data_Management_in_the_Cloud_EN.pdf?1487101351

Berman, N. (2018). The Current State of Cloud Business Intelligence. *Money INC*. Retrieved June 22, 2018 from https://moneyinc.com/the-current-state-of-cloud-business-intelligence/

Bi-survey. (2018). *The Real BI Trends in 2018*. Retrieved May 21, 2018 from https://bi-survey.com/top-business-intelligence-trends

Columbus, L. (2018). The State of Business Intelligence. *Forbes*. Retrieved June 08, 2018 from https://www.forbes.com/sites/louiscolumbus/2018/06/08/the-state-of-business-intelligence-2018/#86ec7d278289

Dudharejia, M. (2018). Four major challenges of adopting cloud business intelligence – and how to overcome them. *Cloudtech*. Retrieved June 20, 2018 from https://www.cloudcomputing-news.net/news/2018/jun/11/four-major-challenges-adopting-cloud-business-intelligence-and-how-overcome-them/

Evelson, B., & Nicolson, N. (2008). Topic Overview: Business Intelligence—An Information Workplace Report. *Forrester*. Retrieved June 08, 2018 from www.forrester.com/report/Topic+Overview+Business+Intelligence/-/E-RES39218

Gartner. (2018). Reviews for Analytics and Business Intelligence Platform. *Gartner Peer Insights*. Retrieved June 23, 2018 from https://www.gartner.com/reviews/market/business-intelligence-analytics-platforms

Gosh, P. (2018). Business Intelligence and Analytics Trends in 2018. *Datavaresity*. Retrieved June 02, 2018 fromhttp://www.dataversity.net/business-intelligence-analytics-trends-2018/

Ilieva, G., Yankova, T., & Klisarova, S. (2015). Cloud Business Intelligence: Contemporary Learning Opportunities in MIS training. *Proceedings of the 2015 Balkan Conference on Informatics: Advances in ICT.*

Louis, C. (2018). The state of business intelligence, 2018. *Forbes*. Retrieved from https://www.forbes.com/sites/louiscolumbus/2018/06/08/the-state-of-business-intelligence-2018/#65e863247828

Market Research Future. (2018). *Business Intelligence Market Research Report – Global Forecast to 2022*. Retrieved May 22, 2018 from https://www.marketresearchfuture.com/reports/business-intelligence-market-2299

Myers, J. (2015). *Analytics in the Cloud. An EMA End Users Research Report*. Retrieved May 14, 2018 from https://www.tableau.com/sites/default/files/media/ema_analytics_in_the_cloud_research_report_2015.pdf

Russom, P., Stodder, D., & Halper, F. (2014). *Real-Time Data, BI and Analytics*. TDWI Best Practices Report. Retrieved June 08, 2018 from https://tdwi.org/research/2014/09/best-practices-report-real-time-data-bi-and-analytics.aspx

SelectHub. (2018), Compare BI Software: Business Intelligence Tools. *SelectHub*. Retrieved July 08, 2018 from https://selecthub.com/business-intelligence-tools/

Teradata. (2018). *Survey: Companies are Bullish on Cloud Analytics, But need to speed up the pace*. Retrieved June 02, 2018 from https://in.teradata.com/Press-Releases/2018/Survey-Companies-are-Bullish-on-Cloud-Analyt

Thornton, G. (2015). *Overcome the 5 challenges of cloud BI*. Retrieved May 23, 2018 from https://www.grantthornton.com/-/media/content-page-files/advisory/pdfs/2015/BAS-Cloud-BI.ashx

Walters, R. (2018). *Business Intelligence vital to employer decision making*. Retrieved May 22, 2018 from https://www.robertwalters.co.uk/hiring/hiring-advice/BI-market-guide-2018.html

Zheng, G. J. (2017). *Data Visualization in Business Intelligence* (M. J. Munoz, Ed.). Global Business Intelligence Taylor and Francis.

Chapter 2
Digital Economy, Business Models, and Cloud Computing

Abbas Strømmen-Bakhtiar
Nord University, Norway

ABSTRACT

From the invention of writing to the steam engine and to computers, human history has been one of technological inventions and change. In our relatively recent past we have witnessed several technological revolutions which rapidly replaced one set of technologies by another, and in the process created what Schumpeter called the creative destruction. Today, we are witnessing a technological revolution that is changing the way we live, work, and communicate. We call this the digital revolution which brings with it new technologies, methods, and business models. This chapter discusses the digital revolution and the platform business model. This business model is used by many "sharing economy" businesses such as Airbnb and Uber. The success of this business model is dependent on the rapid expansion of its user-base. This business model requires infrastructure and applications that can cope with this rapid expansion. Cloud computing has been providing these services.

DOI: 10.4018/978-1-5225-3182-1.ch002

1. INTRODUCTION

Currently, there is considerable discussion in the media, academia, and the official circles about the effects of the latest technological/industrial revolution on how we live, work and communicate. Disintermediation, Digitization, Molecularization, and Prosumption, are just a few themes that explain the processes among many that are changing our world in most profound ways. These changes are occurring so rapidly that lawmakers are unable to address the regulatory implications in a timely manner; consequently, creating large grey areas in statutory laws, which are taken advantage of by innovators and speculators alike. These legal voids have enabled the creation of virtual monopolies and oligopolies on the global scale. Now, a few companies generate more revenue than many countries.

Like the other technological revolutions of the past centuries, this new revolution, named the 'digital revolution', has brought with it a host of new technologies. Technologies such as Cloud Computing, Advanced Mobile Communications, Smart Grids, Internet of Things, 3D printing, Advanced Artificial Neural Networks, Artificial Intelligence, Genetic Technologies, Quantum Computing and a host of other technological advances have given rise to a new economy that is tentatively named the 'digital economy'.

This new economy is changing the old post industrial economy into something unique, with promises of almost science fiction like products and services, such as autonomous vehicles, real time voice translation, genome editing, and many other wonderful products and services that are surpassed by those dreamt up at the turn of the century.

The digital economy is a knowledge economy. It is digitized and networked. It is being disaggregated and replaced by active molecules and clusters of individuals and entities that connect and disconnect at will. Virtualization is exceedingly common, resulting in a shift from analog to digital. People and things, and our relationships with them are changing. The virtual world is highly transactional, without any intermediation. The new economy is global, and consumers demand immediacy irrespective of time and distance.

All these changes have created new opportunities that innovators have turned into new business models such as platform-based Airbnb, Uber, skill share and the like (prosumption). Digitization is reducing marginal costs and, in the process, creating new markets for the unmet needs. Taking advantage of this, Netflix and its analogs are changing the face of movie making and distribution. Companies, using knowledge, digitization, and network technologies, have created augmented automation (augmented automation portal + smart glasses + remote support) to unite experts from various fields such as machine and plant manufacturers with the service and maintenance personnel, delivering higher quality and faster service to the client.

Disintermediation and digitization coupled with the need for immediacy have given the companies such as Amazon, the opportunity to become one of the most dominant one stop retail shopping places on the web. Amazon is one of those companies that has been taking full advantage of the available technologies to create new business models. Amazon's efficient in-house cloud computing was slowly turned into commercial cloud services (Azure). Amazon's check-out solution, warehousing and inventory management, e-commerce sales and payment solutions (Fintech-based), pick-n-pack, fulfillment and return solutions have made the company one the most valued companies (ca $900 billion) in the history. In addition, the logistic services of the company, ship 608 million packages per year.

Google (internet related services and products), PayPal (online payment facilitator), OpenTable (find, explore, reserve, and manage restaurant reservations), SurveyMonkey (online survey), Second Life (virtual world for meeting and engaging with others – not a game), eLance (Finding freelancers), and many others are the result of innovators taking advantage of opportunities offered by the digital economy.

All these businesses rely on the cloud computing for their operations. Cloud computing offers Infrastructure as a Service (IaaS), Platform as a Service (PaaS) and Software as a Service (SaaS). This means scalable infrastructure, virtualized resources, self-service provisioning, device and location independence, managed operations, 24X7 support, lower (total cost of ownership) TCO, lower capital expenditure, security, and much more. Cloud Computing is a darling of the new business model operators because in no small degree it levels the playing field, allowing small businesses to compete with the large corporations.

The new platform business model used by many sharing economy businesses is based on the cloud. Without it, the rapid scaling so vital to these businesses would not have been possible.

Although this chapter will discuss the cloud computing, it will do so as an interrelated subject to the platform business model and the digital economy. This is because cloud computing plays a small part in a much larger event, the new digital revolution. Also, the other chapters delve sufficiently in cloud computing, and this chapter will be complementary to those, adding a scope.

This chapter is composed of the following sections:

2.   A brief review
      2.1. Technological revolutions
      2.2. Digital economy and platform business model
      2.3. Cloud computing

3.   Discussion.
4.   Conclusion.
5.   Further research and direction.

2. A BRIEF REVIEW: FROM GENERAL-PURPOSE TECHNOLOGIES TO CLOUD COMPUTING

Human history is defined, to a certain degree, by the technologies that it invents and uses. Some technologies, such as writing, or electricity have had profound effects on the way we live, work and communicate. Technologies can be classified according to their impact on the society, markets, and economies. We have sustaining (Christensen, 1997), general-purpose/enabling, and disruptive technologies. Sustaining technologies are those that are incremental improvements on the existing technologies. A better mobile phone is an example of sustaining technologies.

General-purpose technology (GPT) is defined as a technology that can affect the whole society. For example, electricity, internal combustion engine, business virtualization, and computers are some of the examples of these GPTs (Lipsey, Carlaw, & Bekar, 2005). One should note that GPTs usually do not deliver productivity gains immediately upon invention (Jovanovic & Rousseau, 2005). GPTs also act as enabling technologies providing "the means to generate giant leaps in performance and capabilities of the user" ("enabling technology," n.d.).

Disruptive technology is defined as a technology "that displaces an established technology and shakes up the industry or a ground-breaking product that creates a completely new industry"("What is disruptive technology?," n.d.). It can also be defined as "a technology that changes the bases of competition by changing the performance metrics along which firms compete" (Danneels, 2004, p. 249). Disruptive technologies initially underperform the established technologies, but over time they will outperform and replace them. Disruptive technologies are children of the GPTs. Historically, GPTs change the society through its enabling function.

When GTP technologies are invented and deployed in a relatively short period of time, they result in a massive and sustained 'creative destruction' (Schumpeter, 1942), i.e., old industries are destroyed as new industries are created. When this happens, it is called a technological or industrial revolution. *Please note that in this chapter we use the terms 'technological revolution' and 'industrial revolution' interchangeably.*

2.1 Technological Revolutions

It is always difficult to state with any certainty the exact date when a technological revolution starts since the effects of a single GT or combination of GTs on society and economies take time to be noticed and recognized. However, various authors seem to agree on the importance of certain GTs such as steam engine, or computerization, and thus tend to categorize the technological revolutions on the diffusion of these technologies. For instance: Freeman and Louca (2001) argue that we have witnessed five technological revolutions since the 1780s (table 1).

Perez (2002) also mentions five technological revolutions but with a slightly different emphasis.

Another categorization is provided by Klaus Schwab (2017). He mentions 4 industrial revolutions beginning with the first industrial revolution (replacement of muscle power by mechanical power, railroad and steam engine) which spanned from 1760 to around 1840. This was followed by the second industrial revolution (electricity, the assembly line, and mass production) which started in late 1800 to early 1900. The third industrial revolution began in the 1960s (development of semiconductors, mainframe computing, 1970-80s personal computing, and 1990s the internet.).

According to Schwab (2017) we are currently going through what he calls the fourth industrial revolution which is causing profound and systemic changes. It

Table 1. Technological revolutions according to Freeman and Luca. Adapted from Freeman and Louca (2001)

Technological Revolutions	Constellation of Technologies	Lead Sector	Life-Cycle
1st	Water-powered mechanization of industry	Cotton spinning, iron products, water wheel	1780s-1815 (1815-1848)
2nd	Steam-powered mechanization of industry	Railways, steam engines, machine tools	1848-1873 (1873-1895)
3rd	Electrification of industry, transport, and homes	Electrical equipment, heavy engineering, and chemicals, and steel	1895-1918 (1918-1940)
4th	Motorization of transport, civil economy, and war	Automobiles, trucks, tractors, tanks, diesel engines, refineries	1941-1973 (1973-??)
5th	Computerization of entire economy	Computers, software, telecommunications equipment, biotechnology	??

Table 2. Technological revolutions according to Perez. Adapted from Perez (2002)

Technological Revolutions	Name	New Technologies or New Redefined Industries	Beginning
1st	Industrial Revolution	Mechanized cotton industry wrought iron, machinery	1771
2nd	Age of steam and railways	Steam engines and machinery, railway construction, rolling stock production, steam power for many industries	1829
3rd	Age of steel, electricity and heavy engineering	Cheap steel, full development of steam engine for steel ships, heavy construction and civil engineering, electrical equipment industry, copper, paper and packaging	1875
4th	Age of oil, the automobile and mass production	Mass produced automobiles, cheap oil fuels, petrochemicals, internal combustion engine, tractors, airplanes, electricity, electrical appliances, refrigerated and frozen food.	19098
5th	Age of information and telecommunications	The information revolution: cheap microelectronics, computers, software, telecommunications, control instruments, computer aided biotechnology, and new materials	1971

is characterized by a much more ubiquitous and mobile internet, by smaller and more powerful sensors that have become cheaper, and by artificial intelligence and machine learning.

He argues that "all new developments and technologies have one key feature in common: they leverage the pervasive power of digitization and information technology" (2017, p. 14). He lists three 'megatrends' of the fourth industrial revolution as physical, digital, and biological. He argues that all are deeply interrelated and benefit from progress and discoveries that each makes.

- Physical mega trend contains autonomous vehicles, 3D printing, advanced robotics, and new materials.
- Digital megatrend contains Internet of Things (IoT) which makes remote monitoring, home security, appliance control, work production, and package transportation monitoring, etc. possible.
- Biological megatrend includes increasing ease of genetic sequencing, genetic therapies, and synthetic biology.

According to Schwab (2017) these technologies are some of the drivers of the fourth technological revolutions.

As can be seen all authors, regardless of their choice of dates and the GPTs, agree on one thing, and that is that the current technological revolution is a digital one. This digital revolution with its technological drivers has changed the factors of competition (e.g., technology, product features and services, price, order lead time, etc.), creating the digital economy.

2.2 Digital Economy and the Platform Business Model

As we have seen in the previous section, the authors faced with this challenge have tended to point to various underlying GPTs and their derivative technologies to describe the effects on the economy and the society.

Similarly, Tapscott (2014) has identified 'themes' that he argues describe the current digital economy. These themes are listed as knowledge, digitization, virtualization, molecularization, integration/internetworking, disintermediation, convergence, innovation, prosumption, immediacy, globalization, and discordant.

Knowledge

At the heart of the digital revolution is knowledge. The digital economy is often referred to as the knowledge economy. To begin with, the knowledge contents of products and services are increasing. Products such as smartphones, smart clothes, smart cards, smart houses, smart cars, smart roads, smart tires, etc., contain significant information and technology. Knowledge creation and sharing are representing an increasing share of the digital economy. In the digital economy, knowledge has become another factor of production along with labor capital and land.

Digitization

The digital economy, to a large degree, is a digitized economy. Knowledge, transactions, communications have been digitized, i.e., computerized. The vast amount of information is stored on digital devices that can be searched in the shortest amount of time. Economic transactions, new products are produced distributed in digital form.

Virtualization

In the digital economy, marketplaces are virtual. In these virtual markets, virtual representations of physical and digital goods are bought and sold without any regard for distance and time. Virtual labor markets for knowledge workers are erasing national barriers to the movement of labor. Also, we have the virtual organization, virtual office, virtual village, virtual reality and more that are changing the way we work and communicate with each other.

Molecularization

Traditional rigid organizational structures are being disaggregated, giving way to a fluid and flexible work environment. A virtual company can have its workers and departments spread across the globe. Many of the new products are digital and are produced by knowledge workers. These workers can be in any place around the world, and hence the new companies can be disaggregated. The workers can cooperate with each other in the virtual offices.

Integration and Internetworking

The internet has changed the world and, in the process, has allowed the new economy to become a networked economy. In this economy, the producers, suppliers, and customers are all interconnected. The internetworking not only allows the small companies to enjoy the advantages of the larger companies (economies of scale and access to resources) but also allows the larger companies to become as agile as the smaller companies.

Disintermediation

In the new economy, intermediaries are on the way out. Online companies have effectively ended the role of the middlemen and in the process have reduced both the cost and prices.

Convergence

In the previous economy the key sectors were the automotive industry, steel, and chemicals. In the new economy, the dominant sectors are those created by the convergence of computing, communications, and content.

Innovation

Innovation in the new economy is increasingly based on information technology to create products and services. Innovation is one of the key drivers of the new economy.

Prosumption

In the new economy, the differences between the consumers and producers are blurred. A clear example of this is Wikipedia.

Immediacy

The Digital world is a world of immediacy. Customers expect to have access to their digital products and services immediately. In the new economy, a product's lifecycle that would have been counted in years is now reduced to months. Many organizations are becoming real-time enterprises, adjusting in real-time to the demands of the marketplace.

Globalization

The new economy is a global economy and companies must compete globally.

Discordant

All these themes are drivers of change and with change comes resistance and subsequent discordance. All the previous technological revolutions had demanded adaption to the new realities; however, none had been compressed in so short a time as the current technological revolution. What used to take place 50 years to be introduced and deployed is now taking five years. Also, the nature of the digital products with its almost zero marginal cost structure allows for the creation of global monopolies in a very short span of time, resulting in a few 'haves' and many 'have nots'. The demand for new skills also creates a similar economic condition in the labor market.

These new themes have changed the old industries' factors of competition and consequently given birth to new industries. Highly innovative businesses have created new business models that take full advantage of these new technologies. A business model in its simplest definition describes how one plans to create value, sell and make money.

There are many business models of which one can mention add-on (Ryan air), auction (eBay), Barter (Pay with a Tweet), Cross-selling (IKEA), Crowdfunding (Pebble Technology), Crowdsourcing (Sisco), Digitization (Jones International University), E-commerce (Amazon), Integrator (Zara), Leverage Customer Data (Google), Orchestrator (Li & Fung), Pay Per Use (Car2GO), Peer to Peer (friendsurance), etc., of which many use the platform as the enabling factor for their business model.

The platform business model utilizes the digitization, virtualization, disintermediation, internetworking and other themes of the digital economy to allow businesses to change the basis of competition and grow at phenomenal rates. Figure 1 displays some of these businesses that use the platform model.

Platform business model facilitates the exchange between buyers and sellers, consumers and producers, while at the same time providing the users with a reputation system addressing the difficult issue of trust (Choudary, 2015; Simon, 2011).

The platform business model deals with information rather than tangible products (virtualization) and hence is highly scalable. This ease of scalability has been one of the primary challenges to the old industries where platforms have made an appearance. For example, Short term accommodation rental platforms such as Airbnb, can easily increase the number of their listing without any substantial extra cost (zero marginal cost), while a similar scaling for a hotel chain would take a long time to achieve (finding suitable land, getting permission to build, build, furnish, and staff).

Figure 1. Some examples of platform-based businesses

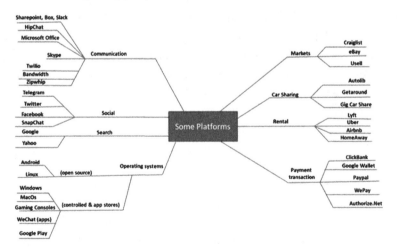

Looking at companies such as Airbnb, we see the speed at which they have gone global. For example, Airbnb, founded by Brian Chesky and Joe Gebbia in 2007, and received capital venture funding in 2010, boasts a listing of 3000,000 in 34000 cities across 191 countries. This phenomenal growth has placed Airbnb at the top of the list of the largest providers of short term rental accommodations in the world, surpassing Marriot International, the largest hotel chain in the world.

Another reason behind this phenomenal growth has been the zero marginal costs. Zero marginal cost means that once the initial cost of manufacturing (set up, etc.), has been paid, the production of new products will be zero. For example, once a book has been written and formatted, the cost of producing new copies of the book will be close to zero. All the platform-based business models rely on zero marginal costs to grow and make a profit. Platform business model has been made possible by the availability of the cloud computing, where low initial cost plus the on-demand expansion makes it possible for the businesses to grow without concerning themselves much about the underlying complexities of running thousands of servers. If cloud computing didn't exist, these companies would have to invent it.

2.3 Cloud Computing

Cloud computing means the sharing of computing resources and services, usually over the internet or private networks to store, manage, and process data. There are five main principles behind cloud computing: pooled computing resources (availability), virtualized computing to maximize utilization (high utilization), elastic scaling (dynamic scaling without Capital Expenditure or CAPEX), automated creation/ deletion of virtual machines (build, deploy, configure, provide, and move, all without manual intervention), and finally, the pay-as-you-go billing.

One of the main attractions of cloud computing for businesses is, of course, the attraction of a marked reduction in expenditure on infrastructure (conversion of capital expenditure or CAPEX to operational expenditure or OPEX). However, outsourcing of IT infrastructure is only one layer, upon which other layers reside; each of which present other cost saving advantages, not to mention the flexibility and agility that they provide. Here we can list the layers as the user applications (Software-as-a-Service or SaaS), the developer (Platform-as-a-Service or PaaS), and of course the above-mentioned IT infrastructure (Infrastructure-as-a-Service or IaaS). The cloud encompasses all these layers, making it one of the ultimate outsourcing systems for all of the users' computing infrastructure and services. (Strømmen-Bakhtiar & Razavi, 2011)

Cloud computing is the IT infrastructure of the future cities. According to Tan (2018), the cloud will also be transformative for companies, especially small and mid-sized businesses, as data analytics, artificial intelligence, and other capabilities become available as services. Because each industry has different needs, there will be Industry Cloud, where thousands of distinct, separate clouds, all working in concert across a digital ecosystem of different industry verticals. For example:

A commercial aviation cloud will help airlines manage ground operations such as maintenance, fueling, baggage handling, and cabin cleaning, thereby increasing efficiency and helping flights take off on time.

A utilities cloud will automatically repair faults in the power grid to ensure that homes and businesses get the electricity they need.

A banking cloud will let financial institutions scan thousands of transactions per second to prevent fraud.

These clouds will be private clouds. The private cloud belongs to and is used by a company. The public cloud is open to anyone who is interested in using its facilities for a fee. Small companies often start with the public cloud, and as they grow larger, they may decide to migrate to their private cloud facilities. Private clouds have shown a tremendous growth rate since 2015 when companies invested a meager $7 billion worldwide on a private cloud. Today, as can be seen from figure 2 they are expected to spend $32 billion on a private cloud.

The public cloud is decidedly larger and especially more important to the small and medium size businesses that either employ the platform business model or would like to have the option of elasticity of use and hassle-free operations. It is not therefore surprising to see that the public cloud is proliferating. Figure 3 shows the share of public cloud services in 2017 by industries.

The revenue of the public cloud computing market (platform as a service PaaS), including business processes, software, platforms, and infrastructure delivered as a service has been growing steadily $26.4 billion in 2012 to $138.4 billion in 2017. It is estimated that by 2020, the revenue will rise to $302.5 billion. The cloud services industry is expected to show a compound annual growth rate of 13.4% over the five years from 2016 to 2020 ("Platform as a Service (PaaS)," 2018). Figure 2 shows this growth according to each sector of the cloud computing industry.

The SaaS vendors are also enjoying sustained growth. It is estimated that the global SaaS vendor revenues will increase from the current $131 billion (2017) to

Figure 2. Enterprise IT spending on the true private cloud market worldwide from 2015 to 2026. Source: Statista (Statista, 2018)

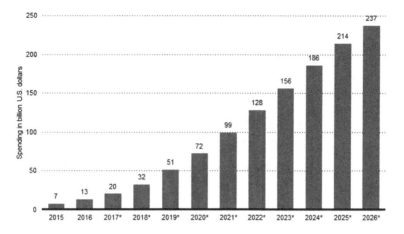

Figure 3. The share of public cloud services and infrastructure vendor revenues in 2017 by industry. Source: Statista (2018)

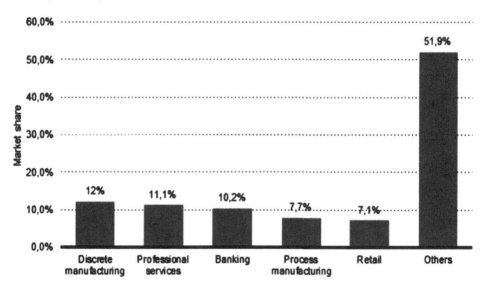

Figure 4. The global market share of cloud infrastructure services (PaaS) in 2017, by the vendor. Source: Statista (2018)

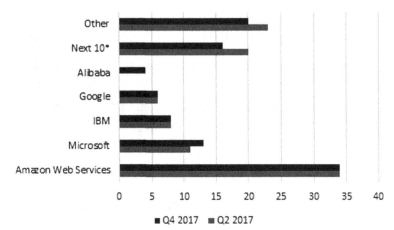

$308 billion by 2026. There are currently many vendors in the SaaS application sector, but it is estimated that, over time, the industry will consolidate, leaving a few large actors to control the sector.

The investment required to create reasonably sized cloud infrastructure is so massive that it has effectively created an oligopoly, dominated by Amazon, Microsoft, IBM, Google, Google, Rackspace, and Alibaba.

One cannot overstate the importance of cloud computing to the digital economy. The digital economy runs on information, and the amount of information that is being produced is increasing exponentially

3. DISCUSSION

Technological revolutions usually start with the invention of a single or several general purpose technologies which tend to have a protracted aggregate impact on the economies and societies. The impact of their derivative methods, products and services are often highly disruptive. We have seen how the first and second industrial revolutions slowly replaced muscle power with mechanical power, subsequently releasing farm workers to migrate to the cities searching for employment, which was in the newly built factories.

Figure 5. Vendor share of the public cloud infrastructure as a service IaaS worldwide. Source: Statista (2018)

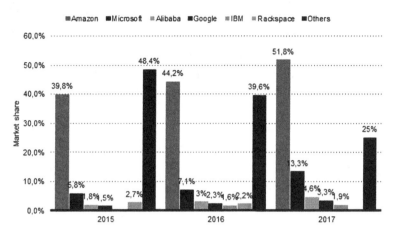

The subsequent technological revolutions such as electricity, automobiles, and mass manufacturing built on the previous technological evolutions to not only make the world a smaller place, but also to release more workers, this time from the manufacturing sector. Here we must stop a moment and reflect on the timing of the diffusion of the products of these technological innovations since it is the products, processes, and services that affect the population at large.

Technological revolutions are often mentioned in such as way as to give the impression that their effects on society are, if not immediate, then rapid. With regard to the earlier technological revolutions, this was far from accurate. For example, the twentieth century is always associated with the age of automobiles, highways, and mechanized warfare. But the truth is that by the start of the Second World War, horses still provided the primary mode of transportation. "In Britain, the most industrialized nation in the world in 1900, the use of horses for transportation peaked not in the early nineteenth century but in the early years of twentieth" (Edgerton, 2011, p. 33).

In agriculture, the horsepower peak was to come later. For example, in Finland the horse population peaked in the 1950s because they were used in logging. The United States provides the most graphic example. Agricultural horsepower peaked in 1915 with more than 21 million on American farms, up from 11 million in 1880, a level to which it had returned by the mid-1930s. (2011, p. 33)

Even by the Second World War, until then, the most mechanized warfare in history, horses played a very prominent role. The horse was the primary means of transport in the German army. Accordingly, each German infantry division had around 5000 horses to move (2011, p. 35).

What all this tells us is that the rate of the diffusion of the technologies was relatively low allowing the population and some businesses time to adapt to the changing environment. But as we see in figure 6, the rate of diffusion has been shrinking rapidly.

For example, it took 50 years for 50% of the US households to own a car and slightly more than five years for the same number to own smartphones. This rapid rate of diffusion is becoming so high that the lifecycle of many high tech products such as mobile phones is being reduced to a mere six months, if not a year. Similarly, other products such as televisions, and cars are being replaced by newer models every one or two years.

This rapid diffusion is putting tremendous pressure on businesses and their many middle-aged and older workers. The older workers are finding it exceedingly hard to adapt. They see their skillsets no longer useful in the new digital economy and are forced to acquire new knowledge continuously or become obsolete.

Figure 6. Fastest growing consumer technologies. Reproduced from (Dediu, 2012)

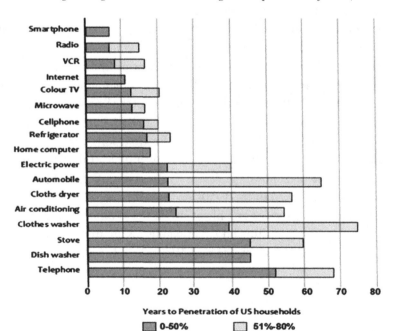

Another problem is task automation. The advent of faster and more powerful computers, cheap sensors, big data, advances in Artificial Intelligence (AI) and the ability to describe how tasks are performed in a precise step by step manner (business process management/reengineering), have made many jobs susceptible to automation. Many jobs have already been automated. For example (in Norway), the bank tellers were replaced by the automatic teller machines (ATM), and then the ATMs are in the process of being obsolete by the digital money or cashless economy. Similarly, the algorithms are replacing many other service jobs.

According to Frey and Osborn (2017) jobs that rely on perception and manipulation, creative intelligence, and social intelligence are, for the time being, safe from automation. These they call the computerization bottlenecks and are listed in table 3.

Another point of worry is the increasing knowledge specialization and differentiation that are rapidly eroding the traditional sources of acquiring knowledge under supervision, i.e., colleges and universities. We are currently using the old

Table 3. Computerization bottlenecks. Source: Frey and Osborn (2017)

Computerisation Bottleneck	O*NET Variable	O*NET Description
Perception and manipulation	Finger dexterity	The ability to make precisely coordinated movements of the fingers of one or both hands to grasp, manipulate, or assemble very small objects.
	Manual dexterity	The ability to quickly move your hand, your hand together with your arm, or your two hands to grasp, manipulate, or assemble objects.
	Crammed workspace, awkward positions	How often does this job require working in cramped work spaces that requires getting into awkward positions?
Creative intelligence	Originality	The ability to come up with unusual or clever ideas about a given topic or situation, or to develop creative ways to solve a problem.
	Fine arts	Knowledge of theory and techniques required to compose, produce, and perform works of music, dance, visual arts, drama, and sculpture.
Social intelligence	Social perceptiveness	Being aware of others' reactions and understanding why they react as they do.
	Negotiation	Bringing others together and trying to reconcile differences.
	Persuasion	Persuading others to change their minds or behavior.
	Assisting and caring for others	providing personal assistance, medical attention, emotional support, or other personal care to others such as co-workers, customers, or patients.

educational system to prepare students for the jobs that as yet don't exist. According to the World Economic Forum ("10 jobs that didn't exist 10 years ago," 2016), the top 10 jobs in demand in 2010 did not exist in 2004. Take marketing for example. In 2004, Facebook was about to be born, and Twitter, WhatsApp, Instagram, and a host of other social media applications did not even exist. Considering this, how could colleges and universities teach digital marketing? Even if they had an inkling of what was in the pipelines, it takes a few years for the professors to learn the materials themselves, and prepare textbooks, before teaching them to the students.

The result is structural unemployment, a gap between what the businesses require and what the educational establishments can deliver. According to a 2016 report by OECD **(OECD, 2016)** states that:

Increased globalization and rapid technological change, but also demographic, migration and labor market developments, have altered considerably the structure of skill requirements in most countries in recent decades – and these trends are expected to continue in the foreseeable future. In such a rapidly changing world, the need for the assessment of existing skill shortages and for forward-looking information on how the labor market and the demand for skills might change has become increasingly acute. Indeed, this chapter demonstrates that i) the costs of "getting it wrong" are substantial, with significant economic costs, for individuals, employers, as well as society as a whole; and ii) the extent of the mismatch and perceived shortages is high, and in some countries even increasing. Yet differences in the extent of mismatch and the prevalence of shortages across countries suggest that skills policies can make a difference. **(OECD, 2016, p. 11)**

As can be seen from the figure 7, skill shortage problem is widespread.

A recent survey of 3958 of CIOs and IT leaders across 84 countries revealed a shortage of skilled workers worldwide. Figure 8 displays the shortage according to specialization

This need has not gone unnoticed. There are currently a few online companies such as Udemy, Udacity, IANAC (Khan Academy), Alison, Big Think, Internet Archive, Academic Earth, edx, Coursera and others that are providing individuals with single courses or programs. Some of these companies such as Coursera have partner up with universities to offer complete degrees. What is interesting about these institutions is that they are market based and provide specialized education that the industries need.

For single, specialized courses, there is no need for the proposal to go through a university's bureaucratic system to be analyzed and considered (if there are enough students, how is the course fit with other courses, should it be an elective or compulsory, etc.) before being accepted. Since these companies are online, the

Figure 7. Skill shortage in selected countries. Source: adapted from (OECD, 2016, p. 22)

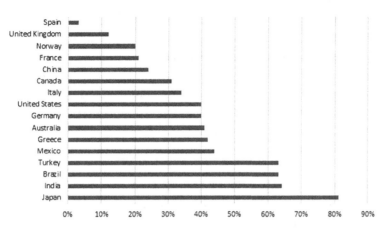

Figure 8. IT skill shortages as of 2017. Source: ("Global IT skill shortages 2017-2018 | Statistic," 2018)

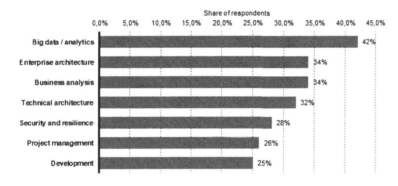

Figure 9. Tech occupation employment outlook. Source: CompTIA(2018)

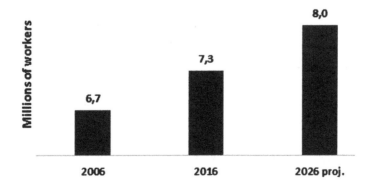

low marginal cost makes it profitable to set up many courses and enroll as many students as possible. The name MOOC or Massive Open Online Courses is an apt name. All MOOCs are based on platform business model. MOOCs not only reduce the cost of education but are also flexible and can offer specialized courses promptly.

Having said all this, we must not forget that even if MOOCs companies succeed and if colleges and universities take up the challenge and offer MOOCs themselves, and somehow provide what is needed by the industry, there will still be a large section of the workers that will be left unemployed, underemployed, or employed at jobs that don't require their level of education.

We should note that every technological revolution brings with it some structural unemployment.

We have seen how the earlier first and second technological revolutions brought with them hydropower and steam engine which replaced muscle power with mechanical power. Subsequent (third and fourth) technological revolutions automated many manufacturing tasks and, in the process, increased the general wealth necessary for the service industry to grow to its present size. Successive technological revolutions brought with them a host of labor hungry industries that were able to absorb those who had lost their jobs in the old industries. Currently, in advance economies, close to 80% of the jobs are in service industries.

Whereas in the previous technological revolutions, the lower level workers were replaced, the new algorithms are replacing both the lower level workers and the middle level managers in many industries from banking to education. But the loss of jobs in the service sector is not being replaced by the creation of the same number of jobs in today's high-tech industries. As can be seen in figure 9, the tech occupation outlook (USA) doesn't look that good at all.

The number of jobs created by the tech industry is very low compared to their revenue. The four top leading U.S. brands in 2017 were high-tech companies. And their revenue per employees surpassed anything that either service or manufacturing could produce.

The hope that the current ongoing technological revolution would somehow create industries that would absorb those lost to automation is highly questionable. Figures 10 and 11 shows that the high-tech companies do not employ people at the level of either manufacturing or service companies. In addition to the increasing automation, we also see a marked increase in sharing/rental economy, with companies like Airbnb, Uber and the like. Over time, if this trend continues at its present rate, it will severely negatively impact not only the manufacturing sector but services as well. If people share cars, then the number of cars sold would decrease, leading to more layoffs in the car manufacturing and associated service industries.

Figure 10. Revenue per employee for selected companies, 2017

(In 1000s)

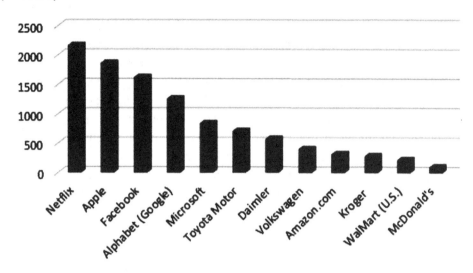

Figure 11. Number of employees in the high-tech, manufacturing, and service industries 2017

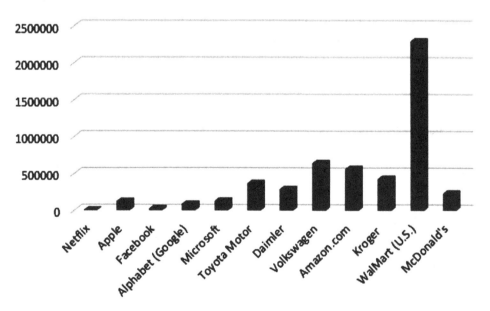

4. FUTURE RESEARCH DIRECTIONS

The computer and associated technologies have been THE single most important invention of the 20th century. It has accelerated the advancement in other areas such as automation, gene sequencing, chemical engineering, aeronautics, pattern recognition, crime detection and protection, and many others.

Today, we are witnessing another important GPT, namely Quantum Computing (QC). QC offers much greater speed and precision that the normal computers.

Researchers are excited about the prospect of using quantum computers to model complicated chemical reactions, a task that conventional supercomputers aren't very good at all. In July 2016, Google engineers used a quantum device to simulate a hydrogen molecule for the first time, and since then, IBM has managed to model the behavior of even more complex molecules. Eventually, researchers hope they'll be able to use quantum simulations to design entirely new molecules for use in medicine. But the holy grail for quantum chemists is to be able to model the Haber-Bosch process – a way of artificially producing ammonia that is still relatively inefficient. Researchers are hoping that if they can use quantum mechanics to work out what's going on inside that reaction, they could discover new ways to make the process much more efficient. (Beall, 2018)

Quantum computing is going to speed up the advancements in many areas, especially in simulations where it may lead to new materials, advancements in AI, process automation, chemicals, medicine and much more. It would also lead to further increases in the current economic inequalities and technological unemployment/ underemployment. Further research into the effects of the current technological revolution on our societies is sourly needed to find solutions not only for the existing problems but also for the coming problems.

5. CONCLUSION

The history shows that each technological revolution is based on several GPTs that facilitates/enables the invention of other technologies that disrupt industries, processes, and methods of communications. For example, the factory system, electricity, and internal combustion engines contributed to the invention of mass manufacturing and automobiles, which in turn allowed the creation of shopping centers, suburbs, the telegraph, etc.

Each technological revolution improved the standard of living of humanity in general. But it did so in a measured slow way. According to Perez (2002), technological revolutions happen at a fifty year interval. The current technological revolution is thought to have been started by the commercialization of the internet in 1991. So, if we follow Perez' fifty-year interval, we should expect the next technological revolution to happen in 2041. But, we see that the new technologies are improving at a rate incomparable with the technological advancements of the past.

We can think of the computer as an augmenting technology, i.e., it is augmenting human brainpower. Today, once a result of an experiment or finding is registered, it becomes accessible to a vast number of researchers across the world. Worldwide collaboration, along with access to relatively high computer processing capability is accelerating technological advancement. Cloud computing is making access to the vast amount of information processing and storage possible at affordable prices.

All these are made possible because of continuous reduction in processing costs. The computer and associated technologies have been THE single most important invention of the 20th century. It has accelerated the advancement in other areas such as automation, gene sequencing, chemical engineering, aeronautics, pattern recognition, crime detection and protection, and many others.

The result of all these advancements has been a marked saving in labor.

The new industries created due to these advancements employ fewer people than those laid off. Also, the requirements of these industries from their employees, in term of education, are very different from those they are replacing. There is a mismatch between knowledge supply and demand. Those with expertise in certain areas such as AI, or analytics, are in demand while traditional system administrators can't find jobs due to the introduction of Cloud Computing.

The unemployment due to a mismatch between supply and demand is called the structural unemployment. When this is due to the adoption of new technologies, it is called technological unemployment. This type of unemployment is difficult to deal with since it requires a reeducation of part of the workforce, usually the older workers. For example, as of August 2018, the Bureau of Labor Statistics ("Job Openings and Labor Turnover Summary," 2018) reported job openings level of 6.7 million, while there was 3.8% unemployment.

Finding an easy solution to the existing technological unemployment is difficult. At the heart of the problem is the existing skill mismatch, something that is going to grow even more with the continuing technological innovations, such as quantum computing, AI, and further automation.

The immediate problem is to address the growing inequality, in general, that this technological revolution creates and reducing hardship on those that have lost their jobs or had to go down in wages because they have had to accept jobs in service industries that pay low wages. A proper unemployment benefit combined with the opportunity for further education can be one way of dealing with the immediate problem. Another problem is to try to change the educational system to be more responsive to the technological changes. This is especially difficult, because those in the position of determining which courses are taught, are often unaware of the full impact of the continuing technological revolution. They often rely on the past or existing market demand. This is analogous to driving forward while looking back.

REFERENCES

Beall, A. (2018, February 16). What are quantum computers and how do they work? WIRED explains. *Wired UK*. Retrieved from https://www.wired.co.uk/article/quantum-computing-explained

Choudary, S. P. (2015). *Platform Scale: How an emerging business model helps startups build large empires with minimum investment* (1st ed.). Platform Thinking Labs.

Christensen, C. M. (1997). *The Innovator's Dilemma: The Revolutionary Book that Will Change the Way You Do Business*. Collins Business Essentials.

CompTIA. (2018, March). 2018 Tech Industry Job Market & Salary Trends Analysis. *Cyberstates by CompTIA*. Retrieved August 9, 2018, from https://www.cyberstates.org/index.html#keyfindings

Danneels, E. (2004). Disruptive technology reconsidered: A critique and research agenda. *Journal of Product Innovation Management, 21*(4), 246–258. doi:10.1111/j.0737-6782.2004.00076.x

Dediu, H. (2012, April 11). *When will smartphones reach saturation in the US?* Retrieved August 1, 2018, from http://www.asymco.com/2012/04/11/when-will-smartphones-reach-saturation-in-the-us/

Edgerton, D. (2011). *Shock of the old: Technology and global history since 1900.* Profile books.

Enabling Technology. (n.d.). In *BusinessDictionary.com*. Retrieved from http://www.businessdictionary.com/definition/enabling-technology.html

Freeman, C., & Louca, F. (2001). *As Time Goes by: The Information Revolution and the Industrial Revolutions in Historical Perspective.* New York, NY: Oxford University Press, Inc.

Frey, C. B., & Osborne, M. A. (2017). The future of employment: How susceptible are jobs to computerisation? *Technological Forecasting and Social Change, 114,* 254–280. doi:10.1016/j.techfore.2016.08.019

Job Openings and Labor Turnover Summary. (2018, August 7). Retrieved August 13, 2018, from https://www.bls.gov/news.release/jolts.nr0.htm

10 .jobs that didn't exist 10 years ago. (2016, June 7). Retrieved August 8, 2018, from https://www.weforum.org/agenda/2016/06/10-jobs-that-didn-t-exist-10-years-ago/

Jovanovic, B., & Rousseau, P. L. (2005). General purpose technologies. In *Handbook of economic growth* (Vol. 1, pp. 1181–1224). Elsevier.

Lipsey, R. G., Carlaw, K. I., & Bekar, C. T. (2005). *Economic transformations: general purpose technologies and long-term economic growth.* OUP Oxford.

OECD. (2016). Getting Skills Right: Assessing and Anticipating Changing Skill Needs. *READ online.* Retrieved from https://read.oecd-ilibrary.org/employment/getting-skills-right-assessing-and-anticipating-changing-skill-needs_9789264252073-en

Perez, C. (2002). *Technological revolutions and financial capital: The dynamics of bubbles and golden ages.* Edward Elgar Publishing. doi:10.4337/9781781005323

Platform as a Service (PaaS). (2018). Retrieved August 6, 2018, from https://www.statista.com/study/31311/platform-as-a-service-statista-dossier/

Schumpeter, J. A. (1942). Capitalism, Socialism, and Democracy (2nd ed.). Impact Books.

Schwab, K. (2017). *The fourth industrial revolution.* Crown Business.

Simon, P. (2011). *The age of the platform: How Amazon, Apple, Facebook, and Google have redefined business.* BookBaby.

Statista. (2018). *Cloud computing.* Retrieved from https://www.statista.com/study/15293/cloud-computing-statista-dossier/

Strømmen-Bakhtiar, A., & Razavi, A. R. (2011). Should the "CLOUD" be Regulated? An Assessment. *Issues in Informing Science and Information Technology, 8,* 219–230. doi:10.28945/1414

Tan, J. (2018, February 25). *Cloud Computing Is Crucial To The Future Of Our Societies -- Here's Why*. Retrieved August 13, 2018, from https://www.forbes.com/sites/joytan/2018/02/25/cloud-computing-is-the-foundation-of-tomorrows-intelligent-world/

Tapscott, D. (2014). *The digital economy*. McGraw-Hill Education.

What Is Disruptive Technology? (n.d.). In *WhatIs.com*. Retrieved from https://whatis.techtarget.com/definition/disruptive-technology

KEY TERMS AND DEFINITIONS

Business Model: A business model is a plan that identifies sources of revenue, the customer base, products, and details of financing. It simply tells how the business makes money.

Cloud Computing: Cloud computing is the sharing of computing resources and services, usually over the internet or private networks to store, manage, and process data.

Digital Economy: Although there is no common definition, one can think of digital economy as economic activities, commercial transactions, and communication based on or enabled by information and communications technologies (ICT).

Disintermediation: Removing intermediaries between producers and consumers is called disintermediation.

General Purpose Technology: General purpose technology (GPT) is a technology that can affect the whole society, for example, electricity.

Platform Business Model: Platform business model by using information and communication technologies facilitates the exchange between buyers and sellers, consumers, and producers while at the same time providing the users with a reputation system addressing the difficult issue of trust.

Sharing Economy: Sharing economy refers to an economic system where individuals (peer-to-peer) share assets or services.

Sustaining Technologies: Sustaining technologies are those that are incremental improvements on the existing technologies. A better mobile phone is an example of sustaining technologies.

Technological Revolution: When in a short period of time a technology or a set of technologies replaces another technology or a set of technologies, it is called a technological revolution.

Section 2
Requirements of Virtual Enterprises

Chapter 3
Cloud–Based Application Integration in Virtual Enterprises

José Carlos Martins Delgado
Universidade de Lisboa, Portugal

ABSTRACT

A key characteristic of a virtual enterprise (VE) is the heterogeneity of the applications that compose its enterprise information systems (EIS), since it builds on the EIS of the individual enterprises that are part of the collaborative network of that VE. This raises an application integration problem, which is even more serious than within any given EIS because a VE has a temporary nature, and therefore, integration requirements can change frequently. Current integration technologies, such as Web Services and RESTful APIs, solve the interoperability problem but usually entail more coupling than needed, since they require sharing data schemas between interacting applications, even if not all values of those schemas are actually used. The fundamental problem of application integration is therefore how to provide at most the minimum coupling possible while ensuring at least the minimum interoperability requirements. This chapter proposes compliance and conformance as the concepts to achieve this goal.

DOI: 10.4018/978-1-5225-3182-1.ch003

INTRODUCTION

Enterprises are always seeking better ways of getting more agile and more efficient, to minimize costs and to maximize profits. The market landscape is increasingly more complex and diversified. Innovation, time to market, and adaptability are key characteristics that any enterprise needs to master to strive in a constant struggle with competitors.

A typical strategy is to concentrate on the core business and to establish collaborative networks (Durugbo, 2016) with other enterprises that have complementary goals. Traditionally, collaborations were long-lasting partnerships. Today, the market changes very swiftly and partnerships are much more limited in their time span, usually for the duration of some project or useful lifetime of a product.

This is the idea underlying the concept of *virtual enterprise* (VE), which corresponds to a temporary partnership between several enterprises with a specific set of goals (Kovács, & Kot, 2017). A VE can encompass several enterprises and the same enterprise can participate in several VEs. This organization provides a better governance of the partnership, since it is governed as an enterprise (although virtual), than having each enterprise govern all its partnerships without clear boundaries.

The goal is also to better support the integration of the applications of the *Enterprise Information Systems* (EIS) of the various enterprises, since there should a mission, a vision, and a strategy of the VE, which are not necessarily the same as those of each of the enterprises. However, if this is already difficult within one enterprise, the challenge is far greater when several enterprises are involved, particularly when creating and terminating VEs can occur within relatively short time spans.

Cloud computing platforms (Toosi, Calheiros, & Buyya, 2014) provide some dynamism in resource and application management, but do not solve basic problems such as enabling applications to understand each other's messages and to perform the intended actions.

An example of a domain in which such collaborations are of primordial importance is the fourth industrial revolution, commonly known as Industry 4.0 (Liao, Deschamps, Loures, & Ramos, 2017), entailing a vision of an intelligent factory where people, machines, processes, customers and suppliers are streamlined to produce and maintain smart products and services, thereby contributing to an improved society.

One of the main challenges that need to be overcome to turn this vision into a reality is *integration* (He, & Da Xu, 2014; Panetto & Whitman, 2016), the ability to meaningfully and efficiently cooperate with other subsystems in order to pursue the goals of the system as a whole. Integration can be seen at all levels of abstraction and complexity, from low-level cyber-physical systems (Zanero, 2017) to high-level enterprise value chains targeting the capabilities required by Industry 4.0 (Schumacher,

Erol, & Sihn, 2016). This chapter focus on the integration of EIS (or simply enterprise integration), a major goal to support the requirements of Industry 4.0 and of VEs in general. The EN/ISO 19439 standard (ISO, 2006) refers to enterprise integration as the process of ensuring the interaction between enterprise entities necessary to achieve domain objectives.

Enterprise integration is a very complex issue, spanning from lower levels, such as data and service interoperability, to the highest levels, including strategy and governance alignment. The former typically resort to technologies based on architectural styles such as Software-Oriented Architecture (SOA) (Erl, Merson, & Stoffers, 2017) and Representational State Transfer (REST) (Fielding, Taylor, Erenkrantz, Gorlick, Whitehead, Khare, & Oreizy, 2017). The latter are mostly dealt with in a tacit way or at the documentation level, in coordination with the enterprise architectures.

The ISO/IEC/IEEE 24765 standard (ISO, 2010) provides the seemingly most cited definition of *interoperability*, as "the ability of two or more systems or components to exchange information and to use the information that has been exchanged".

Interoperability asserts the ability of two systems to understand each other's messages, whereas integration requires collaboration to achieve common goals. Interoperability is thus necessary but not sufficient to achieve enterprise integration (He, & Da Xu, 2014), which usually entails cooperation and coordination at higher abstraction levels.

Just ensuring interoperability is already a daunting task, given the complex, heterogeneous and highly variable enterprise collaboration networks that characterize today's fast-paced enterprise landscape, namely Industry 4.0 scenarios. This is particularly true when recent developments are taken into account, such as cloud computing (Mezgár, & Rauschecker, 2014), big data (Marz, & Warren, 2015) and applications in the context of the Internet of Things (Want, Schilit, & Jenson, 2015).

However, this is not the full picture. Another problem is application *coupling* (Bidve, & Sarasu, 2016), which provides an indication of how much applications are intertwined. Some degree of coupling is unavoidable, since some form of mutual knowledge is necessary to make interoperability possible. However, the two most used integration approaches, SOA (Erl, Merson, & Stoffers, 2017) and REST (Fielding, Taylor, Erenkrantz, Gorlick, Whitehead, Khare, & Oreizy, 2017) achieve interoperability but do not solve the coupling problem, since they require the messages used by the interacting applications to have the same data schemas, even if only some of values of those schemas are actually used. The result is that coupling in integration is higher than actually needed. This chapter shows how to minimize the problem.

The rest of the chapter is structured as follows. It starts by describing the evolution of EIS, from traditional enterprises to virtual enterprises, with emphasis on agility and interoperability. The fundamental problem of integration is then enunciated and models for both the interoperability and coupling are presented. Compliance and conformance are the two concepts proposed to reduce coupling without impairing interoperability. Finally, the chapter lays down the lines of future research and draws some conclusions.

BACKGROUND

The traditional definition of a VE has been a temporary alliance of enterprises (Kovács, & Kot, 2017). More information-oriented circles (Li, & Wei, 2014) define it as a temporary consortium of partners and services, in which services are essentially Internet-based, and take a service-centric integration perspective. Grefen, Mehandjiev, Kouvas, Weichhart and Eshuis (2009) use the "instant virtual enterprise" designation to emphasize the agility of a supplier network.

Virtualization, through dynamic outsourcing and reconfigurability, is very important for enterprise agility (Samdantsoodol, Cang, Yu, Eardley, & Buyantsogt, 2017). However, the automatic (or semi-automatic) design of an EIS from a market of services or processes implies a loss of design control over the outcome, unless the components comply with a general semantic framework or domain defined beforehand, to ensure their compatibility when translating goals into requirements and performing component procurement and composition. That is why most of the examples in this area come from the manufacturing domain (Knoke, Missikoff, & Thoben, 2017), in which the goals and requirements of a component are easier to express, and reconfigurability of the production supply chain is a fundamental objective. The current trend known as Industry 4.0 (Liao, Deschamps, Loures, & Ramos, 2017) is just an example.

This new trend of enterprise collaboration means generating and exchanging more and more data, either at business, personal, or sensor levels. This raises the application integration problem to a completely new level, in which conventional integration technologies expose their limitations since they were initially conceived for human interaction, with text as the main format and subsecond time scales, not for heavy-duty data exchange between computer applications. These new integration problems need new solutions.

Integration (Panetto & Whitman, 2016) can be broadly defined as the act of instantiating a given method to design or adapt two or more systems, so that they cooperate and accomplish one or more common goals. What these words really mean depends largely on the domain to which the systems belong, although there is a pervasive, underlying notion that these systems are active and reacting upon stimuli sent by others, in order to accomplish higher-level goals than those achievable by each single system.

To interact, applications must be interoperable, i.e., able to meaningfully operate together. *Interoperability* (Agostinho, Ducq, Zacharewicz, Sarraipa, Lampathaki, Poler, & Jardim-Goncalves, 2016) is a characteristic that relates systems with this ability and is defined by the 24765 standard (ISO, 2010) as the ability of two or more systems or components to exchange information and to use the information that has been exchanged. This means that merely exchanging information is not enough. Interacting systems must also be able to understand it and to react according to each other's expectations.

Interoperability is distinct from integration. Interoperability is a necessary but not sufficient condition for integration, which must realize the potential provided by interoperability. This is an inherently hard problem, since system interaction occurs at several levels of detail, from very low level (physical communication) to very high level (such as the purpose of the interacting parties to engage in an interaction).

Another problem is *coupling* (Bidve, & Sarasu, 2016), which provides an indication of how much applications depend on each other.

Interoperability and low coupling need to be combined to achieve an effective cooperation in the integration of distributed applications. These issues have been studied in many domains, such as enterprise cooperation (Popplewell, 2014; Rezaei, Chiew, & Lee, 2014), e-government services (Sharma & Panigrahi, 2015), military operations (Hussain, Mehmood, Haq, Alnafjan, & Alghamdi, 2014), cloud computing (Zhang, Wu, & Cheung, 2013), healthcare applications (Robkin, Weininger, Preciado, & Goldman, 2015), digital libraries (Agosti, Ferro, & Silvello, 2016) and metadata (Chen, 2015).

Historically, interoperability has been the main goal in Web-based distributed systems, whereas coupling has been one of the top concerns in software engineering, when developing an application, along with other metrics such as *cohesion* (Candela, Bavota, Russo, & Oliveto, 2016).

Software development methods emphasize decoupling, changeability and agility, which means structuring applications so that a change can be implemented in a very short time and affects the remaining applications as little as possible. Coupling is of paramount importance but has been treated as a side issue in distributed contexts, a best-effort endeavor after achieving the primary goal, interoperability.

This the case of the two most used integration approaches, Software-Oriented Architecture (SOA) (Erl, Merson, & Stoffers, 2017) and Representational State Transfer (REST) (Fielding, Taylor, Erenkrantz, Gorlick, Whitehead, Khare, &

Oreizy, 2017), and of the corresponding technological solutions for distributed interoperability, Web Services (Zimmermann, Tomlinson, & Peuser, 2012) and RESTful APIs (Pautasso, 2014), respectively. These are based on data description languages such as XML (Fawcett, Ayers, & Quin, 2012) and JSON (Bassett, 2015). Although they have achieved the basic objective of interconnecting independent and heterogeneous systems, supporting distributed application interoperability, they are not effective solutions from the point of view of coupling, since they require that the messages' data schemas used by the interacting applications are the same.

Several metrics have been proposed to assess the maintainability of service-based distributed applications, based essentially on structural features, namely for service coupling, cohesion and complexity (Babu, & Darsi, 2013). Other approaches focus on dynamic coupling, rather than static, with metrics for assessing coupling during program execution (Geetika, & Singh, 2014). There are also approaches trying to combine structural coupling and other levels of coupling, such as semantics (Alenezi, & Magel, 2014).

Compliance (Tran, Zdun, Oberortner, Mulo, & Dustdar, 2012) is a concept that can be used as the foundation mechanism to ensure partial interoperability and thus minimize coupling. It has been studied in specific contexts, such as choreography (Capel & Mendoza, 2014), modeling (Brandt & Hermann, 2013), programming (Preidel & Borrmann, 2016), and standards (Graydon, Habli, Hawkins, Kelly, & Knight, 2012).

Conformance (Khalfallah, Figay, Barhamgi, & Ghodous, 2014) is another concept underlying partial interoperability, enabling an application to replace another if it conforms to it (supports all of its features).

THE EVOLUTION OF ENTERPRISE INFORMATION SYSTEMS

The following sections establish several possible scenarios with several types of EIS, establishing a route from a traditional EIS to the concept of what an EIS of a VE should be, in particular in what concerns the interaction between the EIS of the various enterprises in a VE and the integration of the various distributed applications involved. This route can also be viewed as an agility maturity model (Imache, Izza & Ahmed-Nacer, 2012).

The Traditional Enterprise

A traditional EIS is designed and built with classic frameworks and methods. It can be characterized in the following way:

- It deals essentially with an ERP (Enterprise Resource Planning) system.
- There is usually a global data model.
- Processes are the main paradigm and reflect a repeatable workflow design.
- N-tier architecture is the norm.
- The strategy is typically oriented towards well-typified market sectors.
- The goals and objectives rely essentially on past experiences and statistics as a guide for evolution.
- It usually implements most of its components, with outsourcing more the exception than the norm.
- It does not experience frequent changes.
- It does not deal very well with unpredictability and risk.

The EIS is seen as the center of the business world, with suppliers, outsourcees and customers around it. One of the main concerns is integration with the processes of other EIS (Ghobakhloo, Tang, Sabouri, & Zulkifli, 2014).

The Changing Enterprise

EIS are so complex that they start being changed while they are still being conceived. Therefore, an EIS must be designed primarily for changeability, throughout its lifecycle.

Figure 1 depicts a basic system lifecycle, emphasizing changeability, which can be applied to the whole EIS, as it is usually conceived today, or to any of its subsystems. The market represents the rest of the world (namely, other EIS) or the environment in which the subsystem being modeled is immersed.

This model is maximalist, open and non-prescriptive, in the sense that any EIS (or a subsystem thereof) should go through all the stages (conceptually, at least), but the level of emphasis and detail in every stage does not have to be always identical. The higher the level of the subsystem, the more important the vision and strategy will be, but it must go all the way down to operations if it is meant to work. Lower level subsystems will emphasize development and operation, but they also must have an underlying vision and missionl. In the remainder of this chapter, "EIS" should be understood as the whole EIS or any of its subsystems.

Figure 1. The lifecycle of an EIS, emphasizing changeability

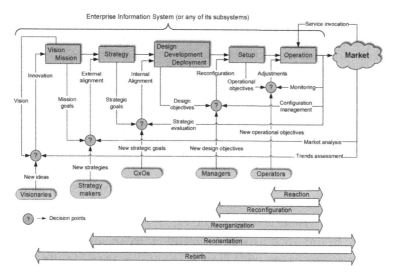

Figure 1 models the lifecycle of an EIS by a pipeline of stages, each more concrete and detailed than the previous one, with several improvement loops. Each of these loops assumes that metrics (indicators) are defined, so that goals and objectives can be assessed. If the difference between the desired and measured indicators is greater than some acceptable measure, the loop should be iterated to decide and implement what needs to be changed in order to improve that difference.

The inner loops deal with lower levels and more detail, whereas outer loops deal with higher levels and less detail. Figure 1 considers the following loops (but others are possible, with a pipeline in which the stages are more detailed):

- **Reaction**: All changes involve state only, so the cost and time to detect (monitoring) and to produce a change (of state) are usually very small. The changes can be very frequent and occur as a reaction to events or to foreseeable trends, in adaptive systems. This is the loop more amenable to automation. However, and not considering self-changing systems (hard to build, particularly in complex systems), every possible change must have been included in the design.

- **Reconfiguration**: Some EIS, such as in the manufacturing domain, particularly in the context of Industry 4.0 (Liao, Deschamps, Loures, & Ramos, 2017), support reconfigurability (Farid, 2017). Reconfiguration does not entail designing a new EIS but involves more than merely changing state. Some of the subsystems will be used in a different configuration or parameterization, for example to manufacture a different product in a production line. This, however, must have been included in the EIS design. Otherwise, a new version of the EIS will be needed, which is the next loop. A reconfiguration can be as frequent as its cost and benefits make it effective.

- **Reorganization**: The EIS needs to be changed in a way that has not been included in the current design. A new version needs to be produced and deployed, which may not be completely compatible with the previous one and may imply changing other subsystems as well.
- **Reorientation**: A reorientation is a profound reorganization, as result of changes in the strategy. This usually is driven by external factors, such as evolution of competitors or customers, but can also be demanded by an internal restructuring to increase competitiveness.
- **Rebirth**: The vision and/or mission can also suffer significant changes, driven by factors such as stiff competition, technology evolution, merges/ acquisitions, or even replacing the person fulfilling the CEO role. This implies so profound changes that, in practice, it has to be rethought and redesigned almost from scratch. This loop can also correspond to a diversification of business areas, making it necessary to build a new EIS or subsystem.

Figure 1 also indicates the typical actors involved in the change/no-change decisions taken at the decision points (the circles with a question mark). Visionaries are hard to come by and do not always exist as such (innovators are more common and frequently take on this role). The strategy makers vary from entrepreneurs, in small enterprises, to a full-fledged team driven by the CEO in large enterprises (including the various chief-level officers, or CxOs). Managers and operators take care of management and day-to-day operations, respectively.

The Agile Enterprise

Typically, a change to an EIS is decided upon when an actor realizes that the benefit of changing (BoC) is higher than the cost of implementing that change (CoC). Agile enterprises need low change costs (McLay, 2014), so that changes can be frequent, either reactively (to market changes) or proactively (anticipating market trends) (Andersen, Brunoe, & Nielsen, 2015).

Since an EIS is not synchronized with its environment (namely, customers and suppliers), it tends to progressively diverge from it, as time goes by. The misalignment of the EIS and the corresponding need for change increase. To realign the EIS, more and more changes will be needed and the CoC will be higher, as illustrated by Figure 2.

Figure 2. Change benefits versus cost of changes: (a) Light EIS (b) Complex EIS

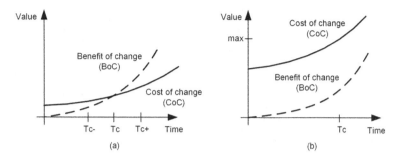

(a)　　　　　　　　　　　　(b)

If the BoC increases faster than the CoC, as in the case of Figure 2a, then the change becomes cost effective and should be made, ideally at time T_c, when the BoC equals CoC. If the change is made too early (at T_{c-}), the cost will outweigh the benefit. If the change is made too late by waiting too much (at T_{c+}), some benefits will be lost.

If, however, the EIS is complex and resorts to diversification (spawning a new version, or introducing an adapter) instead of promoting agility to cope with changing requirements, the CoC gets higher and may never be lower than the corresponding BoC, as illustrated by Figure 2b. In this case, the time to change (T_c) is determined more by the need to limit the CoC (*max*) than by its cost-benefit effectiveness. Having a light EIS, including only what is currently needed so that it becomes reasonably easy to change, is preferable to a complex and very encompassing one, which takes a long time and effort to change.

Note that T_c is just the time at which the change is deemed necessary and ideally required to be complete and in operation. However, the change will take some time to implement and deploy. Suppose that the change starts to be implemented at T_s and is deployed at T_d. This leads to several cases, described in Table 1.

Although proactiveness is a desirable feature, the fact is that guessing the future is still an art and many things can happen between T_s and T_c. In the most unfavorable case, the change made can be completely wrong, given the latest events and market trends, and lead to losses compared to doing no change at all. Therefore, in many cases a fast reactive behavior is the best approach.

In that case, the *change delay* (T_d-T_c) will determine how fast the EIS is able to realign and accommodate a change in requirements. If its average value is small compared to the MTBC (Mean Time Between Changes), the system can be classified as very agile or even real-time.

Table 1. Types of changes

Timings	Type of Change	Description
$T_c \leq T_s < T_d$	Reactive.	Completely reactive change, since its implementation starts only after realizing that it should be in place.
$T_s < T_c < T_d$	Mixed.	Change with a proactive and a reactive part. It starts before T_c, but some time afterwards is still needed to complete the change.
$T_s < T_d \leq T_c$	Proactive.	Completely proactive change, since its implementation starts and finishes even before it is needed. There is no much point in having T_d much before T_c
$T_s < T_d = T_c$	Just in time.	Change is complete precisely when it is needed. The ideal case.

Agility, a desirable EIS property, is generally associated with quick response to a changing environment (Verbaan, & Silvius, 2014), although it has also been defined in terms of low change cost (McLay, 2014) and proactiveness (Andersen, Brunoe, & Nielsen, 2015). However, it is preferable to separate the various factors that characterize a change, with the following definitions (taken as average values) related to EIS changes:

- **Agility**: An indication of the change delay in relation to the rate at which changes are needed $((T_d-T_c)/MTBC)$.
- **Dynamicity**: An indication of the implementation time of a change in relation to the rate at which changes are needed $((T_d-T_s) /MTBC)$.
- **Proactiveness**: An indication of the proportion of the proactive part of the change in its implementation time, or how early the need for change is decided compared to the time required to implement the change $((T_c-T_s)/(T_d-T_s))$. Applicable only when $T_s \leq T_c$
- **Reactiveness**: An indication of the time required to implement the change in relation to the change delay $((T_d-T_s)/(T_d-T_c))$. Applicable only when $T_s > T_c$
- **Efficiency**: An indication of the average ratio between the benefit value of a change and the corresponding implementation cost (BoC/CoC).

Agility should not depend on implementation cost or proactiveness, because it is a necessity caused essentially by external factors, such as competition or technological advances. However, what the market perceives is only whether a given enterprise responds fast enough or slowly to an evolving environment. The cost of that responsiveness, or how much in advance the enterprise has to anticipate the need for change, is an internal matter of that enterprise. Sometimes, it is preferable to pay more for a faster solution and be less efficient in implementing a change, just to beat the competition and gain the competitive edge of being first on the market. If time pressure is not high, optimization can focus on the implementation cost, rather than on minimizing the change delay.

It is also important to acknowledge that these indicators can be measured in each of the loops of Figure 1 but all need to be considered, according to the theory of constraints (Şimşit, Günay, & Vayvay, 2014). If, for example, an enterprise is very agile in innovation and market perception (Reorientation loop) but sluggish in implementing and deploying changes (Reconfiguration loop), the overall agility will be hampered by this slower loop.

The Optimizing Enterprise

Ideally, resources should have 100% utilization, all the time. Unfortunately, customer demand is not constant and supplier capacity is limited. One solution is to own resources planned for an average or higher customer demand, but this translates into wasted capacity when demand is lower and will not be able to satisfy customers when demand is high. Another solution is to design an on-premises EIS for dynamic, on-demand outsourcing (minimum TCO – Total Cost of Ownership – complemented with outsourcing as needed):

- When demand for a module's functionality is higher than its capacity, the requests in excess are dynamically forwarded to one or more alternative modules (with an outsourcing contract foreseeing occasional or seasonal demand).
- When the demand is lower than the module's capacity, the business model is inverted and the module can offer its excess capacity to other enterprises needing its functionality.

This way, load balancing can be achieved both at the demand and capacity ends. The load balancing between consumption and generation should be as much as possible automatic and dynamic, although under previously agreed contractual constraints.

The Resilient Enterprise

Any enterprise should have a backup plan in case any of its EIS modules or resources fails. Resources include not only computers and other equipment, but also humans. Although replacing a sick person that holds specific knowledge is much more difficult than finding an alternative to a broken equipment, the point is that a backup plan must be built into each EIS by proper enterprise architecture design, and not dealt with only when a problem occurs. Resilience is a usual topic in IT, but sometimes enterprises tend to forget that the problem is the same in every aspect of the business (including failing employees, suppliers, outsourcees and customers).

A typical solution for a resource failure is redundancy, either in normal use (in case of failure, only capacity is reduced) or in standby, in which case the alternative resource is only put into service when the normal one fails. In hot standby, the alternative resource exists and is reserved and ready for (almost) immediate use upon failure detection. This is generally too expensive and used only for truly critical resources. The others use warm or cold standby, in which case the situation is foreseen and the actions that need to be done are known. Cold standby is the cheapest alternative solution to implement, but it takes longer to become operational. A failure usually implies a breach of the service dependent on the failed resource, and its impact and allowed recovery time should be part of the EIS design.

The Cloud-Oriented Enterprise

Cloud computing platforms (Ritter, May, & Rinderle-Ma, 2017) are now pervasive among EIS and most likely including hybrid clouds, integrating the enterprise's owned infrastructure with one or more public clouds.

Mobile cloud computing (Abolfazli, Sanaei, Sanaei, Shojafar, & Gani, 2016) is also a very relevant topic, particularly given the ever-increasing pervasiveness of smartphones and tablets that created a surge in the BYOD (Bring Your Own Device) tendency (Weeger, Wang, & Gewald, 2016).

The Internet of Things (Botta, de Donato, Persico, & Pescapé, 2016), is experiencing an explosive development rate that raises the need to integrate enterprise applications with the physical world, including sensor networks (Iyengar & Brooks, 2016). Al-Fuqaha, Guizani, Mohammadi, Aledhari, and Ayyash (2015) provide estimates that indicate that the number of Internet-capable, autonomous devices greatly outnumber human-operated devices, which means that the Internet is no longer dominated by human users, but rather by small computer-based devices that require technologies adequate to them, rather than to full-fledged servers supporting web sites.

Given the huge variety and complexity of today's application scenarios, and the need to integrate many and heterogeneous applications, running on a wide range of platforms, it is only natural that enterprises resort to cloud computing as a means to provide a dynamic platform with as few constraints as possible and to simplify application integration (Mezgár & Rauschecker, 2014). Clouds run applications as services, entailing a service delivery model characterized by the usual cloud properties:

- **Self-Service**: The customer is a heavy co-producer.
- **Automation**: The customer does not have to deal with the management of resources, provisioning of services, application patches and updates.
- **Virtualization**: The customer has no notion of where and how the service is implemented.
- **Elasticity**: The apparent service capacity shrinks or grows dynamically as the customer requires.
- **Pay-Per-Use**: No investment upfront, no minimum consumption.
- **Multi-Tenancy**: The resources are shared by many customers, transparently, with security and load balancing, which reduces maximum capacity and hence the service costs.

An application is a set of software modules with synchronized lifecycles, i.e., compiled and linked together. Applications are the unit of system distribution and their interaction is usually limited to message exchange. Applications are independent and each can evolve in ways that the others cannot predict or control.

The interaction between modules belonging to the same application can rely on names to designate concepts in the type system (types, inheritance, variables, methods, and so on). A name can have only one meaning in a given scope, which means that using a name is equivalent to using its definition. A working application usually assumes that all its modules are also working and use the same implementation language and formats, with any change notified to all modules. The application is a coherent and cohesive whole.

The interaction between different applications, however, is a completely different matter. Different applications may use the same name for different meanings, be programmed in different languages, be deployed in different cloud platforms, use different formats and, without notifying other applications, migrate from one server to another, change its functionality or interface, and even be down for some reason, planned or not.

This raises an interoperability problem, not only in terms of correctly interpreting and understanding exchanged data but also in keeping behaviors synchronized in some choreography. The typical solutions involve a common protocol (such as HTTP), self-describing data, at the syntactic and sometimes semantic levels, and many assumptions previously agreed upon. For example, XML-based interactions, including Web Services, assume a common schema. REST proponents claim that client and server are decoupled, since the client needs just the initial server´s URI – *Universal Resource Identifier*. However, RESTful applications do require previously agreed media types (schemas) and implicit assumptions by the client on the behavior of the server when executing the protocol verbs.

It is virtually impossible for one application to know how to behave in the interaction with another application if it knows nothing about the latter. Not even humans are able to achieve it. Some form of coupling (shared and agreed knowledge, prior to interaction) needs to exist. The goal is to reduce coupling as much as possible while ensuring the minimum level of interoperability required by the problem that motivated the interaction between applications.

Figure 3 provides an example of the sort of problems that need to be tackled in order to achieve this goal, in the context of distributed, cloud-based applications.

Figure 3 can be described as follows, with the scenario of Figure 3a until step 7:

1.   Application *A* resorts to a directory to find a suitable application, according to some specification.
2.   The directory has a reference to such an application, *B*.
3.   The directory sends that reference to *A*.
4.   Application *A* sends a message to *B*, which it must understand, react and respond according to the expectations of *A* (note the bidirectional arrow).
5.   If is unreachable, *A* can have predefined alternative applications, such as *B1* and *B2*. Resending the message to them can be done automatically or as a result from an exception.
6.   If *B* is reachable but somehow not functional, *B* itself (or the cloud that implements it) can forward the message to an alternative application, such as *B3*.
7.   Application *B* can be migrated dynamically to another cloud, yielding the scenario of Figure 3b.
8.   *B* leaves a reverse proxy as a replacement, which means that if *A* sends another message to *B* (step 4) it will be automatically forwarded to the new *B*.

Figure 3. Illustration of some interoperability aspects. (a) – Before migration of application B. (b) – After migration

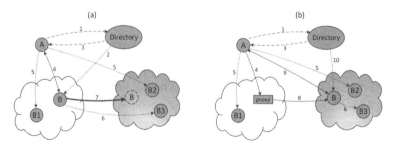

9.   The response, however, will be sent to the original sender, *A*, including information on the new location of *B*, which *A* will use for subsequent messages (the message protocol must support this).

10.   The proxy could be garbage-collected, but this is not easy to manage in a distributed system that is unreliable by nature. Therefore, the proxy can be maintained for some time, under some policy, and destroyed afterwards. If some application still holding a reference to the old *B* sends a message to it, the protocol should respond with a suitable error stating that *B* does not exist. *A* can then repeat steps 1 and 3, obtaining the new location of *B* from the directory.

Figure 3 raises some interesting interoperability problems, such as those mentioned in Table 2, which also hints a few solutions. Many more problems could be identified, in particular at the non-functional level, such as security and SLR (*Service Level Requirements*), but this chapter cannot tackle them all and concentrates on the basic interoperability issues.

The Virtual Enterprise

The meaning of virtual enterprise (Esposito, & Evangelista, 2014) has evolved from a classical partnership of strategic outsourcing and collaboration, in a timescale of weeks to years, to a dynamic, cost optimizing service networks and collaborations, valid for a time span as small as a single business transaction. Cloud computing platforms and tools are the enablers that support such virtual and dynamic environments (Patrignani, & Kavathatzopoulos, 2016).

In an era where everything is seen as a service (Li, & Wei, 2014), a virtual enterprise can be conceived as a small-grain collaborative network (Durugbo, 2016), which can extend and retract, defined dynamically at the process or even at the transaction level, according to the current needs and to the functionality that needs to be implemented.

This concept, designated here VEaaS (Virtual Enterprise as a Service), can be characterized by the following guidelines:

- There must be a definition of a VEIS (Virtual Enterprise Information System), which is the EIS of the VEaaS and defines the possible variations of the configuration of the collaborative network.
- Instead of guessing what and how much the customer demand will be (introducing provisions for it in the VEIS in advance, in a static way), the

Table 2. Interoperability problems and possible solutions

Topic	Problems	Possible Solutions
Heterogeneity (types/schemas)	How can an application understand message types/ schemas from another independent application?	• Self-description. • Structural compatibility.
Decoupling	Do applications need to share their entire interfaces or just the features that they actually use to interact?	Partial compatibility.
Reliability	If a service becomes unavailable, how can suitable alternatives be provided, in order to maintain the overall system working, as much as possible?	Foreseen alternatives, in either at the consumer or provider sides of an interaction, with automatic redirection.
Migration	If an application migrates from one cloud to another (due to load-balancing, maintenance, better performance or lower cost, or some other reason), how can other applications continue to interact with it transparently?	• Reverse proxy left at the original place with automatic message forwarding. • Repeat search for application (updated location returned)
Heterogeneity (portability)	How can an application be deployed to different clouds, with different APIs, platforms and processors?	• Portable platform (for interpreted languages). • Application includes several implementations.
Heterogeneity (management)	How can an application managing other applications in different clouds deal with different cloud management APIs?	Each application becomes manageable (wraps what it needs from the cloud API in its own API).

VEIS should be designed so that it can assembled and/or reconfigured on the fly in reaction to concrete customer demand and requests, with a high degree of customization.

- Instead of considering the VEIS as merely a part of a value chain, see it as a value creator, or an adapter between what the customer wants and what other enterprises can provide.
- Instead of seeking static collaboration with other enterprises, build the VEIS dynamically and virtually on top of a library of services, using outsourcing as the main organizational paradigm.
- Instead of investing a lot in defining an elaborate strategy, build the entire VEIS for agility, so that strategy is easily and quickly adaptable to the fast-evolving business world.

The VEaaS builds upon a menu-based VEIS, in the sense that a new, specialized and customized VEIS can be built for each business transaction (or class of transactions), with smaller granularity and higher agility than traditional EIS. Unlike traditional scenarios, outsourcing is the main service delivery mechanism of the VEaaS model and is meant to be used with all service types, including human roles.

Although VEaaS may seem similar to SaaS (Software as a Service), these are two orthogonal concepts. SaaS is essentially a service delivery mechanism, whereas VEaaS is an EIS building paradigm. SaaS offers full applications remotely, hiding management problems, but has no idea of how an EIS should be organized, and indeed current SaaS offerings (ERPs, in particular) are not that easy to configure and to integrate with other subsystems. VEaaS, on the other hand, advocates smaller granularity and promotes the dynamic interoperability of services more than their static integration into an EIS. Instead of one large application, it is better to use a library of smaller, customizable services. Agile adaptability to the customer requirements is the main tenet.

Figure 4 depicts the lifecycle of the VEIS of a VEaaS, reflecting a changeability model more dynamic than that of Figure 1, which reflects the EIS of a traditional enterprise. Customers are at the center by design.

The VEaaS model divides the VEIS lifecycle into two parts, with the customer precisely at the middle. The customer is the most important actor in the lifecycle, around which everything cycles. Again, this is a maximalist model, and real cases can optimize some of the aspects. This model can be briefly explained as follows:

- **The Market Making Part**: This involves not only assessing what the customer wants but also influencing him by showing how a customized

Figure 4. The lifecycle of the VEIS of a VEaaS (Virtual Enterprise as a Service)

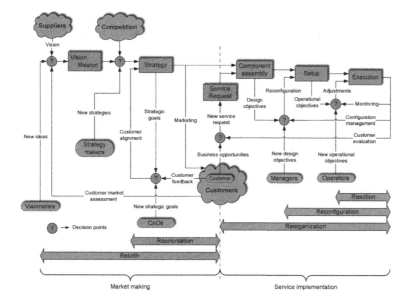

solution can solve his problems. The VEaaS must make its own customers, not just wait for them to appear. It involves two loops:

- ○ **Reorientation**: This essentially recognizes business patterns and tries to contribute to the organization and structure of the service library, to capitalize on service reuse and minimize the customization effort and implementation time. On the other hand, the customer does not always know what exactly he needs, and the service library, based on proven business patterns, can be a precious help. In other words, it contributes to the mutual alignment between the service library and the customer needs.

- ○ **Rebirth**: Necessary when new technologies, innovative ideas, or competition changes appear. The VEaaS develops its market vision from the gap between the customer needs and the suppliers offerings, which define the business opportunities, in particular when innovative ideas are available. Strategy, which must be light and agile, must also be attentive to competition, which has to be assumed agile as well.

- **The Service Implementation Part**: The VEaaS should be able to provide a new VEIS design for each customer request. Naturally, most of these requests will follow common business patterns and therefore the VEIS will actually be variants of pre-established VEIS, adequate to those patterns. How easy will be to adapt these patterns to concrete cases depends on how well the library is designed. This involves the following loops:

  - ○ **Reaction**: This is essentially the same as in a traditional EIS, but keep in mind that the VEaaS must be flexible to be adaptable, which means that monitoring and control techniques may be made more specialized and adapted to each case.

  - ○ **Reconfiguration**: This is less relevant than in a traditional EIS because reorganization, the next loop, becomes a feasible and more flexible alternative, given the customization philosophy of a VEaaS. Nevertheless, the VEIS of a VEaaS must be able to cater for situations that require frequent choice among a fixed set of configurations.

  - ○ **Reorganization**: This needs to be done in each change of pattern of customer requests. The design, development, and deployment box of Figure 1 has been replaced here by an assembly box, to make clear that this essentially involves assembling services from reusable services in the library. Adapting services and in particular developing new ones should be the exception, rather than the norm.

INTEGRATING APPLICATIONS IN THE CONTEXT OF VIRTUAL ENTERPRISES

In the context of this chapter, in which a VEIS is built as a dynamic mesh of applications provided by the collaborating enterprises, application integration is of paramount importance. Changing one of the enterprises, even if not changing anything else, will most likely mean changing objectives, processes, data formats, and so on. Therefore, reducing coupling between EIS, while ensuring the minimum business requirements for interoperability, is a fundamental factor in increasing the agility of a virtual enterprise.

The Fundamental Problem of Application Integration

Interoperability and coupling are two facets of the same problem, application integration, which revolves around two conflicting goals:

- **Interoperability**: Applications need to interact to accomplish collaboration, but it necessarily entails dependencies, since some form of mutual knowledge and understanding is required. This may hamper the evolution of these applications, since a change may prevent one application from understanding the messages from another.
- **Decoupling**: Applications can only evolve freely and dynamically if they do not have dependencies on others. Unfortunately, independent applications do not understand each other and are not able to interact, which means that some form of coupling is unavoidable to establish interoperability.

The fundamental problem of application integration is therefore how to provide *at most* the minimum coupling possible while ensuring *at least* the minimum interoperability requirements. The main goal is to ensure that each interacting application knows just enough about the others to be able to interoperate with them but no more than that. Unnecessary dependencies and constraints should be avoided. This is consistent with the information hiding principle, which itself is an instance of the principle of least knowledge (Hendricksen, 2014).

Existing data interoperability technologies, such as XML (Fawcett, Ayers, & Quin, 2012) and JSON (Bassett, 2015), assume that interacting applications share the same message schema, as illustrated by Figure 5. This can be referred to as *symmetric interoperability* and is reminiscent of the first days of the Web and HTML documents, in which the client read the document produced by the server and both needed to use the same data specification. Today, data have been separated from their specification (schema), but both client and server still work on the same information. Coupling has not diminished.

The problem is that a server may need to serve several potentially different clients and a client may need to send requests to several potentially different servers. Sharing a schema couples both client and server for the whole set of messages that the schema can describe, even if the client only uses a subset of the admissible requests and the server only responds with a subset of the admissible responses.

The net effect of this symmetry is that, in many cases, client and server are more coupled than needed and changes in one application may very likely imply changing the other as well, even if a change does not affect the actually exchanged messages.

A Layered Model of Application Interoperability

Most interoperability technologies, such as Web Services (Zimmermann, Tomlinson, & Peuser, 2012) and RESTful APIs (Pautasso, 2014), usually consider only the syntactic format of messages, or at most the semantics of its terms (Verborgh, Harth, Maleshkova, Stadtmüller, Steiner, Taheriyan, & Van de Walle, 2014; Wang, Gibbins, Payne, Patelli, & Wang, 2015). However, the ability to meaningfully interact involves higher levels, naturally including behavior. Table 3 establishes a linearized systematization of interoperability in several levels of abstraction. The higher levels are particularly relevant when complex, enterprise-class applications are involved.

The abstraction levels of interoperability can be described as follows:

- **Symbiotic**: Expresses the purpose and intent of two interacting applications to engage in a mutually beneficial agreement. This can entail a tight

Figure 5. Schema sharing in symmetric message-based interaction between two distributed applications

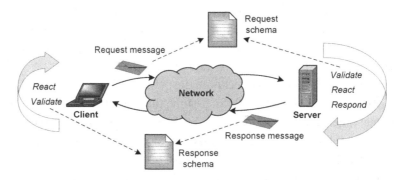

Table 3. Abstraction levels and layers of interoperability in application interactions

Abstraction Level	Layers	Description
Symbiotic (purpose and intent)	• Coordination • Alignment • Collaboration • Cooperation	• Motivations to interact, with varying levels of mutual knowledge of governance, strategy and goals.
Pragmatic (reaction and effects)	• Contract • Workflow • Interface	• Management of the effects of the interaction at the levels of choreography, process and service.
Semantic (meaning of content)	• Inference • Knowledge • Ontology	• Interpretation of a message in context, at the levels of rule, known application components and relations, and definition of concepts.
Syntactic (notation of representation)	• Structure • Predefined type • Serialization	• Representation of application components, in terms of composition, primitive components and serialization format of messages.
Connective (transfer protocol)	• Messaging • Routing • Communication • Physics	• Lower level formats and network protocols involved in transferring a message from the context of the sender to that of the receiver.

coordination under a common governance (if the applications are controlled by the same enterprise), a joint-venture agreement (if the two applications are substantially aligned), a collaboration involving a partnership agreement (if some goals are shared), or a mere value chain cooperation (an outsourcing contract). Enterprise engineering is usually the topmost level in application interaction complexity, since it goes up to the human level, with governance and strategy heavily involved. Therefore, it maps mainly onto the symbiotic layer, although the same principles apply (in a more rudimentary fashion) to simpler applications.

- **Pragmatic**: The effect of an interaction between a client and a server is the outcome of a contract, which is implemented by a choreography that coordinates processes, which in turn implement workflow behavior by orchestrating service invocations. Languages such as Business Process Execution Language (BPEL) (Juric & Weerasiri, 2014) support the implementation of processes and Web Services Choreography Description Language (WS-CDL) (Ebrahimifard, Amiri, Arani, & Parsa, 2016) is an example of a language that allows choreographies to be specified.
- **Semantic**: Interacting applications must be able to understand the meaning of the content of the messages exchanged, both requests and responses. This implies interoperability in rules, knowledge and ontologies, so that meaning

is not lost when transferring a message from the context of the sender to that of the receiver. Semantic languages and specifications, such as OWL (Matentzoglu, Parsia, & Sattler, 2017) and RDF (Tzitzikas, Manolis, & Papadakos, 2017), map onto this category.

- **Syntactic**: Deals mainly with form, rather than content. Each message has a structure, composed of data (primitive resources) according to some structural definition (its schema). Data need to be serialized to be sent over the channel as messages, using data description languages such as XML (Fawcett, Ayers, & Quin, 2012) or JSON (Bassett, 2015).
- **Connective**: The main objective is to transfer a message from the context of one application to the other's, regardless of its content. This usually involves enclosing that content in another message with control information and implementing a message protocol (such as SOAP or HTTP) over a communications network, according to its own protocol (such as the Transmission Control Protocol/Internet Protocol – TCP/IP) and possibly involving routing gateways.

All these abstraction levels are always present in all application interactions (Figure 5), even the simplest ones. There is always a motivation and purpose in sending a message, an effect stemming from the reaction to its reception, a meaning expressed by the message, and a format used to send it over a network under some protocol. However, what happens in practice is that some of these levels are catered for *tacitly* (implicitly assumed) or *empirically* (explicitly hidden behind some existing specification).

Also relevant is non-functional interoperability. It is not just a question of invoking the right operation with the right parameters. Adequate service levels, context awareness, security and other non-functional issues must be considered when applications interact, otherwise interoperability will be less effective or not possible at all. The abstraction levels of Table 3 must be considered for each of these concerns.

It is also important to realize that all these interoperability levels constitute an expression of application coupling. On the one hand, two uncoupled applications (with no interactions between them) can evolve freely and independently, which favors adaptability, changeability and even reliability (if one fails, there is no impact on the other). On the other hand, applications need to interact to cooperate towards common or complementary goals, which means that some degree of previously agreed mutual knowledge must exist. The more they share with the other, the easier interoperability becomes, but the greater coupling gets.

The Meaning of Application Coupling

Considering the graph of all the possible interactions between applications, any application that is not initial (does not receive requests from any other) or terminal (does not send requests to any other) will usually take the roles of both client and server.

Any interaction entails some form of dependency, stemming from the knowledge required to establish that interaction in a meaningful way (Figure 5), which translates to application coupling that expresses:

- How much an application depends on (is affected by changes in) the servers it uses.
- How much its clients depend on (are affected by changes in) it.

Coupling can be assessed by the fraction of the features of one application that impose constraints on another application. Features can be operations, messages, data types, semantic terms, and so on. From the point of view of a given application, two coupling metrics can be defined:

- C_F (*forward coupling*), which expresses how much an application is dependent on its servers:

$$C_F = \frac{\sum_{i \in S} \dfrac{Us_i}{Ts_i \cdot N_i}}{|S|} \tag{1}$$

where:

S - Set of servers that this application uses, with $|S|$ as its cardinality

Us_i - Number of features that this application uses in server i

Ts_i - Total number of features that server i has

N_i - Number of servers with which this application is compatible as a client, in all uses of features of server i by this application

- C_B (*backward coupling*), which expresses how much impact an application has on its clients:

$$C_B = \frac{\sum\limits_{i \in C} \dfrac{Uc_i}{Tc \cdot M}}{|C|} \tag{2}$$

where:

C - Set of clients that use this application as a server, with $|C|$ as its cardinality

Uc_i - Number of features of this application that client i uses

Tc - Total number of features that this application has

M - Number of known applications that are compatible with this application and can replace it, as a server

These coupling metrics yield values between 0, expressing completely unrelated and independent applications, and 1, in the case of completely dependent applications, constrained by all features. These metrics can be interpreted in the following way:

- Equation (1) indicates that the existence of alternative servers to a given application reduces its forward coupling C_F, since more applications with which this application is compatible (as a client) dilute the dependencies.
- Equation (2) means that having alternatives to an application, in its role as a server, reduces the overall system dependency on it, thereby reducing the impact that application may have on its potential clients (its backward coupling C_B).
- Both equations (1) and (2) also express the fact that a smaller fraction of features used induces a lower coupling.

Alternative server applications can be found not only by designing and building them on purpose, but also by reducing the fraction of features needed for compatibility to the minimum required by the interaction between applications. The smaller the number of constraints, the greater the probability of finding applications that satisfy them.

Therefore, both factors on which coupling depends (the fraction of features used, as a client, and the number of server alternatives available) work in the same direction, with the first reinforcing the second. Reducing coupling means reducing the fraction of features used, or the knowledge of one application about another. Therefore, the integration of applications designed with these issues in mind will be easier.

Technologies such as Web Services (Zimmermann, Tomlinson, & Peuser, 2012) and RESTful APIs (Pautasso, 2014) constitute poor solutions in terms of coupling, since Web Services rely on sharing a schema (a WSDL document) and RESTful APIs are usually based on previously agreed upon media types. These technologies support the distributed interoperability problem, but do not solve the coupling problem.

Compliance and Conformance as a Means to Reduce Application Coupling

Conventionally, searching for an interoperable application is done by schema matching with similarity algorithms (Elshwimy, Algergawy, Sarhan, & Sallam, 2014) and ontology matching and mapping (Anam, Kim, Kang, & Liu, 2016). This may find similar server schemas, but does not ensure interoperability and manual adaptations are usually unavoidable.

The goal in this chapter is to be able to integrate applications with exact, not just approximate, interoperability even if the client and server schemas are not identical, as long as certain requirements are verified. This does not mean being able to integrate any set of existing applications, but rather being able to change an application, due to a normal evolution in specifications, while not impairing an existing interoperability. Less coupling means greater flexibility for accommodating changes.

In this respect, two application relationships are of relevance:

- **Client-Server**: *Compliance* (Tran, Zdun, Oberortner, Mulo, & Dustdar, 2012). The client must satisfy (*comply with*) the requirements established by the server to accept requests sent to it, without which these cannot be validated and executed (Figure 6). It is important to note that any client that complies with a given server can use it, independently of having been designed for interaction with it or not. The client and server need not share the same schema. The client's schema needs only to be compliant with the server's schema in the features that it actually uses. Since distributed applications have independent lifecycles, they cannot freely share names, and schema compliance must be tested structurally, feature by feature, between messages sent by the client and the interface offered by the server. Note that in a response the roles of schema compliance are reversed.

- **Server-Server**: *Conformance* (Khalfallah, Figay, Barhamgi, & Ghodous, 2014). The issue is to ascertain whether a server 1, serving a client, can be replaced by another server 2 such that the client-server relationship enjoyed by the client is not impaired. This is illustrated by Figure 7, presented below. In other words, the issue is whether server 2 is replacement compatible with server 1. Conformance expresses the replacement compatibility between two servers. Server 2 must possess all the characteristics of server 1 (and probably more), therefore being able to take the form of (*to conform to*) of server 1 and fulfill the expectations of the client regarding what it expects the server to be. In particular, the schema of server 2 cannot include any additional mandatory component, regarding the schema of server 1, otherwise it would impose more requirements on the client and the interoperability could break. The reasons for replacing a server with another may be varied, such as switching to an alternative in case of failure or lack of capacity, evolution (in which case server 2 would be the new version of server 1), or simply a management decision.

The compliance-based interoperability mechanism of Figure 6 can be described in the following way:

- The server publishes a request *type schema*, which describes the type of request message values that the server can accept.
- The actual request message, sent by the client, is described by a *value schema*. This is simply a self-description and, unlike type schemas, includes no variability (range of structured values).
- When the request message arrives at the server, the message's value schema is validated by checking it for satisfaction of, or compliance with, the type schema of the server, in the *compliance checker*. If compliance holds, the request message is one of those that satisfy the server's request type schema and is accepted.
- The request message's value is structurally assigned to the *data template*, which is a data structure that satisfies the server's type schema and includes

Figure 6. Compliance-based interoperability; only the request message validation is shown

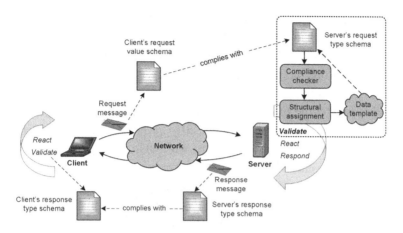

default values for the components in the type schema that are optional (minimum number of occurrences specified as zero).

- Structural assignment involves mapping the request message to the server's request type schema, by assigning the message to the data template, component by component, according to the following basic rules:
  - Components in the message that do not comply with any component in the data template are not assigned but simply ignored.
  - Components in the data template that are also present in the message have their values set to the corresponding message's component values, otherwise maintain their default values.
  - Structured components are assigned by recursive application of these rules.

After this, the data template is completely populated and ready to be accessed by the server. Each request message populates a new instance of the data template. Note that this mechanism is different from the usual data binding of existing technologies, since the server deals only with its own request message schema. It does not know the actual schema of the request message and there is no need for a data binding stub to deal with it. The mapping between the request message and the data template is done in a universal manner and does not depend on the schemas used by either the client or the server. As long as compliance holds, the structural assignment rules can be applied. This means that coupling is reduced in comparison with symmetric interoperability (Figure 5), with the following advantages:

- Coupling is limited to the actually used features of a schema and not to the full set of features of that schema.
- A client is more likely to find suitable servers based on a smaller set of features, rather than on a full schema.
- A server will be able to serve a broader base of clients, since it will impose fewer restrictions on them.

Figure 7 completes the application integration scenario by including conformance (Khalfallah, Figay, Barhamgi, & Ghodous, 2014), which expresses the ability of one application to replace another it conforms to, without impairing interoperability with existing clients. This can be useful when an application evolves (the new version replaces the old one, as long as it is conformant to it), migrates to another cloud (Figure 3), eventually with differences in its interface, or an alternative application is used due to a failure or simply to balance the load of requests.

Figure 7. Compliance and conformance in application interoperability

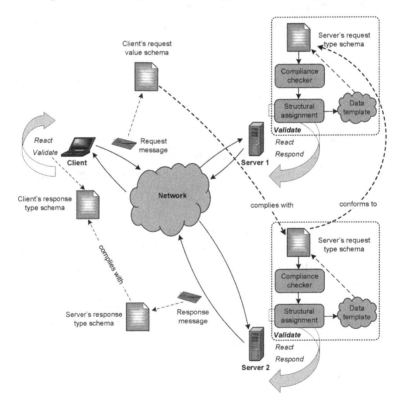

Given the huge variability possible in application interfaces, compliance and conformance are not universal solutions to find a server adequate for any given client, but can cater for client and/or server variants while supporting the substitution principle. An application can be replaced by another (as a server) without breaking the service, delegation can be used to implement part of the interface that is missing, and a server can remain in service while a variant serves new clients.

FUTURE RESEARCH DIRECTIONS

Compliance and conformance are basic concepts in application integration and can be applied to all domains and levels of abstraction and complexity. Although work exists on its formal treatment in specific areas, such as choreographies (Yang, Ma, Deng, Liao, Yan, & Zhang, 2013), an encompassing and systematic study needs to be conducted to formalize the meaning of compliance and conformance at each of the interoperability layers of Table 3. Their formal definition, across all layers, needs to be made in a systematic way.

Cloud interoperability (Kostoska, Gusev, & Ristov, 2016) is also a huge problem with increasingly importance, in which compliance and conformance can play a role. Cloud providers favor standardization but not homogeneity, since they need differentiation as a marketing argument. A study needs to be carried out on the suitability of compliance and conformance as partial interoperability solutions for cloud-based applications.

Non-functional interoperability and coupling are also important, namely in context-aware applications and in those involving the design and management of SLR (Service Level Requirements). Detailing how compliance and conformance can be applied in these cases requires additional research.

CONCLUSION

This chapter has revisited the application integration problem, in particular in cloud computing environments and at the level of virtual enterprises, with their collaborative networks. Enterprises need to interact to be able to pursue common or complementary goals. Their information systems need to be integrated in the best possible way, which means providing the minimum interoperability requirements while minimizing application coupling.

SOA and REST are the most common architectural styles that try to address this problem, but they focus more on the interoperability side of the issue than on coupling. Both require previous knowledge of the types of the resources involved in the interaction, which entails more coupling than actually required, since data schemas must be shared by the interacting applications. SOA-based technologies usually provide a link to the schema, shared by the consumer and by the provider, whereas REST-based technologies usually agree on a given schema prior to the interaction of the applications. If an application changes the schema it uses, those interacting with it must follow suit, to avoid breaking the interaction.

This chapter contends that both aspects, interoperability and coupling, need to be dealt with in a balanced way. The fundamental problem of application integration is how to achieve the minimum possible coupling, so that dependencies between applications that hinder changeability are kept to a minimum, while ensuring the minimum interoperability requirements, so that applications are able to effectively interact.

The solution preconized by this chapter is to use structural compliance (Tran, Zdun, Oberortner, Mulo, & Dustdar, 2012) and conformance (Khalfallah, Figay, Barhamgi, & Ghodous, 2014), relaxing the constraint of having to share message schemas. Two applications that share at least the characteristics actually required by interoperability can interoperate, independently of knowing the rest of the characteristics, at design, compile or runtime. This minimizes coupling with regard to both SOA and REST. Reducing the number of features of an application on which another depends not only reduces the perceivable width of the interface but also increases the number of providers that are compatible with a consumer, and vice-versa. Coupling metrics have been defined, which show that these effects reinforce each other in the goal of reducing coupling.

Although an implementation of compliance and conformance has not been discussed, it could be conceived with Web Services, for example, by including a structural section in WSDL documents. The goal is not to replace existing application integration approaches, such as SOA or REST, but rather to evaluate what can be gained, particularly in the context of virtual enterprises, including the Industry 4.0 endeavor.

REFERENCES

Abolfazli, S., Sanaei, Z., Sanaei, M. H., Shojafar, M., & Gani, A. (2016). Mobile Cloud Computing. In S. Murugesan & I. Bojanova (Eds.), *Encyclopedia of Cloud Computing* (pp. 29–40). Chichester, UK: John Wiley & Sons, Ltd. doi:10.1002/9781118821930. ch3

Agosti, M., Ferro, N., & Silvello, G. (2016). Digital library interoperability at high level of abstraction. *Future Generation Computer Systems, 55,* 129–146. doi:10.1016/j. future.2015.09.020

Agostinho, C., Ducq, Y., Zacharewicz, G., Sarraipa, J., Lampathaki, F., Poler, R., & Jardim-Goncalves, R. (2016). Towards a sustainable interoperability in networked enterprise information systems: Trends of knowledge and model-driven technology. *Computers in Industry, 79,* 64–76. doi:10.1016/j.compind.2015.07.001

Al-Fuqaha, A., Guizani, M., Mohammadi, M., Aledhari, M., & Ayyash, M. (2015). Internet of things: A survey on enabling technologies, protocols, and applications. *IEEE Communications Surveys and Tutorials, 17*(4), 2347–2376. doi:10.1109/ COMST.2015.2444095

Alenezi, M., & Magel, K. (2014). Empirical evaluation of a new coupling metric: Combining structural and semantic coupling. *International Journal of Computers and Applications, 36*(1). doi:10.2316/Journal.202.2014.1.202-3902

Anam, S., Kim, Y., Kang, B., & Liu, Q. (2016). Adapting a knowledge-based schema matching system for ontology mapping. In *Proceedings of the Australasian Computer Science Week Multiconference* (p. 27). New York, NY: ACM Press. 10.1145/2843043.2843048

Andersen, A., Brunoe, T., & Nielsen, K. (2015). Reconfigurable Manufacturing on Multiple Levels: Literature Review and Research Directions. In S. Umeda, M. Nakano, H. Mizuyama, N. Hibino, D. Kiritsis, & G. von Cieminski (Eds.), *Advances in Production Management Systems: Innovative Production Management Towards Sustainable Growth* (pp. 266–273). Cham, Switzerland: Springer International Publishing.

Babu, D., & Darsi, M. (2013). A Survey on Service Oriented Architecture and Metrics to Measure Coupling. *International Journal on Computer Science and Engineering, 5*(8), 726–733.

Bassett, L. (2015). *Introduction to JavaScript Object Notation: A to-the-point Guide to JSON.* Sebastopol, CA: O'Reilly Media, Inc.

Bidve, V. S., & Sarasu, P. (2016). Tool for measuring coupling in object-oriented java software. *IACSIT International Journal of Engineering and Technology*, *8*(2), 812–820.

Botta, A., de Donato, W., Persico, V., & Pescapé, A. (2016). Integration of cloud computing and internet of things: A survey. *Future Generation Computer Systems*, *56*, 684–700. doi:10.1016/j.future.2015.09.021

Brandt, C., & Hermann, F. (2013). Conformance analysis of organizational models: A new enterprise modeling framework using algebraic graph transformation. *International Journal of Information System Modeling and Design*, *4*(1), 42–78. doi:10.4018/jismd.2013010103

Candela, I., Bavota, G., Russo, B., & Oliveto, R. (2016). Using cohesion and coupling for software remodularization: Is it enough? *ACM Transactions on Software Engineering and Methodology*, *25*(3), 24. doi:10.1145/2928268

Capel, M., & Mendoza, L. (2014). Choreography Modeling Compliance for Timed Business Models. In *Proceedings of the Workshop on Enterprise and Organizational Modeling and Simulation* (pp. 202-218). Berlin, Germany: Springer. 10.1007/978-3-662-44860-1_12

Chen, Y. (2015). A RDF-based approach to metadata crosswalk for semantic interoperability at the data element level. *Library Hi Tech*, *33*(2), 175–194. doi:10.1108/LHT-08-2014-0078

Durugbo, C. (2016). Collaborative networks: A systematic review and multi-level framework. *International Journal of Production Research*, *54*(12), 3749–3776. doi:10.1080/00207543.2015.1122249

Ebrahimifard, A., Amiri, M., Arani, M., & Parsa, S. (2016). Mapping BPMN 2.0 Choreography to WS-CDL: A Systematic Method. *Journal of E-Technology*, *7*, 1–23.

Elshwimy, F., Algergawy, A., Sarhan, A., & Sallam, E. (2014). Aggregation of similarity measures in schema matching based on generalized mean. In *Proceedings of the IEEE International Conference on Data Engineering Workshops* (pp. 74-79). Piscataway, NJ: IEEE Computer Society Press. 10.1109/ICDEW.2014.6818306

Erl, T., Merson, P., & Stoffers, R. (2017). *Service-oriented Architecture: Analysis and Design for Services and Microservices*. Upper Saddle River, NJ: Prentice Hall PTR.

Esposito, E., & Evangelista, P. (2014). Investigating virtual enterprise models: Literature review and empirical findings. *International Journal of Production Economics*, *148*, 145–157. doi:10.1016/j.ijpe.2013.10.003

Farid, A. (2017). Measures of reconfigurability and its key characteristics in intelligent manufacturing systems. *Journal of Intelligent Manufacturing, 28*(2), 353–369. doi:10.100710845-014-0983-7

Fawcett, J., Ayers, D., & Quin, L. (2012). *Beginning XML*. Indianapolis, IN: John Wiley & Sons.

Fielding, R., Taylor, R., Erenkrantz, J., Gorlick, M., Whitehead, J., Khare, R., & Oreizy, P. (2017). Reflections on the REST architectural style and principled design of the modern web architecture. In *Proceedings of the 2017 11th Joint Meeting on Foundations of Software Engineering* (pp. 4-14). New York, NY: ACM Press. 10.1145/3106237.3121282

Geetika, R., & Singh, P. (2014). Dynamic coupling metrics for object oriented software systems: A survey. *Software Engineering Notes, 39*(2), 1–8. doi:10.1145/2579281.2579296

Ghobakhloo, M., Tang, S., Sabouri, M., & Zulkifli, N. (2014). The impact of information system-enabled supply chain process integration on business performance: A resource-based analysis. *International Journal of Information Technology & Decision Making, 13*(05), 1075–1113. doi:10.1142/S0219622014500163

Graydon, P., Habli, I., Hawkins, R., Kelly, T., & Knight, J. (2012). Arguing Conformance. *IEEE Software, 29*(3), 50–57. doi:10.1109/MS.2012.26

Grefen, P., Mehandjiev, N., Kouvas, G., Weichhart, G., & Eshuis, R. (2009). Dynamic business network process management in instant virtual enterprises. *Computers in Industry, 60*(2), 86–103. doi:10.1016/j.compind.2008.06.006

He, W., & Da Xu, L. (2014). Integration of distributed enterprise applications: A survey. *IEEE Transactions on Industrial Informatics, 10*(1), 35–42. doi:10.1109/TII.2012.2189221

Hendricksen, D. (2014). *12 More Essential Skills for Software Architects*. Upper Saddle River, NJ: Addison-Wesley Professional.

Hussain, T., Mehmood, R., Haq, A., Alnafjan, K., & Alghamdi, A. (2014). Designing framework for the interoperability of C4I systems. In *International Conference on Computational Science and Computational Intelligence* (102–106). Piscataway, NJ: IEEE Computer Society Press. 10.1109/CSCI.2014.102

Imache, R., Izza, S., & Ahmed-Nacer, M. (2012). An enterprise information system agility assessment model. *Computer Science and Information Systems, 9*(1), 107–133. doi:10.2298/CSIS101110041I

ISO. (2006). *Enterprise integration -- Framework for enterprise modelling. ISO/CEN Standard 19439:2006*. Geneva, Switzerland: International Organization for Standardization.

ISO. (2010). *Systems and software engineering – Vocabulary. ISO/IEC/IEEE 24765:2010(E) International Standard* (p. 186). Geneva, Switzerland: International Organization for Standardization.

Iyengar, S., & Brooks, R. (Eds.). (2016). *Distributed sensor networks: sensor networking and applications*. Boca Raton, FL: CRC Press.

Juric, M., & Weerasiri, D. (2014). *WS-BPEL 2.0 beginner's guide*. Birmingham, UK: Packt Publishing Ltd.

Khalfallah, M., Figay, N., Barhamgi, M., & Ghodous, P. (2014). Model driven conformance testing for standardized services. In *IEEE International Conference on Services Computing* (pp. 400–407). Piscataway, NJ: IEEE Computer Society Press. 10.1109/SCC.2014.60

Knoke, B., Missikoff, M., & Thoben, K. D. (2017). Collaborative open innovation management in virtual manufacturing enterprises. *International Journal of Computer Integrated Manufacturing, 30*(1), 158–166.

Kostoska, M., Gusev, M., & Ristov, S. (2016). An overview of cloud interoperability. In *Federated Conference on Computer Science and Information Systems* (pp. 873-876). Piscataway, NJ: IEEE Computer Society Press. 10.15439/2016F463

Kovács, G:, & Kot, S. (2017). Economic and social effects of novel supply chain concepts and virtual enterprises. *Journal of International Studies, 10*(1), 237–254. doi:10.14254/2071-8330.2017/10-1/17

Li, G., & Wei, M. (2014). Everything-as-a-service platform for on-demand virtual enterprises. *Information Systems Frontiers, 16*(3), 435–452. doi:10.100710796-012-9351-3

Liao, Y., Deschamps, F., Loures, E., & Ramos, L. (2017). Past, present and future of Industry 4.0 - a systematic literature review and research agenda proposal. *International Journal of Production Research, 55*(12), 3609–3629. doi:10.1080/00207543.2017.1308576

Marz, N., & Warren, J. (2015). *Big Data: Principles and best practices of scalable realtime data systems*. Greenwich, CT: Manning Publications Co.

Matentzoglu, N., Parsia, B., & Sattler, U. (2017). OWL Reasoning: Subsumption Test Hardness and Modularity. *Journal of Automated Reasoning*, 1–35. PMID:30069069

McLay, A. (2014). Re-reengineering the dream: Agility as competitive adaptability. *International Journal of Agile Systems and Management*, 7(2), 101–115. doi:10.1504/IJASM.2014.061430

Mezgár, I., & Rauschecker, U. (2014). The challenge of networked enterprises for cloud computing interoperability. *Computers in Industry*, 65(4), 657–674. doi:10.1016/j.compind.2014.01.017

Panetto, H., & Whitman, L. (2016). Knowledge engineering for enterprise integration, interoperability and networking: Theory and applications. *Data & Knowledge Engineering*, 105, 1–4. doi:10.1016/j.datak.2016.05.001

Patrignani, N., & Kavathatzopoulos, I. (2016). Cloud computing: The ultimate step towards the virtual enterprise? *ACM SIGCAS Computers and Society*, 45(3), 68–72. doi:10.1145/2874239.2874249

Pautasso, C. (2014). RESTful web services: principles, patterns, emerging technologies. In A. Bouguettaya, Q. Sheng, & F. Daniel (Eds.), Web Services Foundations (pp. 31-51). New York, NY: Springer.

Popplewell, K. (2014). Enterprise interoperability science base structure. In K. Mertins, F. Bénaben, R. Poler, & J. Bourrières (Eds.), *Enterprise Interoperability VI: Interoperability for Agility, Resilience and Plasticity of Collaborations* (pp. 417–427). Cham, Switzerland: Springer International Publishing. doi:10.1007/978-3-319-04948-9_35

Preidel, C., & Borrmann, A. (2016). Towards code compliance checking on the basis of a visual programming language. *Journal of Information Technology in Construction*, 21(25), 402–421.

Rezaei, R., Chiew, T., & Lee, S. (2014). A review on E-business interoperability frameworks. *Journal of Systems and Software*, 93, 199–216. doi:10.1016/j.jss.2014.02.004

Ritter, D., May, N., & Rinderle-Ma, S. (2017). Patterns for emerging application integration scenarios: A survey. *Information Systems*, 67, 36–57. doi:10.1016/j.is.2017.03.003

Robkin, M., Weininger, S., Preciado, B., & Goldman, J. (2015). Levels of conceptual interoperability model for healthcare framework for safe medical device interoperability. In *Symposium on Product Compliance Engineering* (pp. 1–8). Piscataway, NJ: IEEE Computer Society Press. 10.1109/ISPCE.2015.7138703

Samdantsoodol, A., Cang, S., Yu, H., Eardley, A., & Buyantsogt, A. (2017). Predicting the relationships between virtual enterprises and agility in supply chains. *Expert Systems with Applications, 84*, 58–73. doi:10.1016/j.eswa.2017.04.037

Schumacher, A., Erol, S., & Sihn, W. (2016). A maturity model for assessing industry 4.0 readiness and maturity of manufacturing enterprises. *Procedia CIRP, 52*, 161–166. doi:10.1016/j.procir.2016.07.040

Sharma, R., & Panigrahi, P. (2015). Developing a roadmap for planning and implementation of interoperability capability in e-government. *Transforming Government: People. Process and Policy, 9*(4), 426–447.

Şimşit, Z., Günay, S., & Vayvay, Ö. (2014). Theory of Constraints: A Literature Review. *Procedia: Social and Behavioral Sciences, 150*, 930–936. doi:10.1016/j.sbspro.2014.09.104

Toosi, A., Calheiros, R., & Buyya, R. (2014). Interconnected cloud computing environments: Challenges, taxonomy, and survey. *ACM Computing Surveys, 47*(1), 7. doi:10.1145/2593512

Tran, H., Zdun, U., Oberortner, E., Mulo, E., & Dustdar, S. (2012). Compliance in service-oriented architectures: A model-driven and view-based approach. *Information and Software Technology, 54*(6), 531–552. doi:10.1016/j.infsof.2012.01.001

Tzitzikas, Y., Manolis, N., & Papadakos, P. (2017). Faceted exploration of RDF/S datasets: A survey. *Journal of Intelligent Information Systems, 48*(2), 329–364. doi:10.100710844-016-0413-8

Verbaan, M., & Silvius, A. (2014). The Impact of IT Management Processes on Enterprise Agility. *Communications of the IIMA, 12*(1), 7.

Verborgh, R., Harth, A., Maleshkova, M., Stadtmüller, S., Steiner, T., Taheriyan, M., & Van de Walle, R. (2014). Survey of semantic description of REST APIs. In C. Pautasso, E. Wilde, & R. Alarcon (Eds.), *REST: Advanced Research Topics and Practical Applications* (pp. 69–89). New York, NY: Springer. doi:10.1007/978-1-4614-9299-3_5

Wang, H., Gibbins, N., Payne, T., Patelli, A., & Wang, Y. (2015). A survey of semantic web services formalisms. *Concurrency and Computation*, *27*(15), 4053–4072. doi:10.1002/cpe.3481

Want, R., Schilit, B., & Jenson, S. (2015). Enabling the Internet of Things. *IEEE Computer*, *48*(1), 28–35. doi:10.1109/MC.2015.12

Weeger, A., Wang, X., & Gewald, H. (2016). IT consumerization: BYOD-program acceptance and its impact on employer attractiveness. *Journal of Computer Information Systems*, *56*(1), 1–10. doi:10.1080/08874417.2015.11645795

Yang, H., Ma, K., Deng, C., Liao, H., Yan, J., & Zhang, J. (2013). Towards conformance testing of choreography based on scenario. In *Proceedings of the International Symposium on Theoretical Aspects of Software Engineering* (pp. 59-62). Piscataway, NJ: IEEE Computer Society Press. 10.1109/TASE.2013.23

Zanero, S. (2017). Cyber-physical systems. *IEEE Computer*, *50*(4), 14–16. doi:10.1109/MC.2017.105

Zhang, Z., Wu, C., & Cheung, D. (2013). A survey on cloud interoperability: Taxonomies, standards, and practice. *Performance Evaluation Review*, *40*(4), 13–22. doi:10.1145/2479942.2479945

Zimmermann, O., Tomlinson, M., & Peuser, S. (2012). *Perspectives on Web Services: Applying SOAP, WSDL and UDDI to Real-World Projects*. New York, NY: Springer Science & Business Media.

ADDITIONAL READING

Baker, T., Ugljanin, E., Faci, N., Sellami, M., Maamar, Z., & Kajan, E. (2018). Everything as a resource: Foundations and illustration through Internet-of-things. *Computers in Industry*, *94*, 62–74. doi:10.1016/j.compind.2017.10.001

Barros, A. (2015). Process Choreography Modelling. In J. vom Brocke J., M. Rosemann (Eds.) Handbook on Business Process Management (pp. 279-300). Berlin, Germany: Springer. doi:10.1007/978-3-642-45100-3_12

Bora, A., & Bezboruah, T. (2015). A Comparative Investigation on Implementation of RESTful versus SOAP based Web Services. *International Journal of Database Theory and Application*, *8*(3), 297–312. doi:10.14257/ijdta.2015.8.3.26

Dahiya, N., & Parmar, N. (2014). SOA AND REST Synergistic Approach. *International Journal of Computer Science and Information Technologies*, 5(6), 7045–7049.

Fielding, R. (2000). *Architectural Styles and the Design of Network-based Software Architectures*. Doctoral dissertation. University of California at Irvine, CA.

Käster, T., Heßler, A., & Albayrak, S. (2016). Process-oriented modelling, creation, and interpretation of multi-agent systems. *International Journal of Agent-Oriented Software Engineering*, 5(2-3), 108–133. doi:10.1504/IJAOSE.2016.080892

Kumari, S., & Rath, S. (2015). Performance comparison of SOAP and REST based Web Services for Enterprise Application Integration. In *International Conference on Advances in Computing, Communications and Informatics* (pp. 1656–1660). Piscataway, NJ: IEEE Computer Society Press. 10.1109/ICACCI.2015.7275851

Romero, D., & Vernadat, F. (2016). Enterprise information systems state of the art: Past, present and future trends. *Computers in Industry*, *79*, 3–13. doi:10.1016/j.compind.2016.03.001

Sungkur, R., & Daiboo, S. (2015). SOREST, A Novel Framework Combining SOAP and REST for Implementing Web Services. In *Proceedings of the Second International Conference on Data Mining, Internet Computing, and Big Data* (pp. 22-34). Red Hook, NY: Curran Associates, Inc.

Sungkur, R., & Daiboo, S. (2016). Combining the Best Features of SOAP and REST for the Implementation of Web Services. *International Journal of Digital Information and Wireless Communications*, 6(1), 21–33. doi:10.17781/P001923

Thakar, U., Tiwari, A., & Varma, S. (2016). On Composition of SOAP Based and RESTful Services. In *Proceedings of the 6th International Conference on Advanced Computing* (pp. 500-505). Piscataway, NJ: IEEE Computer Society Press. 10.1109/IACC.2016.99

KEY TERMS AND DEFINITIONS

Agility: The capacity of an enterprise to adapt (reactively and/or proactively) to changes in its environment in a timely and cost-efficient manner.

Compliance: Asymmetric property between a consumer C and a provider P (C is compliant with P) that indicates that C satisfies all the requirements of P in terms of accepting requests.

Conformance: Asymmetric property between a provider P and a consumer C (P conforms to C) that indicates that P fulfills all the expectations of C in terms of the effects caused by its requests.

Consumer: A role performed by a resource A in an interaction with another B, which involves making a request to B and typically waiting for a response.

Coupling: A measurement of how much an application is dependent on the interface of another application.

Interoperability: Asymmetric property between a consumer C and a provider P (C is compatible with P) that holds if C is compliant with P.

Provider: A role performed by a resource B in an interaction with another A, which involves waiting for a request from A, honoring it and typically sending a response to A.

Service: The set of operations supported by an application that together define its behavior (the set of reactions to messages that the application is able to receive and process).

Chapter 4

A Requirements Approach for Building an Enterprise Cloud Service Catalog

R. Todd Stephens
AT&T Corporation, USA

ABSTRACT

In the context of cloud computing, the service catalog is a critical component of the cloud computing architecture. Most cloud computing projects will invariably begin with a discussion of what IT services an enterprise needs. Even when end users have a cloud environment, the business still wants to know which cloud services we need and how much does it costs. Information Technology Infrastructure Library (ITIL) service design defines a service catalog as a list of technology-enabled services that an organization provides, often to its employees or customers. More specifically, the service catalog is an expression of the operational capability of a service provider or enterprise within the context of an end customer, a market space, or an internal business unit stakeholder. Unfortunately, most service catalogs are built by technologists for technologists. This design methodology is fine assuming the user of the catalog is an information technology professional.

DOI: 10.4018/978-1-5225-3182-1.ch004

INTRODUCTION

In the context of cloud computing, the service catalog is a critical component of the cloud computing architecture. Most cloud computing projects will invariably begin with a discussion of "what IT services does an enterprise need?" Even when end users have a cloud environment, the business still wants to know which cloud services do we need and how much does it cost? Information Technology Infrastructure Library (ITIL) service design defines a service catalog as a list of technology-enabled services that an organization provides, often to its employees or customers (Cisco, 2011). More specifically, the service catalog is an expression of the operational capability of a service provider or enterprise within the context of an end customer, a market space, or an internal business unit stakeholder.

Unfortunately, most service catalogs are built by technologists for technologists. This design methodology is fine assuming the user of the catalog is an information technology professional. Most service catalogs require a tremendous amount of training and education before the user can be proficient. However, one potential user of the catalog is the business user or cloud architect who is designing an infrastructure for a specific set of business requirements. These users shouldn't be forced into extensive training programs due to the high degree of complexity of the application. Good design techniques will help reduce this complexity and provide real business value for the enterprise. The key is to get your service customers to understand what cloud-based services are available, what they cost, and what they provide for greater customer satisfaction. Increased satisfaction leads to greater utility and an increase in service utilization.

This paper will review the foundational background which will include the basics of cloud computing, usability and design concepts, and the traditional functionality of a technology register. We will also introduce a collection of business requirements for a cloud service registry with a specific focus on the end user experience. An end user service cloud catalog will bridge the gap from the design requirements to the technology delivery organization. Once in the hands of IT, a more traditional service catalog can be used to leverage the service orchestration and delivery components. Finally in this paper, we will look at an actual case study to review the impact of this research. Success will be measured by reviewing the business metrics in order to show the criticality of great design techniques and using familiar models like e-commerce.

BACKGROUND

The background section is going to take a look at several different areas of the technology spectrum as they relate to this research paper. We will begin by taking a look at basics of cloud computing and the impact this technology is having on the businesses. Next, the paper will review a few of the usability frameworks and design considerations that can impact the utility of the application itself. Finally, we will review the traditional cloud service registry and the basic functional requirements needed by large organizations.

Cloud Computing Overview

In many ways, cloud computing offers up an alternative to the infrastructure ownership paradigm that is so prevalent today. Business and Information Technology organizations assumed they needed dedicated computers and software for their business needs. Over time this methodology creates infrastructure that has a lower utilization rate and limits the flexibility that is needed in today's rapidly changing environment. Cloud computing comes into focus only when you think about the core business drivers within Information Technology today. Some of these requirements include ways to increase capacity or add capabilities on the fly without investing in new infrastructure, training new personnel, or licensing new software. Cloud computing encompasses any subscription-based or pay-per-use service. Cloud computing is a model for enabling convenient, on-demand network access to a shared pool of configurable computing resources (such as networks, servers, storage, applications, and services) that can be rapidly provisioned and released with minimal management effort or service provider interaction (Akende, April, & Belle, 2013)

The service models of Infrastructure as a Service (IaaS), Platform as a Service (PaaS) and Software as a Service (SaaS) have generally become well accepted, as well as the notions of public, private and hybrid clouds. Some authors have suggested a further division of IaaS to include Hardware as a Service (Haas), Data as a Service (DaaS) and Communication as a Service (CaaS). (Butrico, M., Silva, D., & Youseff, 2008). SaaS may be the most common Cloud technology that you have used in the past. Take for example, Turbo Tax that runs in the cloud and you simply interact with the software via your computer. Nothing is actually stored on your computer and you can access the information from any device. PaaS is a little more complicated since it focuses its attention on the development of applications. Salesforce.com is an example of a company providing PaaS where you can develop applications on their platform that interact with the core Salesforce application and data. Here, the cloud service is a development platform. The final area is IaaS in which the infrastructure for your application is a cloud utility. By infrastructure, we mean databases, servers, power, and network equipment is provided for you for a utility fee. You have no long term commitment and you can simply pay for the computing service based on your usage. For instance, a cloud provider might also host its own customer-facing services on cloud infrastructure. From a hardware provisioning and pricing point of view, three aspects are new in cloud computing. The appearance of infinite computing resources available on demand, quickly enough to follow load surges, thereby eliminating the need for cloud computing users to plan far ahead for provisioning. The elimination of an up-front commitment by cloud users, thereby allowing companies to start small and increase hardware resources only when there is an increase in their needs (Armbrust, Fox, Griffith, Joseph, Katz, Konwinski, Lee, Patterson, Rabkin, Stoica, & Zaharia, 2010.)

Like any emerging paradigm of information technology, cloud computing present several research challenges that need to be addressed. While the literature reporting research challenges in cloud computing is growing quite fast, there has not been much attention paid to identify and report software engineering related challenges for designing, developing, and deploying solutions for cloud computing. We have observed that while several dozens of cloud based services are being offered, the landscape is still fragmented and there are no comprehensive guidelines for designing, developing and deploying solutions to leveraging cloud computing. Moreover, we have also observed that there is hardly any guidance available for migrating existing systems to cloud computing in terms of software engineering aspects (Babat & Chauhan, 2011).

Usability and Design Standards

The idea of usability as a key theme in the Human-Computer Interaction (HCI) literature is not new. Research in this area has been reviewed for several decades now. The basic idea is that study of human factors is a critical component in all software applications. The main goal of HCI is to propose and review techniques, methods, and guidelines associated with designing better and more usable interfaces. Research of web site usability, application usability, and now mobile interfaces all share a common goal which is to provide a better end user experience. Some research focuses on the existence or non-existence of specific functional components. Other research reviews the environment based on the emotions of the end user as well as the ability to provide a positive or negative experience. This paper is going to focus time and energy on the functional and design elements of a web application.

The goal of this paper is to ask the question does usability have an impact on a cloud registry environment. Can you apply usability principles to a cloud registry environment and see an improvement in end user engagement? First, we need to define what usability actually is or is not. The importance of usability is well documented. Lecerof and Paterno (1998) defined usability to include the concepts of relevance, efficiency, user attitude, learnability, and safety. The ISO organization defines usability as the extent to which a product can be used by specified users to achieve goals with effectiveness, efficiency, and satisfaction within a pattern of contextual use (Karat, 1997). Usability is the broad discipline of applying sound scientific observation, measurement, and design principles to the creation and maintenance of web applications in order to bring about the greatest ease of use, ease of learnability, amount of usefulness, and least amount of discomfort for the humans who use the application (Pearrow, 2000). Shackel (2009) describes usability as "a technology's capability to be used easily and effectively by the specified range of users, given specified training and user support, to fulfill the specified range of tasks, within the specified range of environmental scenarios". Usability refers to terms such as ease of use and ease of learning that implied providing users with systems requiring minimum cognitive and physical effort to accomplish users' needs and expectations (Sindhuja & Surajith, 2009). All of these definitions focus on the ability of the user to leverage the application for value creation.

There are various schools of thought on which design elements make a successful web site. Scanlon, Schroeder, Snyder, and Spool (1998) collected qualitative and quantitative data on key design factors, which included: searching, content, text links, images, links navigation, page layout, readability, graphics, and user's knowledge. Each of these design elements makes an important contribution to a successful website. Attractive websites are visually pleasant, and appeal the interest of the users, whether it is functionality or information. Appearance of a website is a crucial factor that improves the perception of information in order for subjects to perform better cognitive mapping and assessment of decisions for execution. The same study suggests that the graphical representations such as icons, colors, images and animations, give website a higher attractiveness. This could improve the degree of users' satisfaction with the website (Mentes & Turan, 2012). Websites are built to provide information or sell a product or service. Experts indicate that usability is about making sure that the average person can use the site as intended. Well-chosen names, layout of the page, text, graphics, and navigation structure should all come together to create instantaneous recognition (Krug, 2000). Becker and Mottay (2001) developed a usability assessment model used to measure a user's experience within a web environment. The authors defined eight usability factors, which included page layout, navigation, design consistency, information content, performance, customer service, reliability, and security. Usability and design can play an important role within the electronic commerce market. Design consistency has been defined as the key to usability (Nielsen, 1998). Karvonen (2000) reported that experienced users admitted to making intuitive and emotional decisions when shopping online. Some users simply stated, "If it looks pleasant then I trust it". Even if developing trust is not that simple, the research clearly shows how important design is in the area of trust.

There are a variety of web design elements that can have a positive impact on a website's image, effectiveness, and trustworthiness. Design elements like well-chosen images, clean and clear layout, careful typography, and a solid use of color can create an effective site. In addition, a solid navigation structure and continuity in design can provide the user with the control and access required within an electronic commerce interface (Andres, 1999). Although, design elements may take on the form of a visual cue, the true value comes from a combination presentation, structure, and interactivity. A solid website is a collaboration of design, content, usability, and a back end system that is integrated into the processes of the business (Veen, 2001). Krug (2000) defines a set of tools as location indicators, which are design elements of the site that tells the user where they are. This can be in the form of a page name, header, sitemap or page utility. The page utility should be used within a list type program, which allows the user to know where they are within the list of elements. Indicators like "Page 1 of 12" can be extremely helpful informing the user of their location. Nielsen (2000) describes the need for the user to know where they are, where they have been and where they can go.

Usability is increasingly recognized as an essential factor that determines the success of software systems. Practice shows that for current software systems, most usability issues are detected during testing and deployment. Fixing usability issues during this late stage of the development proves to be very costly. Some usability-improving modifications such as usability patterns may have architectural implications. We believe that the software architecture may restrict usability. The high costs associated with fixing usability issues during late-stage development prevent developers from making the necessary adjustments for meeting all the usability requirements (Bosch, J., Folmer, E., & Gurp, J., 2004)

Traditional Services of a Cloud Registry

A cloud service registry may also be known as a metadata repository in that it does not contain the actual service but the associated metadata describing that service. The external service registries store and maintain various types of service specifications for a certain service including structural specifications represented in WSDL, behavioral specifications represented in BPEL4WS, quality specification represented in different XML-based schema, and context specification represented in specific XML-based ontologies (Dooley, Spanoudakis, & Zisman, 2008). The cloud service registry is a critical component for developing trust and enabling a successful cloud deployment (Muchahari & Sinha, 2012). Many researchers understand that service discovery is critical to the success of a cloud implementation by providing that single point of access to multiple services (Bratanis, Braun, Paraskakis, Rossini, Simons, & Verginadis, 2014).

The automated provisioning of services in cloud computing environment present several challenges to any organization. Users can request virtual machines from cloud infrastructure providers, but these machines have to be configured and managed properly. This article describes an architecture that enables the automated deployment and management of the virtual infrastructure and software of services deployed in the cloud. The architecture takes a template description of a service, which encapsulates requirements, options, as well as behavior for a collection of resources and orchestrates the provisioning of this service into a newly created set of virtual resources. The template is used for integrating the deployment and reconfiguration behavior of a service in which logical components are described along with options to scale them and appropriately change their configuration. Services are described through a set of components, which can easily be mapped and remapped to dynamically created resources, letting services take full advantage of flexible cloud resources (Kirschnick, J., Alcaraz Calero, J., Wilcock, L. & Edwards, N., 2010). The implementation of a cloud service catalog can provide some simplifications for the end user where the complexity of the cloud environment is hidden.

With cloud computing, service providers enjoy greatly simplified software installation and maintenance and centralized control over versioning and offload these problems to cloud computing provider The diversity of the services hosting on the infrastructures or platforms provided by clouds brings a challenge: how to discover the most suitable service cater to the discovery request of service consumer which includes functional requirements and nonfunctional requirements (Chen & Li, 2010). Much has been written in the literature about automatic discovery based on functional requirements. However, most early implementations of cloud computing rarely review the catalog from an end user perspective. In this perspective, the service catalog is an integral and critical component of the cloud computing architecture. By reviewing the landscape of vendor offerings, most service registries focus on the service orchestration or deployment automation of the services. Unfortunately, the usability of these applications are poor and can only be used with extensive training. The gap in the architecture is having the ability for the traditional information worker to review and order services. The cloud services approach focuses on a positive user experience while shielding the user from the complexity of the underlying technology. Each cloud service progresses through a well-defined life cycle: The cloud service provider defines the cloud services to be offered and exposes them via a service catalog; service requesters instantiate the services, which are managed against a set of service-level agreements; and finally the cloud service is destroyed when it is no longer needed (Breiter, G., & Behrendt, M., 2009).

RESEARCH REVIEW

Based on the research provided in this paper, there is a need for a cloud service registry build on solid usability principles that can be used by the average end user. From the traditional services research section, we see a very complex cloud registry design is used in today's solutions. This makes sense when you think about the main requirement of automation and integration. However, business users that leverage this type of registry find very difficult to understand and a lot of training is required in order to be able to perform even the simplest of functions. When users want cloud services provided in a seamless and clear understanding way, traditional design is flawed.

Business Oriented Cloud Service Catalog

During the latter part of 2009 and early 2010, the AT&T cloud program interviewed a collection of information technology professionals on what they would like to see in a cloud service catalog. The results of this interview and documentation of business requirements provided a different set of needs than the one's traditionally found in the information technology area. In this case project managers, business users, and architectural planners wanted to focus more on the service catalog functions provided by the application. The following is a result of the documented business requirements needed by this group of users:

- The users wanted a single location to get cloud services regardless if those services were virtualized cloud environments or dedicated hardware.
- The users wanted to be able to search, filter and sort services based on their needs.
- The users wanted to be able to view the detailed specifications of the cloud services or any associated content that would provide additional information.
- The users wanted to be able to bundle cloud services into a single order.
- The users wanted to be able to get a price based on the quantity of services ordered.
- The users wanted to be able to get a total price for all the services ordered.
- The users wanted to be able to complete the order with a one button click.
- The users wanted to be able to do duplicate an order as well as change it.
- The users wanted online support, help, and a click to chat function.
- The cloud managers wanted to be able to update the offerings without relying on developers.
- The users wanted integrated workflow and approvals

From these business requirements we can see that the end-user is more focused on features and functionality versus the integration of backend systems. That is to say that while information technology focuses on integration and orchestration, the end-user was more concerned about what services were available, how they can get them, and how fast they can get a functional environment up an operational. The overall goal of the information technology department is to move to a much more seamless environment. An environment that is customer focused and one that can fulfill the needs of the customer as quickly as possible. By leveraging this type of cloud service registry, the end-user has the ability to fulfill those obligations and get their cloud infrastructure configured ordered configured set up and completed within days or even hours.

Business Layer of the Cloud Service Catalog

Figure 1 provides an overview of the business requirements presented in the prior section. The left side of the diagram is the service administration area while the right side represents the business functions associated with the information worker. The middle section represents the cloud service catalog which integrates with the service orchestration application at the bottom of the diagram. The service catalog acts like an ordering platform for cloud services and any specific conditions associated with the services themselves. With the service catalog, we can leverage the system for demand management as well as a governance platform for controlling the services available and service level agreements.

Starting with the left side, there are many administration type functions that a cloud service catalog could perform. The first box represents the service inventory which is the inventory of IaaS, SaaS, and PaaS services that the end user can order. These services can be bundled in order to build a complete vertical environment designed for the specific business need. The specification section is the detailed service information that can be used to describe the service. This content would include sizing information, various pricing models and a variety of categorical classifications. The metadata of the service could be segmented into the database or included in the more detailed specification. There is really no limit to the information that can be captured and then shared back to the end user. Even obscure information like service retirement data, transactions processed, or frequency of use could be leveraged by the end user to decide on a particular service.

With all of this metadata, the service catalog can leverage this information to provide functional services which create a better end user experience. Everything from search to service classifications, the catalog can make it easy to locate and

Figure 1. Cloud registry functionality structure

Service Administration	Service Catalog	Information Workers
Service Inventory	Service Catalog	Bundling Services
Service Specifications	Service Location	Project Requests
Service Metrics	Service Associations	Cost Estimation

Service Orchestration

procure the cloud services. Other features such as notifications, sorting, and bundling can extend the service catalog's utility to the community. Specifications may also include sizing options and any custom configurations are available. Specifications are usually more detailed documentation for the service which include usage rates, pricing, and service level agreements.

Metrics have always been an important part of information technology. Unfortunately for the most part, metrics are an afterthought of the project or application itself. The natural progression of a system that moves from innovation, incubation, and migration (or the SDLC of choice) is to eventually measure the impact and value-add to the business. Some metrics are simply irrelevant to the cloud work being done or do not have a direct impact on the long term success of the program. Information gets gathered, but no action is taken as a result. Take a look at the performance metrics in the service catalog and ask yourself, "When was the last time we took an action, based on this number?" Many times metrics are used as a weapon against the staff member. Dr. Edward Deming often said, "We need to drive fear out of the workplace" but most performance measurement systems do exactly the opposite. Two key categories of metrics include content and usage based metrics. Content metrics describe what information we have inside the repositories. Without considering how the data is used; content focuses on the what. Perhaps the most obvious example of content metrics is the service count. A service count sounds like a simple concept except for fact that there are multiple methods for defining what classifies as a service. We can measure the breath and scope of these service metadata elements for each object type as well as the percentage of completeness for the model itself. Some objects may have an extended meta-model with 20 metadata elements while others may only contain only a few. The number of attachments is another measurement that we can take on a specific asset. The thinking here is that objects that have extended unstructured documentation are better understood than those with only a few attachments. Examples of attachments could include service level agreements, service models, user guides, installation instructions, etc. The relationship is another content metric that most implementations fail to measure. Relationships between service assets can follow into a wide variety of classifications: assimilation, classification, semantic, and activity based. The most obvious relationship between assets is the assimilation relationship which basically states that one asset is directly, systematically, and purposefully related to another. The classification relationship is a basic domain based relationship. The activity base relationships are created by reviewing the usage metrics which in turn create relationships like "Most Popular" or "Top Ten Downloads". Content metrics should be captured on a monthly basis and evaluated by utilizing trend analysis software which evaluates the information over an extended period of time. Ideally, the process of collection should be automated and have the ability to capture at any point in time. What growth percentage should be applied to the content metrics? Again, long term success is not defined by the explosion of growth in the first year but by the subsequent 3-5 years. The other key metric is usage. Remember, you can have all of the content in the world but without usage you haven't done much more than build a nice inventory. Usage is the key to delivering long term value-add to the organization. The first usage metric class is focused on the user. Many web based applications utilize three high-level classifications for user traffic. A "hit" is each individual file sent to a browser by the web server. A "page view" can be described as each time a visitor views a webpage on your site, irrespective of how many hits are generated. Web pages are comprised of files. Every image in a page is a separate file. When a visitor looks at a page (i.e. a page view), they may see numerous images, graphics, pictures etc. and generate multiple hits. For example, if you have a page with 10 pictures, then a request to a server to view that page generates 11 hits (10 for the pictures, and one for the html file). A page view can contain hundreds of hits. This is the reason that we measure page views and not hits. Additionally, there is a high potential for confusion here, because there are two types of 'hits'. The hits we are discussing in this article are the hits recorded by log files, and interpreted by log analysis. A second type of 'hits' are counted and displayed by a simple hit counter. Hit counters record one hit for every time a webpage is viewed, also problematic because it does not distinguish unique visitors. The third type of class is a visitor which is a human being, and their actions are 'human' events, because only humans navigate the internet. We can also track the length of time a person stays on the service catalog, what time of day is most popular, and which day compromises the heaviest traffic. These time based metrics are important to ensure the repository is up and operational 100% of the time, especially during high traffic periods. Now, if we move away from the user and focus the attention on the actual page or artifact, other metrics provide insight. We can tell which of the asset pages is viewed the most and which artifact has the highest download rate. These simple metrics may alter the way you present artifacts and even generate new classifications. Having links on the repository that represent "Most Popular", "Most Downloaded" or "Latest Additions" add value to the metadata environment. These classifications are defined as usage based classifications. In other words, the use of the repository actually defines the classification of the assets. Assuming your repository has some advanced features, you can measure how many subscriptions per asset you have, how many transactions may be processed by the component, or what is the reuse level within the application. Remember, you can generate any number of metrics but we should only focus on the ones that can generate action, support the expansion of the brand, and help managers understand the environment.

On the information worker side, we start with the idea to bundle services together. We could bundle the services based on size; such as a large server collection. Users may also bundle services associated with the business function. For example a business unit that needs a Web server might select a small database with a couple Web server applications on top these bundling type activities to be preconfigured. Another function of bundling service is the idea of associating orders with past orders. This would allow the end-user to duplicate or replicated an order for a future application or project. The second area, project requests, would allow for things such as project approval, verification a budget, and executive oversight that would be required. The final area would include the cost estimation with service pricing. An end user can get a cost estimate which they can then take back to their business unit to gain approval. The lower circle in figure 4 indicates the need for the catalog to integrate with service orchestration piece of the infrastructure. Service orchestration is the applications that will create the virtual environments.

USABILITY CRITERIA FOR APPLICATION SYSTEMS

Criteria for evaluating the usability of cloud registry systems should follow similar usability issues with traditional web applications and business systems. A common set of criteria needs to be developed which could be used across all cloud registry applications. Singh and Wesson (2009) provide some of the common usability criteria including the following items:

- Ease of use
- Usefulness
- Task Support
- Navigation
- Guidance
- Flexibility
- Image Design
- Customization
- Memorability
- Accuracy and Completeness
- Learnability
- Performance and Stability
- Visual Appeal

- System Reliability
- System Responsiveness
- UI Presentation
- Output Presentation

In order to simplify the research, this paper will condense the list into five basic categories of usability constructs in order to evaluate improvements made on the cloud registry application. These will include the following:

- Visual Appeal of the application and cloud registry functionality
- System Performance of the cloud registry tool
- Ease of Use which will include the concepts of customization and navigation
- Learnability of the cloud registry application
- Task Support which includes workflow, form management, and basic cloud registry functionality

The aim of this paper is to propose a set of characteristics that are specific to cloud registry applications. This is necessary to address the inconsistent engagement of most cloud registry environments. The following sections will look at these five criteria and how they can be applied to cloud registry environments. In order to measure usability, we will define a set of heuristics or descriptors to manage the improvements. This will allow us to define specific criteria that can be evaluated in order to show the improved usability. Based on the criteria we can then measure the improvements in the cloud registry environment.

Visual Appeal

Visual appeal is a phrase used for application components that impact the presentation of information. Many technical solutions focus on putting as much information on the screen as possible with little regard to how that presentation provides context and meaning. Visual appeal includes components such as page layout, image quality, color palette, font selection, dialog boxes, controls, and form elements. Visual appeal can be reviewed by the following heuristics:

- Visual layout of the information
- Image Quality
- Measuring the accuracy and understanding of the information being presented
- Intuitiveness of the interface
- Consistency of the design

System Performance

System performance is a measurement of the how the system performs in handling the user requests. We can measure the performance by the speed by which processes requests and the number of concurrent users within a specific environment. Research suggests that performance impacts usability with a positive correlation in the areas of efficient access, search success, flexibility, understanding of content, relevant search result, and satisfaction (Janecek & Uddin, 2007). System performance can be evaluated by the following heuristics:

- Transaction Processing Speed
- End User Task Accomplishment
- Expected Results (i.e. search results)
- Learning Times
- End User Satisfaction

Ease of Use

Perceived ease of use is the extent to which a person believes that using a technology will be free of effort. Perceived ease of use is a construct tied to an individual's assessment of the effort involved in the process of using the system (Venkatesh, 2000). Ease of use can be reviewed by the following heuristics:

- Navigation Elements
- End User Task Accomplishment
- Learning Times
- End User Satisfaction
- Ability to locate specific information
- Timeliness of information presented

Learnability

Learnability is in some sense the most fundamental usability attribute of cloud registry applications (Nielsen, 2000). The system should be easy to learn so that the user can rapidly start getting value from the application. As Dzida, Herda, and Itzfelt (1978) reported, learnability is especially important for novice users. Learnability can be described as the amount of effort in using a new Web site and to measure how easy a site for new visitors to orient themselves and get a good overview of what the site offers (Jeng, 2005). Ease of use can be reviewed by the following heuristics:

- Time required to learn the application
- Access to online help and community support
- Ability to actively contribute to the conversation is a short period of time
- Consistency of the design
- Complexity of the core tasks

Task Support

The idea of task support is an alignment between the technical world and the business environment. Does the technology support the business environment by ensuring tasks are started, completed, and communicated effectively? Task support deals with how well a product or system enables users to perform their typical tasks to achieve their goals with the product (Anschuetz, L., Keirnan, T. & Rosenbaum, S., 2002). Task support can be reviewed by the following heuristics:

- Consistent terminology is used in the application
- Consistent use of imagery and style based on the organizational style
- Information is real and contextual in nature
- Confirmation of tasks
- Tasks process support and state communication
- Automation of redundant tasks
- Personalization of content and context

CASE STUDY

The research methodology was designed to provide a basis for usability along with a heuristic evaluation. The goal of the study is to demonstrate that improvements in usability will increase the usage and utility of a cloud registry environment. Usage can be defined as the number of times an end user consumes the information which is represented by the number of visits, downloading documentation and actual service orders. Utility or utilization is measured by the number of changes in the environment which come in the form of information updates. Updates can be measured by the number of adds, changes, and deletes across all of the content containers within the online environment. Table 1 provides a detailed mapping of the design elements presented in this paper and how they were implemented in the actual project.

Design Review

With the design information, the organization setup out to build a common cloud portal which would house information about cloud computing. This information would come in the form of written content, social media platforms, online videos, and other interactive components. The goal of the design was to increase the end user experience by implementing the usability criteria defined above. Additionally, the design would include a common cloud service catalog which would drive the deployment of cloud services throughout the enterprise.

Figure two provides a visual example of the home page for the cloud portal. The main focus of the design on the informational style pages is in the visual design, use of images, and ease of use. The rotating banner allows the cloud organization to spotlight a variety of touch points for the end user as well as enhancing the graphical user interface. Cloud users can find the latest information on the services in the catalog, a collection of training materials, access to the social media environment

Table 1. Table type styles

Design Elements	Implementation	
	How the Technique Was Implemented	
Visual Appeal	Overall Design of the Portal Professional Cloud Images Consistency of Design	
System Performance	Build upon SharePoint Infrastructure Leverage XML Data Exchange Local JQuery Responsive Design for Mobile Devices	
Ease of Use	Leverage Shopping Cart Patterns Consistent Navigation Feedback Integrated Shopping Cart Inventory	
Learnability	Online Help Social Media Community for Support Visual Progression for Online Orders Saving Cloud Service Cart	
Task Support	Order Confirmations Email Confirmations Consistent Use of Cloud Related Images Site Map for all Cloud Resources	

Figure 2. Example home page

for the cloud organization, and access to the latest communications. The variety of information available helps the site focus on task support related to accessing cloud services as well as other features of a cloud environment. Additional integration elements, such as RSS, are present to allow for information exchange with different tools such as native RSS readers, outlook, and web browsers. Users also have the ability to subscribe for email alerts in the social media environment which provides a greater sense of integration. By making the site easy to use and ensuring a consistency in design, we address many of the learnability issues related to internally developed web applications.

Figure 3 contains the actual service catalog. The service catalog contains all of the PaaS, SaaS, and IaaS services available for purchase. The site provides a "Show Me" filter that allows the services to be filtered by type, category, size, and operating system. Each service contains metadata information pertaining to the actual service including category, type, operating system, size, number of CPU's, memory, storage, and cost breakdown. The service specification can be downloaded to provide a physical copy of what the end user can see on the screen. The catalog leverages the traditional shopping cart methodology which is familiar to most information

Figure 3. Product view

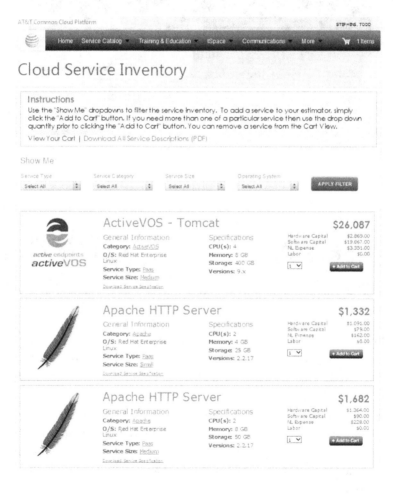

technology professionals. End users can add the different services along with the quantities to the shopping cart. The catalog leverages a consistent look and feel with the rest of the site to ensure users follow a pattern of usability. Once a user has completed selecting which services they need, they can then click the shopping cart to get a final price. The right side of figure 3 provides a visual of the shopping cart screen. The primary purpose of this screen is to provide the end-user a last chance to review the services they placed into the cart, quantities of those services they asked for as well as the pricing breakdown. The user will also be able to update the quantities of services or delete the service from the card from this particular screen. Review Impact of a Functional Business Cloud Service

The main research question was to determine if these design elements can make a difference to the number of services or quantity of cloud environments that are being built? While the cloud program was operational for 12 months prior to the implementation, the correlation of impact may be elusive but the success is difficult to be ignored.

Take a look at Figure 4 where the number of cloud environments have been charted with a resulting linear trend line. The base metric was the actual number of cloud environments constructed. During the first full-year about 240 cloud environments were created by the deployment teams. We have taken the first 12 months of cloud deployments and mapped that along a linear progression to estimate where this number should be over the next three years. The lower line or blue line, in Figure 4, shows this trend. As an example by the end of the second year an estimated 1,000 cloud environments should have been built. By the end of the fourth year, we should have upwards of 2,200 cloud environments constructed.

Figure 4. Cloud implementations over four years

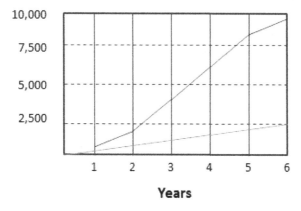

The second trend line (red) starts the environment calculation after the cloud portal was implemented; after the first 12 months of deployment. Notice that by the end of the second quarter of the second year, we exceeded 2,500 environments. Today, we have over 9,700 cloud environment created. Clearly, the introduction of the cloud portal and service catalog influenced the number of environments constructed during the second and third years. This indicates that the ability to integrate the end-user business requirements as well as getting cost estimations actually makes it easier to do business with the cloud environment. This translates into more cloud environments and more conversions to the cloud infrastructure. The two trend lines indicate a divergence between the original estimate and the new trend line. By the end of year five, this difference was upwards of 7,000 sites.

Now the question that remains, what would have the infrastructure growth had been if this education portal, information design elements and integration had not taken place. Clearly they would be some element of growth because as with all programs early in their nature may or may not take off that will eventually continue to move forward. That is to say that the assumptions on the linear trend line may not have continued but more of an exponential growth would be seen. However, with the limited amount of data and not having a comparison environment, we have to assume the increase in environments is influenced by the ease of use as well as the information presented in the portal.

Based on subject matter expert interviews with the cloud program leadership, the cloud information portal benefited the program greatly on three different fronts. The first front was the online communications, education and training that was provided to the community. The ability to communicate the benefits of the cloud program including the cost advantages was an critical step in the deployment plan. End users needed to know what the cloud was as well as why they should migrate to this new type of infrastructure. Having the information was important but having it easy to locate and consume was just as critical. Many of the interviewees commented on how professional the application looked which in turn gave the program more credibility. This was important during the early stages when many of the automated pieces were not in place. Other comments focused on the familiarity of the end user shopping cart paradigm. Most people understand how the shopping cart works and the transition from physical goods to cloud services was relatively easy.

The second area which was aided by the design function was of course the service catalog itself. Normally services would have included a Word document to describe the specific of the service. The service catalog provided the end-user with a list of services and the ability to filter, search, and categorize them. This creates the ability to find services which increases the desire to actually move into the cloud environment. This front end environment also enables cloud service managers the ability to edit service metadata such as prices sizing configurations memory and storage very easily. This means that price shifts or price changes are automatically updated. For example a price that may change in the backend but then requires a programmer effort in order to get that price implemented. This was accomplished by leveraging feeds from the orchestration element so that the prices and quantities and sizing all always up-to-date

The final area of improvement is the ability to integrate the application with the project management systems as well as the orchestration environment. Project management here means the ability to get a budget, get approvals, and then process the order within the cloud environment. By integrating the cloud portal with the backend applications, we reduced the length of time that it took to process an order for a cloud service to drop. The next major task in the process is the ability to build the physical infrastructure. Cloud orchestration powers the self-service portals that allow end users to employ a browser interface to rapidly provision services and resources available from a catalog of standardized offerings. With orchestration software, we can streamline the process and reduce the time required to implement a cloud solution. Based on the results, the studied organization reduced the time required to build the virtual cloud environment by 85%. This decrease was in large part based on the increased integration and the automation putting both to update pricing as well as to integrate the prices into the backing orchestration applications. The largest gap in time is for the budget approvals which are still manual in that an individual must approve the order. Unlike external cloud environments that can take an order without budget approval, large organizations still have this oversight in place.

FUTURE RESEARCH DIRECTIONS

The design structure and case study introduced in this paper provides a natural guide to future research. Typically, case studies have a much narrower domain due to the nature of business. That is to say, businesses generally do not allow for multiple iterations in order to produce a working product. Additional case studies would provide a much broader perspective and analysis which will expand the body of knowledge in this space. This paper set out to show how solid design principles could be applied to an end user cloud service catalog. The results of which have been positive but additional research needs to be done as cloud computing moves toward a more mature technology. The transition from an information technology perspective to one based on general knowledge workers comes with maturity of the technology itself. Therefore, additional research needs to be done to aid this transition.

CONCLUSION

Cloud computing offers several opportunities of using IT infrastructures as a utility with the possibility of scaling up or scaling down depending upon the needs an organization. However, like most of the emerging IT technologies, cloud computing has raised several technical and design challenges. The research question that this paper wanted to address was to determine if good design based on human factors would improve the deployment of cloud services. Can we leverage other design research and improve how cloud services are defined, discovered, and selected in order to expand the value to the business? While this paper only focused on a single implementation, it is clear that great design does help the deployment of cloud based services. From the simple education and expansion of knowledge around cloud computing to the actual ordering process, design elements improve the overall experience from the end users perspective. We have not observed much literature on software engineering aspects of developing and evolving cloud-enabled catalog systems that focus on the end user versus the core integration and orchestration tasks. During this project, we studied the common cloud portal which allowed us to test the design elements and then review the impact by the number of orders and cloud infrastructure environments. This paper aimed at sharing our experiences and observations gained through this project and critical analysis of the literature with those who intend to move toward a more user friendly service catalog.

REFERENCES

Akande, A., April, N., & Belle, J. (2013). Management Issues with Cloud Computing. In *Proceedings of the Innovative Computing and Cloud Computing*. Wuhan, China: The Association of Computing Machinery.

Alcaraz, J., Calero, J., Edwards, N., Kirschnick, J., & Wilcock, L. (2010). Toward an architecture for the automated provisioning of cloud services. *Communications Magazine, IEEE, 48*(12), 124–131. doi:10.1109/MCOM.2010.5673082

Andres, C. (1999). *Great Web Architecture*. Foster City, CA: IDG Books World Wide.

Anschuetz, L., Keirnan, T., & Rosenbaum, S. (2002). Combining Usability Research with Documentation Development for Improved User Support. In *Proceedings of the SIGDOC*. Toronto, Canada: The Association of Computing Machinery.

Armbrust, A., Fox, A., Griffith, R., Joseph, A., Katz, R., Konwinski, A., ... Zaharia, M. (2010). Above the Clouds: A View of Cloud Computing. *Communications of the ACM*, *53*(4), 50. doi:10.1145/1721654.1721672

Babat, M., & Chauhan, M. (2011). A Tale of Migration to Cloud Computing for Sharing Experiences and Observations. In *Workshop on Software Engineering for Cloud Computing*. Honolulu, HI: IEEE.

Becker, S., & Mottay, F. (2001). A global perspective on website usability. *IEEE Software*, *18*(1), 61–54. doi:10.1109/52.903167

Behrendt, M., & Breiter, G. (2009). Life Cycle Characteristics of Services in the World of Cloud Computing. *IBM Journal of Research and Development*, *53*(4), 527–534.

Bratanis, K., Braun, S., Paraskakis, I., Rossini, A., Simons, A., & Verginadis, Y. (2014). Advanced Service Brokerage Capabilities as the Catalyst for Future Cloud Service Ecosystems. In *Proceedings of the Cross Cloud Brokers*. Bordeaux, France: The Association of Computing Machinery.

Butrico, M., Silva, D., & Youseff, L. (2008). Toward a unified ontology of cloud computing. In *Grid Computing Environments Workshop*. Austin, TX: IEEE.

Chen, H., & Li, S. (2010). SRC: A Service Registry on Cloud Providing Behavior-aware and QoS-aware service discovery. In *International Conference on Service-Oriented Computing and Applications*. Perth, Australia: IEEE.

Cisco. (2011). *The Need for Service Catalog Design in Cloud Services Development*. Corporate White Paper.

Dooley, J., Spanoudakis, G., & Zisman, A. (2008). Proactive Runtime Service Discovery. In *Proceedings of IEEE 2008 International Service Computing Conference*. Honolulu, HI: IEEE.

Dzida, W., Herda, S., & Itzfelt, W. (1978). User-perceived quality of interactive systems. *IEEE Transactions on Software Engineering*, *SE-4*(4), 270–276. doi:10.1109/TSE.1978.231511

Folmer, E., Gurp, J., & Bosch, J. (2004). Software Architecture Analysis of Usability. *The 9th IFIP Working Conference on Engineering for Human-Computer Interaction*.

Janecek, P. (2007). Faceted classification in web information architecture: A framework for using semantic web tools. *The Electronic Library, 25*(2), 219–233. doi:10.1108/02640470710741340

Jeng, J. (2005). Usability assessment of academic digital libraries: Effectiveness, efficiency, satisfaction, and learnability. Libri. *International Journal of Libraries and Information Services, 55*(2/3), 96–121.

Karat, J. (1997). User-centered software evaluation methodologies. In M. Helander, T. K. Landauer, & P. Prabhu (Eds.), *Handbook of Human-Computer Interaction* (pp. 689–704). New York: Elsevier Press. doi:10.1016/B978-044481862-1.50094-7

Karvonen, K. (2000). The beauty of simplicity. In *Proceedings of the ACM Conference on Universal Usability*. Arlington, VA: The Association of Computing Machinery.

Krug, S. (2000). *Don't Make Me Think*. Indianapolis, IN: New Riders Publishing.

Lecerof, A., & Paterno, F. (1998). Automatic Support for Usability Evaluation. *IEEE Transactions on Software Engineering, 24*(10), 863–888. doi:10.1109/32.729686

Mentes, A. & Turan, A. (2012). Adressing the Usability Of University Websites: An Empirical Study On Namik Kemal University. *Tojet, 11*(3).

Muchahari, M., & Sinha, S. (2012). A New Trust Management Architecture for Cloud Computing Environment. *2012 International Symposium on Cloud and Services Computing (ISCOS)*, 136-140 10.1109/ISCOS.2012.30

Nielsen, J. (1998). Introduction to web design. In *Proceedings of the SIGCHI on Human Factors in Computing Systems*. Los Angeles, CA: The Association of Computing Machinery.

Nielsen, J. (2000). *Designing Web Usability. Indianapolis, IN: New Riders Publishing. Nielsen, J. & Tahir, M. (2002). Homepage Usability: 50 Websites Deconstructed.* Indianapolis, IN: New Riders Publishing.

Pearrow, M. (2000). *Web Site Usability Handbook*. Independence, KY: Charles River Media.

Scanlon, T., Schroeder, W., Snyder, C., & Spool, J. (1998). Websites that work: Designing with your eyes open. In *Proceedings of the SIGCHI on Human Factors in Computing Systems*. Los Angeles, CA: The Association of Computing Machinery.

Shackel, B. (2009). Usability-context, framework, definition, design and evaluation. *Interacting with Computers, 21*(5), 339–346. doi:10.1016/j.intcom.2009.04.007

Sindhuja, P., & Surajith, G. (2009). Impact of the factors influencing website usability on user satisfaction. *The IUP Journal of Management Research*, *8*(12), 54–66.

Singh, A., & Wesson, J. (2009). Evaluation Criteria for Assessing the Usability of ERP Systems. In *Proceedings of the 2009 Annual Conference of the South African Institute of Computer Scientists and Information Technologists*. Vaal River, South Africa: The Association of Computing Machinery.

Veen, J. (2000). *The Art & Science of Web Design*. Indianapolis, IN: New Riders Publishing.

Venkatesh, V. (1985). Determinants of Perceived Ease of Use: Integrating Control, Intrinsic Motivation, and Emotion into the Technology Acceptance Model. *Information Systems Research*, *11*(4), 342–365. doi:10.1287/isre.11.4.342.11872

Section 3
Business Models in the Cloud Computing Environment

Chapter 5
Cloud Computing for E-Governance

N. Raghavendra Rao
FINAIT Consultancy Services, India

ABSTRACT

Multidisciplinary experts are required to develop a model for resource management in a country. Various concepts in information and communication technology are required to be applied in designing and developing a model for the management of natural resources. The concepts such as cloud computing along with social media play an important role. Case illustrations are discussed in this chapter stressing the role of cloud computing along with the concepts of collaborative technology in developing models for the benefit of citizens in a country.

DOI: 10.4018/978-1-5225-3182-1.ch005

INTRODUCTION

Economic development has helped to raise the standard of living and has also led to mismanagement of natural resources. This has resulted in environmental issues. Wisdom is used in maintaining a balance between the needs of human beings and supplies from natural resources so that the delicate ecological balance is not disturbed. Governments in many countries in their zeal to go ahead with ambitious plans of development, integration of knowledge relating to environmental sciences, economics, space technology and information and communication technologies has escaped the attention of the governments.

The advancements in information and communication technologies have resulted in new concepts being developed in this discipline. Cloud computing is one among the number of other concepts. Cloud computing is a concept generally defined as the clusters of scalable and virtualized resources such as distributed computers, storage, system software and application software which make use of the internet to provide on-demand services to the user.

This chapter explains the components of natural resources and the human activities on natural resources. Further, it recommends a model for making use of space technology and Cloud computing to create a knowledge-based system for natural resources. This model will mainly be useful to the various government departments which are involved in the management of natural resources and environmental issues. Further, it also suggests a model for handling the damage caused by natural disasters.

GOVERNMENT AND GOVERNANCE

Governments in both developed and developing countries aim at protecting the interests of their people and preserving the resources of their Country. They pass laws to implement their plans. In this process, they also recommend new policies and propose changes as needed in the existing policies and programs.

One needs to be clear about the distinction between government and governance. A quotation going back to 1656 is relevant in understanding the distinction. "Wise princes ought not to be admired for their Government, but governance". The distinction that is drawn at present briefly runs as follows: While Government refers to actions carried out within a formal legal setting, governance involves all activities of government along with informal activities, even outside a formal government setting that are meant to achieve goals.

COORDINATION FOR E-GOVERNANCE

UNESCO defines E-Governance as: "Governance refers to the exercise of political, economic and administrative authority in the management of Country's affairs, including citizen's articulation of their interests and exercise of their legal rights and obligations. E-governance may be understood as the performance of this governance via the disseminating information to the public, and other agencies, and for performing government administrative activities."

UNESCO definition indicates the importance of coordination among the Government departments to provide and improve the Government services, transactions with citizens, business, and other departments of government. E-Governance in the area of natural resource management in any country will be successful only when there is coordination among the various government departments.

Framing policies pertaining to natural resource and managing them will not be with one department under any government. An e-governance consisting of a multidisciplinary expert is required to develop a model for resources management in a country (Kaushik A and Kaushik C P, 2006). Electronic governance will help the members of the core team and the various departments in the government to facilitate in managing their resources. When they work as a team, they need to have centralized data pertaining to geographical information both quantitative and textual content. Then only it will be possible to develop a knowledge based system for natural resources management. Further the knowledge based system will be useful for environmental management and natural disaster management. Cloud computing is more useful for data-intensive application such as a knowledge based system for natural resources management. This application has to manage data replication for facilitating data recovery and responding dynamically to changes in the volume of data in databases. Cloud computing supports the above requirements (Buyya & Sukumar, 2011).

CLOUD COMPUTING FOR E-GOVERNANCE

Cloud computing has a real advantage over other conventional systems. Technological benefits and cost advantage together makes it a viable Technology. Cloud computing has inbuilt features like scalability, virtualization, rapid elasticity, pay as per usages, on demand access to software, storage, network and other platform services. Many governments across the world have realized the importance of Cloud computing in e-governance. The analyst firm Gartner has predicted that Cloud Computing will be the top most technology area in information technology.

The Japanese Government has undertaken a major initiative to bring all the Government ministries under Cloud Computing, known as "KASUMIGASEKI CLOUD" and is likely to be completed by 2015. Accordingly, to Japan's ministry of internal affairs and communication it will have benefits like integrated and consolidated hardware, shared platform services and security. It will greatly reduce the Government's efforts in terms of electronic governance related to development and operating cost.

The United Kingdom Government has accepted the proposal of creation of "G-CLOUD" for Government wide Cloud Computing as a strategic priority. The Digital Britain report prepared by the department of business innovation and skills and the department of culture, media, sports outlined the benefits of Cloud and supported this national initiative. According to UK Government, they have identified the initiatives under this plan such as standardization and simplification of the desktop, standardization of networking, realization of the data centre estate, making use of open source, open standards and reuse strategy, green IT, information security and assurance.

The United States Government has also started efforts for shifting information systems to the Cloud across the US Federal Government. It may be noted that the efforts in this direction have already been started by the general services administration, national aeronautics and space administration, department of health and human services, census bureau and White House.

ECONOMIC DEVELOPMENT

Generally, economic development and natural resources management; are considered mutually antagonistic. Promotion of one would inevitably mean damage to the other. In the present globalization scenario, it has become a necessity for integrating natural resources concerns into economic development activities. If the agenda of any government is to concentrate only on urban development, there will be a risk of losing natural resources. This is because the former will take over the latter. The stress on the earth's surface requires careful assessment. A new natural resources management agenda is needed for reducing the stress on natural management. The type of information required for the purpose of analysis and framing policies for natural resources management varies from country to country. It also depends on the resources available and their usage in the respective areas in a country.

ADVANTAGES OF CLOUD COMPUTING FOR GOVERNMENT

Cloud computing based systems are better alternative systems to high capacity and high computing power hardware at each department in the government. There would be reduction in investments and in operating cost of Cloud computing environment. Every department in the government can make use of the services such as storage, platform, and software as per its needs. Infrastructure at a remote central will help the government to minimize the investment in software and its licenses. Further, it helps to reduce the power consumption. Darrel M. West, Vice President and Director of Governance Studies at Brookings, has reported Cost Savings Estimates from various sources. The Cost Saving Analysis based on its reports says a minimum of 40% cost reduction in almost all the cases.

SCALABILITY

Changing needs in the conventional architecture, scaling requires procurement, deployment and configuration of hardware and software. Generally, there will be delays in the procurement process in the government. To avoid delays in the procurement process, each department procures the information Technology infrastructure, more than its needs within the Budget sanctioned limit. In most of the cases there will be under utilization of its resources.

The Cloud computing architecture is designed in such a way that additional requirement can be provided to each department at any time. The size of Cloud architecture can be scaled up or down effectively. Internally, the resources can be shared by the different government departments. Distribution of resources can be determined on the basis of each department's needs. This provides elasticity within the systems wherein each department gets its requirement fulfilled.

USEFULNESS TO GOVERNMENT

Generally the data are largely not utilized by the government except for preparation of few departmental reports under the conventional E-Governance procedure. Cloud based e-governance model facilitates to monitor the centrally managed data center of the government, stores the vital information pertaining to the various departments. This will have the real time as well as the historic data. Software tools can be used for analyzing the data at the centralized government data center for framing policies and planning strategies (Levin, 2013).

DISASTER MANAGEMENT

Disaster is inevitable and unpredictable. It can be either natural disaster or human error. Any disaster leads to loss of lives, property or data security and safety of electronic data is vital in e-governance. Disaster management is an integral part of Cloud based architecture which provides data protection and fault tolerance to the client as a part of its service. Internal Cloud service providers replicate their data at multiple locations so the loss of one data center's data due to any disaster does not lead to loss of information for its clients. Similarly the government in a Country can have their data centers in different locations in their Country.

IMPLEMENTATION

It is easier to implement e-governance application at one location under Cloud computing-based architecture compared to a similar application being implemented in multiple locations. The latter approach requires a uniform infrastructure at all locations which can be expensive and may not be available in certain situations. Even if it is available it may lead to inconsistency due to variations in versions of the software.

MIGRATION TO NEW TECHNOLOGY

Generally, the government polices of various ministries change from time to time requiring appropriate changes in e-governance applications. Many times it may need to migrate to new technology. Migration is a challenging task in the distributed computing environment. Comparatively migration to new technology is relatively easier and faster in the Cloud based architecture. This is because changes at one location alone ensure migration to a new application by the concerned department (Majumdar, 2011).

GREEN COMPUTING

Traditional infrastructure requires personal computers, number of servers, printers and other related devices in every government department. Maintaining environmental condition will be required at least in Server Rooms. It is not considered to be a healthy practice for the environment to have more systems in the various departments in government. It also accumulates large stock of obsolete hardware waste that need to be destroyed properly over the years. The Cloud computing architecture optimizes utilization of resources cleverly ensuring the lower consumption of electricity, less emission of harmful gases and lower stockpiles of obsolete hardware.

EXISTING E-GOVERNANCE PRACTICE

E-governance adopted by many government departments is in isolation and scattered pattern. This procedure lacks an integrated approach towards e-governance. Information available with one department is not easily accessible by the other departments. This is due to lack of standardization and uniformity in platform, data and software instead of sharing the data, departments go for the creation of their own data.

CASE ILLUSTRATION 1

Managing natural resources and economic development in a country are considered mutually antagonistic, because promoting one would result in damaging the other and economic development is given more importance to remain competitive in the globalization scenario. It is important that a Government in a Country should realize the necessity for integrating natural resources concerns into economic development activity. Careful assessment is required to assess the stress on the earth's surface. A better natural resources management agenda is needed, especially in the developing countries. The agenda should concentrate to reduce the stress on natural resources and to manage environmental issues in urban areas. The type of data and information for the purpose of analysis and framing policies for natural resources management varies from country to country. It also depends on the availability of natural resources and its uses in the respective areas in a country. A well structured database and information systems is required by the authorities who are involved in planning and framing the policies for managing the natural resources under their control. Developing countries need a model that helps them to manage their country's resources judiciously (Glynn Henry J, and Cary WHeinke, 2004). It is a general practice in many countries that the government assigns the responsibility to one department or two or more departments for managing the components of natural resources. In most of the cases there will not be coordination among departments for handling the issues related to natural resources management. So a core team consisting of multidisciplinary experts to develop a model for managing natural resources is needed. The concept of cloud computing and other collaborative technologies will be the backbone for this model (Tiwari, 2010).

COMPONENTS OF NATURAL RESOURCES

It is needless to say that nature belongs to all of us. It is important that the authorities who are involved in managing the natural resources are expected to be aware of the structural composition and functions of natural resources. These components play an important role as life supporting systems. The structural components of life systems are land, mines, water resources and forest resources. These components are otherwise known as natural resources. It is to be remembered that natural ecosystem operates themselves under natural conditions without any interference by human beings (V.N., 2006). Misuse of natural resources will affect the human beings on the planet earth.

E-GOVERNANCE

Natural resource management is interdisciplinary, where coordination is required among the various government departments. It is advisable to form a core team consisting of the representatives of the various departments along with environmental and bio-technology experts, professionals in the areas of space, information and communication technologies will provide their expertise to the e-governance for the creation of knowledge based model for natural resources. Members of the core team can analyze and draw conclusion from the knowledge based model. This model will help them framing policies pertaining to the usage of natural resources.

KNOWLEDGE BASED MODEL

This Model can be created with five sub modules. They are 1) Geographical data for a Country 2) Quantitative and textual contents of geographical data 3) Data for environmental management 4) Knowledge base for natural resources and 5) Disaster Management Data

1. Geographical data for a Country: GIS Software is required for creating geographical data of a Country.
2. Quantitative and textual contents of geographical data: Geographical data is the base for converting into quantitative and textual data. This data will be useful for analysis and framing policies and issues related to natural resources.
3. Data for environmental Management: The type of data required for Analysis for environmental issues related to urban areas can be stored under this module.
4. Knowledge base of natural resources The data related to an analysis done under the sub mode 1 and 2 can be stored in this sub module.
5. Disaster Management Data: Places prone to natural disaster can be identified from this submodule. The information on this sub module will be useful for handling the natural disasters.

CLOUD DEPLOYMENT FOR E-GOVERNANCE

Cloud Computing can be classified and deployed under four ways. They are 1) Private Cloud 2) Public Cloud 3) Community Cloud and 4) Hybrid Cloud

1. **Private Cloud:** The Cloud infrastructure is owned or leased by single enterprise. It is operated solely for that organization.
2. **Public Cloud:** The Cloud infrastructure is owned by an organization which provides the Cloud services for a fee. Generally, these services are made use by the general public and business enterprises.

3. **Community Cloud:** The Cloud infrastructure is shared by several organizations and supports a specific community.
4. **Hybrid Cloud:** The Cloud infrastructure is composed of two or more Clouds such as private, community or public that remains unique entities. They are bound together by standardized or proprietary technology that enables data and application portability.

DATA INTENSIVE APPLICATIONS

Cloud Computing is more useful for data intensive application. Data for natural resource management falls under this category. The core team members require the data for sharing and analyzing data across a Country. Data related to land, mines, forest and rivers need to be maintained in the database consisting Region wise and country wide data replication of the above components is required to be maintained in the system. Further, it will have the facility of data recovery and responding dynamically to changes in the volume of data in databases (Krutz & Vines, 2010).

PRIVATE CLOUD

Data related to natural resources is considered to be sensitive data for any Country. A Government in a Country should have its own data center. Private Cloud is the best solution for a Government data center. High volume and sensitive data of a government can be maintained in the private cloud.

With the growing use of the internet, there is no need to limit group collaboration to a single department's network environment. Users from multiple locations within the government and multiple governments can collaborate on data and information related to natural resources stored in private cloud environment with ease. Many leading manufacturers in the area of infrastructure are offering to build the cloud network.

Similarly, the software companies are offering the cloud based software applications. Essence of cloud computing concepts is to facilitate users of any device which has an internet feature such as mainly mobile phones and laptops. It is clear from the above that cloud computing concept make e-governance reasonably simple (Sahoo G, Shabana Mehfuz, and Rashmi Rai, 2013).

GEOGRAPHICAL INFORMATION SYSTEM

Geographical Information System is associated with basic terms such as geography and information system. The literal interpretation of geography is "Writing about the Earth". Geography is the base for identifying the relationship of land with human beings (A., 2009; Kraak & Ormelling, 2004).

Geographical information system is a tool for handling geographic (Spatial and Descriptive) data. It is an organized collection of computer hardware, software with geographic data. This is designed efficiently to capture, store, retrieve, update and manipulate data. This data can be used for analysis and displaying all forms of geographically referenced information as per the user defined specifications. One can visualize the real world consisting of much geography such as topography, land use, coverage of land, soil, crops, forests, water bodies, districts, and towns (A. H. & C. P., 2006).

GEOGRAPHICAL DATA FOR A COUNTRY

The details of natural resources, population, and location of industries, educational institutions, town and cities are available in the various departments in a government. Most of the above information is not available in the integrated system. Many Governments do not have integrated system due to heavy investment in infrastructure. Many governments across the world find it very difficult to frame policies in respect of management of natural resources in their countries.

Geographical Information System (GIS) facilitates to know the inventory of natural resources, and exact location of the resources. Once the data obtained by GIS System are stored in the database under the cloud computing environment, then it can be accessed by many government departments across the country.

COMPONENTS OF NATURAL RESOURCES

The components of natural resources can be classified as renewable resources and nonrenewable resources. Renewable resources have the inherent ability to repair or replenish themselves by recycling, reproduction or replacement. These renewable resources are water, plants, animals, soil and living organisms. Non renewable resources are the earth's geologic environment such as minerals and fossil fuels. These resources are available in the fixed quantity in the environment. It is required that every member of the core team needs to be aware of this.

QUANTITATIVE AND TEXTUAL CONTENTS IN THE SUB MODEL

A quantitative and textual data in reference to geographical data can be classified and stored in the sub modules. They are the following:

1. **Forests:** Data related to different types of forests such as moist tropical forests, dry tropical forests, mountain subtropical forests, mountain temporal forests, sub alpine forests and alpine scrubs. Classification of forest varies from country to country.
2. **Water Resources:** Data related to fresh water, lakes, rivers, ground water and oceans falls under this category.
3. **Minerals:** Data related to metallic and nonmetallic are stored under this category.
4. **Agricultural Land:** Data related to cultivable and non cultivable land will be stored under this category.
5. **Industrial Areas:** This will contain data pertaining to various industries such as automobile, textiles, pharmaceuticals, consumer durables and consumer related products. This is not an exhaustive list.
6. **Urban Areas:** Data related to residential, roads, transport, infrastructure and utility falls under this category.
7. **Rural Areas:** Data related to the areas which do not fall under the category of urban areas can be considered under this category.
8. **Service Units**: Data related to educational institutions, healthcare units and other related units fall under this category.
9. **Business Units:** Data related to trading organizations, financial institutions, hospitality units and other similar units fall under this category.

The above category of data in the sub modules of the database in the cloud computing will be useful for framing policies to manage the resources of a Country.

NATURAL RESOURCES AND ENVIRONMENTAL MANAGEMENT

Industrialization and urbanization have become a worldwide phenomenon. Industrialization and urbanization raise many environmental issues. It is because of the requirements of people living in urban and industrial areas are increasing. Managing their requirements need to be accessed properly.

The relationship between the availability of natural resources and its consumption can be established from the quantitative and textual data in any particular area. Further, it helps to address the environmental issues (Thakur I S, 2006). This also helps the policy makers to understand, minimizing environmental hazards and avoiding the depletion of resources. The details pertaining to water usage, solid waste products, dispose of package materials and other related information can be made available for this model. This will be more useful for environmental management. The type of data required for analyzing environmental issues is 1) Underground composition of urban areas 2) Water usage 3) Disposition of wastage and 4) Air pollutants.

1. **Underground Composition of Urban Areas**: Earth is being dug up in the developing countries very frequently for the purpose of laying lines of communication, electricity, water mains, sanitary and sewage lines. Generally it is not well planned activity, especially in the developing countries. The details of the information pertaining to every area in cities and sub-urban parts are required for analysis and developing urban areas. The data in the module in Cloud computing environment will help the town planners for action (Golden, 2012).

2. **Water Usage:** The data related to water consumption by residents and industrial, service and business sectors can be ascertained and stored in this module. This will be useful in accessing the requirements of consumption of water by these sectors. The contingency plan at the time of shortage of water can be prepared on the basis of information in this module.

3. **Disposition of Wastage:** The advancement in the package industry has created a good scope of marketing of the products manufactures across the globe. Demand for packing materials for products is on the rise in the developing countries. Disposal of left over packaging material are to be carried out by the civic authorities. Statistics of discarded packaging material are required for allocation of places in cities and suburban areas. This module will provide the required information.

4. **Air Pollutants:** Oxygen and nitrogen are the major constituents of the atmosphere. Coal, fuel oil and gasoline used by us emit carbon monoxide. This human activity is contributing to changes in the atmosphere. The largest single source of this emission from automobile pollution in the air is from the above factors. The health of human beings is affected by this pollution. The data in this Model will help the policy makers to think of workable solutions.

REMOTE SENSING FOR EARTH RESOURCES MANAGEMENT

Remote sensing data and image have been used to derive thematic information on various natural resources and environment. The type and level of information extracted depends on the expertise of the analyst's requirements. The utilization of remote sensing data can be broadly classified into three categories 1) To identify the category to which the earth's surface expresses belongs 2) To infer a particular parameter or phenomenon using the part of data for suitable modeling 3) under the third category, surface expressions are the indicators of certain resources, which are not directly observable by remote sensing.

DATA FOR NATURAL DISASTER MANAGEMENT

It is said that global warming causes climatic changes and natural disasters. Unprecedented rains, floods, earthquakes, tsunami, severely dry and wet weather are considered as natural disasters. It is the responsibility of governments in a country to have a proper "Disaster Management" plan. It is required under this plan to provide services to the victims of natural disasters whenever they acquire.

The stress caused on planet earth needs a careful assessment of the use of natural resources. Satellite systems facilitate to observe atmospheric changes and disturbances (Raja Rao K N, 2005). High resolution remote sensing

Satellites,integrated GPS system provides the inputs at the various phases of natural disasters for preparedness, prevention, mitigation and disaster management.

Any disaster management needs data. The past data can be used as guidance for preparing to handle disasters. Same approach is needed for managing natural disasters. Disaster prevention measures can be improved in three ways. They are 1) Mapping the disaster prone areas 2) Forecasting impending areas and 3) Disaster affected areas.

Geostationary satellite data are capable of providing information every half an hour and is useful in monitoring short term disaster by cyclones and tornadoes. It is felt that the combination of high spatial, temporal and spectral resolution data would certainly be beneficial in disaster management.

DISASTER MANAGEMENT

It is said that natural disasters are likely to occur more often due to global warming. Information pertaining to the type of help and services rendered is to be stored in the information system. This will be more useful for taking action in an emergency.

The kinds of services needed are medical services, transporting people from the affected areas to safe places and organizing food and provisions to the people in distress. The macro level data and information in the disaster management system are given below:

The experiences of the people who have been directly involved in providing services to the victims of disaster will be the inputs for creating this database.

RESOURCE ALLOCATION MODULE

This Module will have the list of basic supplies such as food items, clothes, raincoats and umbrellas required to help the victims of natural disasters. Addresses of the volunteer rescue team, medical doctors and paramedical professionals are to be stored in this module.

TRANSPORT MODULE

The details of heavy transport vehicles that can wade through water, boats and aerial survey aircrafts should be available in this module.

EVACUATION MODULE

Vulnerable areas and safe regions' exact locations are to be stored in this module by using GIS applications.

SHELTER MODULE

This module will contain the details of resources of various shelter locations.

DEPRIVATION MODULE

This module will contain the details of short supply of food items in the earlier disaster affected areas and statistics of the number of people infected with diseases. This information will be useful for avoiding such type of situations.

DISASTER MODULE

This module will contain the details of handling the various situations at various disaster management operations. Success and failure of the rescue operations can be derived from information from this Module. It will be useful for the future operations.

CLOUD BASED NATURAL RESOURCES DATA MODEL

Experts in the areas of information technology, space technology, domain and functional experts and executives in the government departments are the backbone of the e-governance. The role of the e-governance is to design cloud based natural resources data module. This model will take care of the basic data of the natural resources of a Country. The e-governance's analysis and solutions can be stored in this model. Data and information in this model can be made available to the executive of the various governments who are associated with the natural resources management, environmental issues and natural disaster management systems. Access to this module by them will be through e-governance.

Remote sensing systems and geographical systems are used for acquiring data of natural resources in a Country. Private Cloud can be made use of storing and organizing data (Schulz, 2012). The type of and level of information required depends on the expertise of analysts. Data pertaining to geography, quantitative and textual in respect of natural resources will be the base for graphical, data warehouse and text database in this model. This model will have the data at a Country, state, region, city, town and village levels. This will provide a good scope for analyzing the various aspects of natural resources.

Software tools such as GIS analysis, data mining and text mining can be made use of analysis (Pujari, 2010). The data analyzed by the specialists identified by the E-Governance will be available in this Model. The analyzed data will help the policy makers to frame policies for their Country. This model stresses the importance of a systematic approach in the creation of this Model. The exponential increase in computing power under the cloud environment and advancements in space technology have led to design this conceptual model.

The data in this Model will also be useful for managing environmental issues and managing natural disasters. *Figure 1.* gives an idea of a model at the macro level.

Figure 1. Classification of data of a country

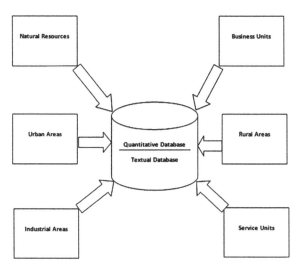

Figure 2. talks about the macro level contents for analyzing for environmental issues.

Figure 3 explains the macro level data and information needed in the disaster management system.

Social Media

Social media is changing the public interaction within the society. It is setting new trends and agendas in topics. The enormity and high variety of information propagates through larger user communities.It provides a good opportunity for harnessing that data for specific purposes. Social media sites can be used to promote good environmental practice, sharing ideas of best practices, awareness of government policies and plans. Business enterprises are already using social media channels for the promotion of their business activities. Similarly, government and non government organizations should involve the citizens of their country to express their ideas and suggestions on the issues related to their country. These discussions will facilitate the government to understand the views and concerns of the people. Further, it will help the government for framing the policies in the context of natural resource management, natural disaster management, and issues related to urban areas.

Figure 2. Environmental data

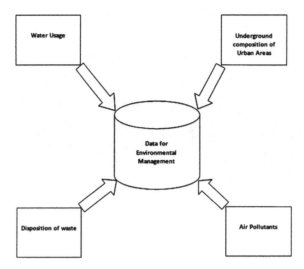

The classification of data of a country is available in the data in the data warehouse under the private cloud computing maintained by the government. A government may not have the required experts or specialists in every sphere under

Figure 3. Modules in disaster management system

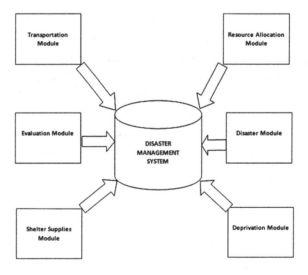

natural resources management. Generally agriculture sector needs the attention of the government. The government has the required data in textual and quantitative format in respect of agriculture sector. On the basis of this data many schemes and benefits are announced. Many times the farmers are not aware these announcements. It would be better to engage the services of the experienced agriculture scientists to guide the farmers in taking advantage of the schemes and benefits announced by the government. The following case illustration-2 explains the important role played by the agricultural scientists in helping the farmers in their activities.

CASE ILLUSTRATION 2

Farmers in the rural part of South India mainly concentrate on growing a particular type of crop. Most of them are not familiar with the new techniques of agricultural production. They are eager to learn and make use of the new techniques in the agricultural crop production. Unfortunately, they do not know when they are expected to contact for guidance. The locations of cultivable land are scattered in the different parts in the rural area of South India. The output of the agricultural products varies on the basis of various reasons. Some of the reasons are improper irrigation facilities, not familiar with the use of pesticides and fertilizers.

A team of agricultural scientists with doctorate degrees in agricultural science has decided to render their services to the farmers who would need guidance in the cultivation and marketing. This team has rich experience and knowledge in the various aspects of agricultural production and marketing. The team has planned to visit the farm lands for assessing the actual requirements for guidance. Most of the agricultural land is located at the various locations. They felt it was a time consuming process to visit the various locations of the agricultural land. They would want to discuss with the farmers, after getting an idea of the physical location of various agricultural land.

The Approach Followed by the Agricultural Scientists

The agricultural scientists have decided to use a device to know the physical appearance and location of the agricultural land. They felt drone could be used for scanning the area of cultivable land. They have hired a drone. Four cameras are fixed in the drone. The images of the various areas have been captured. They have made use of drone in the different locations for capturing the images of cultivable land (A., 2009).

Action Plan

The agricultural scientists have studied the images captured by them in the cameras fitted in the drone. On the basis of their study, they have prepared a tentative plan. They sought the head of village heads for convening a meeting with the farmers. The meeting took place at a convenient place agreed with all of them.

The agricultural scientists had a talk with the farmers. During the course of their interaction, images of their land shown to them. The agricultural scientists understood their problems and their requirements. They have explained many aspects of new techniques in the agricultural production. The agricultural scientists felt that it would be better to provide PDAs (Personal Digital Assistants) with the information for their use. The farmers may not remember all the aspects related to new techniques discussed at the meeting. PDAs have been provided with the information to the farmers. They have also organized farmers tractors for cultivation. They are made available on the payment of nominal hire charges.

A farmer's tractor is fitted with GPS units inside the cabin of a farmer's tractor. The GPS unit will help them for spraying less fertilizer and fewer pesticides. This will benefit the farmers in these times of rising costs of fuel, seed, and fertilizers (K., 2010).

The following useful information to farmers has been loaded in the PDAs.

1. **Good Agricultural Practices**: Dissemination of knowledge pertaining to low cost technologies is provided.
2. **Deteriorating Soil Health**: Appropriate measures such as diversification, balanced fertilizers and use of B.T.O. Fertilization are explained.
3. **Supplemental Life Saving Irrigation**: Life-saving irrigation facilities are explained to harvest and manage rain water through BIO industrial watersheds as against exploitation of ground water.
4. **Critical Inputs**: The importance of inputs such as BIO fertilizers, sulfur, Zinc, and Bio pesticides is explained. The need for starting co-operative societies for getting the above inputs at economical prices is suggested.
5. **Village Level Seed Distribution System**: Low cost, innovative seed systems will be encouraged through public and private participation models.
6. **Minimize Post-Harvest Losses**: Scientific storage practices are explained.
7. **Storage Policy Point**: Innovative, value chains for the agricultural products and strategies for improving marketing and best practices are explained.
8. **Marketing**: Making an investment in the market infrastructure and information systems are explained.

DISCUSSION

Farmers who live in the rural parts of South India do not have the required support and guidance in acquiring the latest technology in the agricultural production and marketing. Qualified and experienced agricultural scientists have identified the devices such as PDAS, drone and farmer's tractors with GPS fitted for the benefit of farmers. The group has created an open innovation agricultural model in updating the knowledge required for the farmers in their agricultural activities.

Many Non Government Organizations (NGOs) are willing to associate themselves with any scheme for implementing to the benefit of a particular set of people and society in general. They can be invited by the government to visit specific rural areas to educate the rural people in general health care, preserving trees, and literacy programs. Their services can also be made use in developing the untapped skills of the rural people. The following illustration-3 explains the benefits derived by the workers in tea plantations. The initiative of the social workers helped them to improve their standard of living.

CASE ILLUSTRATION 3

A group of social workers visited a tea plantation in south India. They went with the idea of giving talks related to health care, particularly in the context of hygiene to plantation workers. After their regular conducting health related programs, they used to go round tea plantations. They have noticed the locals were depleting the forest of foliage and destroying the soil. During their interaction with forest dwellers, they came to know that it was the lack of lively hood they were forced to cut the trees. The social workers felt that the forests need to be saved. It is not an easy task to grow trees. They have decided to consult for preserving forests. At the same time they would like to provide alternative livelihood to the forest dwellers. The social workers sent emails to their friend's advice for finding an alternative livelihood to the forest dwellers. This would help to preserve the forest. Their friends posted the issue on their social media sites. At the request of their friends more information and data related to the issue are provided to them.

There were responses to the message on social media sites by some experts who are familiar with soil management and agricultural techniques. The experts are keen to advise them without demanding any consultancy fees. The experts have suggested to grow bamboo. It is because those bamboo thickets can be grown in just three months. A tree needs thirty years to grow.

At the suggestion of the experts the social workers advised the forest dwellers to grow bamboo and restore the quality of their soil. Further bamboo is a cash crop that will help them to earn money. This suggestion has appealed to the forest dwellers. They have started acting on the advice of the experts.

Open Innovative Initiative

The social workers observed that many of the forest dwellers are eager to learn new things. Some of them are keen to get trained in new vocation also. Their enthusiasm prompted the social workers to inform their friends through email about their observations about the forest dwellers. The latest news related to forest dwellers has been uploaded in their social media sites.

Response to the messages posted on social media sites is encouraging. Trainers who are good at designing products with bamboos have agreed to train the forest dwellers in making jewelry, bags and utility products from bamboo. Further, they have trained them in making use of other forest produce for better commercial purposes. The social workers have started contacting private marketing agencies as well as the government agencies for marketing the products produced by the forest dwellers. Some of the forest dwellers have displayed unique skills while making the products from the bamboo. The social workers felt that their unique skills need to be encouraged. Special training programs have been organized. Many new products have emerged from their innovative design skills. Now they are planning to market their products in the global market. The social workers are also planning to create an exclusive social media site for marketing the products produced by the forest dwellers.

Observation

It is interesting to note a group of social workers who visited the tea plantations in south India to educate basic hygiene to forest dwellers, has felt that they need to create better livelihood opportunities to the forest dwellers. Interaction with their friends on social media has given an opportunity to create an open innovation initiative approach. It is the involvement of friends, well wishers and experts on the social media sites have changed the standard of living of the forest dwellers. Further the untapped skills of the forest dwellers got recognition. It has given pride to their workmanship. It is a good example of making use of contacts on social media sites for the open innovation initiative.

The government has data related to qualified youth from the rural areas. Most of them have engineering degrees in the disciplines such as civil, electrical, electronics, and other related engineering subjects.

They need to be encouraged by providing the facilities and support to start business ventures. The following illustration-4 gives an insight into the start up ventures in the rural areas.

CASE ILLUSTRATION 4

Many villages in India have agricultural land, cattle and poultry. Villagers own their agriculture land and market the produce of their land. Farmers own cows and poultry. Produce from the agricultural land is rice, wheat, and other staple food products, vegetables and fruits (Chapin, F S, Kofinas G P & Floke C, 2009). Production of the above products is sold in the local market. They also sell these products at nearby towns and cities. Children of the villagers study at schools and colleges situated in towns and cities close to their villages. After completion of their education, many of them take up the jobs in the places, they are offered. Migration to towns and cities is taking place to better their prospects. Most of them are engineers in different disciplines of engineering. Some have additional qualification in the discipline of business administration.

A group of young engineers felt that they should do something different in their lives. Instead of taking up jobs in the towns and cities, they have decided to make use of the knowledge gained in schools and colleges for the improvement of economic activities in their village (Chiras Daniel D & Reganold John P, 2010).

The electrical engineers in their group have suggested that it would be better to generate electricity with the resources available in their village. Resources available in plenty are cow dung, poultry waste, vegetables and fruit wastes. In addition to these resources rice husk and rice straw are also available in huge quantity (Conroy, Michael J & Paterson James T, 2013). Other members of the group have accepted their suggestion. The group has felt that the electrical engineers are familiar the concepts only. They do not have the actual experience in the process of generating electricity with the kind of resources in their village.

The group has created a social media site exclusively for getting the process know how from the experienced people. They have sent personal emails to their friends to visit the social media site created by them. They have requested them to spread their message to their friends and experts in the fields. Response to their request has been encouraging.

The details pertain to setting up the plant; the type of machinery required and the total costs of the project have been provided by senior professionals in the power generation field. They felt that they should not demand any consultancy fees. The reason being, the project is being started by a first generation people in a rural basic ground. But the group felt that it was not fair on their part to receive expert's advice without any payment. They have decided to pay them later when their project starts earning income.

The group has started a mini power plant with the financial resources provided by their families. Their enthusiasm and hard work has helped them to achieve their business venture. After the success of the power plant venture, they have planned to start an automobile ancillary unit by making use of the electrical power generated by them. Once again this message has been posted on their social media sites. Their college classmates, who are working with the leading automobile manufacturers, have happened to visit their social media sites. They have provided the salient features and general requirements to manufacture automobile components. The group name has been suggested to the management of the company where they are employed. Their reverence has helped the group to get the orders for manufacturing auto components as per their requirements. The group has sought help from their friends through social media sites for organizing training program for skilled and semi-skilled workers in their village. This venture has created confidence in them to start some more engineering ancillary units in their village. They have been able to improve their business prospects with their contacts through their social media sites (Ho V & Wong S, 2009).

Observation

It may be noted that the young engineers with their education background have started business ventures in a village in South India.

Their open innovation approach has provided an opportunity to think differently in making use of agricultural product wastage for the generation of electricity (A.K., 2010). Another initiative has helped them to venture into other related manufacturing units. Further the social media sites have facilitated them to get ideas for their open business innovative initiative. Ultimately, their ventures have created many economic activities in their village (Christensen, Clayton M, Baumann Heiner, Ruggles Rudy & Sadtler Tomas M, (December 2006).

Need for Social Media Channels for Citizens in India

It would be better if the government indicates their tentative plans and policies relating to deforestation in hilly areas, preserving wildlife animals, use of pesticides, mining, wasteland reclamation, and disposal of waste materials. Once the government uploads their tentative approach to the above matters on the social media channels, citizens can express their views and narrate the incidents taken place in the various locations in India.

Following are some of the issues related to natural resources management in India have been discussed by a group of research scholars among themselves for their academic interest in their social media sites. It would be better the government creates a social media site exclusively for the citizens to discuss and express their views on the issues related to their country. The government can know the issues related natural resources, environment, noise pollution and other related issues from the citizens' perspective.

Deforestation in a Hilly Area

A hilly region near Chotta Nagpur used to be a good forest area toward the turn of the century and used to receive fairly frequent afternoon showers favoring tea plantations. Following the destruction of forest rainfall declined in the Chotta Nagpur area to such an extent that tea gardens also disappeared from the region.

Waning Rainfall in Ooty

The abnormal rainfall at Ooty in Nilgiris Mountains has been found to be closely associated with declining forest cover in these regions. Earlier the Nilgiris had luxuriant forest cover and annual rainfall used to be much higher.

Deforestation in the Himalayas

Deforestation in Himalayas, involving the clearance of natural forests and plantation of monocultures like a piano's barge, eucalyptus camadulenis and other related plantations of monocultures have upset the ecosystem by changing various soil and biological properties. Nutrient cycling has become poor, original rich germ plasma is lost and the area is covered by exotic weeds. These areas are not able to recover and are losing their fertility.

Wayanad Wildlife Sanctuary

The Wayanad wildlife sanctuary was affected by the displacement of tribal families living in that area. They were promised to allocate land in some other area of their dwelling. In the process of allocation of land, some tribal families got and many others did not get the land as promised to them. As a result of this the tribal felt cheated and they encroached into the forest in large numbers, cutting down the trees and started constructing huts and digging wells, causing a violent encounter with the forest officials, ultimately causing injuries and deaths to the people.

Valmiki Tiger Reserve

The tribes living in the Valmiki tiger reserve area in Bihar state felt that they have been deprived of their legitimate ancestral rights to collect firewood and fodder from the forest. Their employment was also lost due to the "Project Tiger". The jobless villagers felt cheated and started indulging in the destruction of the forest and started engaging themselves in unsocial activities.

Waste Land Reclamation

Economically unproductive land is generally used for dumping waste materials. This type of usage of land creates health problems of people who are living nearby.

Plastic Materials

Plastic has become a part of modern living. Right from packaging to making toys and various other items are made out of plastic. Normally they are petroleum products where alkaline oxides are polymerized to form plastics such as polyethene. They are non-bio degradable being novel to the environment and hazardous to the earth.

Noise Pollution During Diwali

Diwali is the festival of lights in India. There has been concern over the noise levels generated during Diwali. It is required that the manufacturers of fireworks should mention the noise levels on the labels of crackers.

Environmental Awareness

Making environmental education as a part of a subject at the school stage will inculcate a feeling respecting the mother earth among the students.

Discussion of Natural Disasters on Social Media Platforms

Chennai is a city in India. This city has experienced heavy rains in the last week of November and the first week of December 2015. This year's monsoon particularly has created havoc in Chennai. A group of architects, urban planners and environmental specialists discussed about the disaster created by the heavy rains in Chennai on their social media group channel. The following is the gist of the professionals' views regarding the reasons for the damage suffered by the city due to natural disaster. One of the participants has expressed that the citizens of Chennai are paying the price for unscrupulously developing real estate on the city's natural reserves, lakes and marshlands. The fact remains that the increasing population has forced the city to reclaim land and expand its boundaries. The challenge lies in executing infrastructure development of this expanded city in a smart and sustainable manner.

Other participants indicated that permanent solutions are ignored and looking instead only for quick, and patchwork alternatives. They felt that the government authority can use the guidance of the institute of town planners of India and Indian Institute of Architects for plans constructing buildings. Increasing density within the city and expanding its boundaries with better connectivity in a scientific manner is the way forward. The reason behind the current water logging is because most water bodies have filled up and have lost their internal links. Rivers and lakes are to flourish their flow. Their needs are to be respected. The problem is house construction sites are becoming smaller and buildings are getting closer. Any construction activity during the monsoon is a threat to neighboring buildings as the soil is likely to slide.

In Chennai it can be seen imbalanced, sporadic growth areas driven by economics and opportunity rather than by cohesive master plan. A cohesive master plan is required that takes into account a holistic approach by placing nature, environment and urban expansion on equal pedestals. Developing residential and commercial projects in low lying areas need to be avoided. If developments are to take place storm water and sewage provisions should be designed to withstand double the normal capacity.

Recycle Demolition Debris

The global average contribution of construction and demolition waste is set to be around 50% of total solid waste generated in major cities. The numbers in Indian metros are not tracked, but safe estimate will be fairly close to this general worldwide statistics.

Construction and demolition waste can be broadly categorized based on the sources of generation, such as extracted soil, road and infrastructure, waste, demolition waste and other complex wastes generated from project sites. The problem is further intensified with the general landfills. There is a pressing need for our building industry to recognize the global best practices in the area of construction and demolition of waste recycling.

It is usually the most land scarce areas that are first to innovate successfully. Hongkong and Singapore are considered pioneers in this area and manage to divert between 60-90% of their construction and demolition wastes from landfills. These high numbers are largely due to legal processes that are put in place along with the incentives required to ensure success in implementation. Their laws often describe step-wise processes for demolition, the codes on the use of recycled aggregates and building standards that mandate inclusion of recycled construction and demolition materials.

While waste management is one part of the concern, there is a larger worry about the availability of resources. There is indiscriminate sand mining in the river beds and beaches that causes extensive damage to the environment. Strategies to recycle construction and demolition of wastes would lower the demand on river sand. The reduced demand will in turn preserve our natural ecology.

The above ecologic issue in respect of construction and demolition of waste requires the attention of the government. An architect feels that the Indian standards for construction, project construction management have some indications on the inclusion of recycled material in constructing projects. These standards are required to be standardized and passed as benchmarks for using recycled construction and demolition materials in the construction projects. This will improve the ecology in the construction sector.

Role of Social Media in Natural Calamities This is another a gist of the discussion on social media channel pertaining to recycling of demolition debris.

When Chennai was to face with rains and floods in November & December 2015, social media came to the rescue of the residents. As phone networks remained jammed, most people have made use of what's app twitter and Facebook to share information, pictures, and extending help. The role of social media has been a life saver, as several people were given help, while others came forward to do it.

People of Chennai turned crusaders in many places. Citizens took to twitter to offer their homes to strangers seeking shelter from the rain and floods. Images and videos of helpful Samaritans were soon uploaded in social media sites. Live updates of the situation in the social media sites saved many people from getting caught unguarded. When there was no access to news, these social media were information providers. Several help groups used the online media, as it was the only virtual communication room to get in contact with emergency numbers of ambulance. The constant stream of what's app forwards and other social media channels also helped to distribute a substantial amount of food items and other requirements of the people who are stuck in the flood affected areas. Another group of citizens played a crucial role in providing weather forecasts and updates in the various social media groups.

The government data related to urban areas. The details pertaining to constructing buildings and constructing other infrastructure are available to them. Waste management needs the attention of the government. Before framing polices it would be better to engage the citizens for obtaining their views and opinion.

Discussion

It may be noted that the social media channels provide a lot of information about the various activities taking place in every part of the country. The discussions and other related information need to be captured by the government and stored in their data warehouse in their private cloud environment. This data will be more useful for framing policies and providing guidance to parts of the country where they similar issues.

FUTURE TRENDS

It is becoming the practice of creating a private cloud environment by a government in a country. The data related to natural resources and their utilization. Even the government has the required data, many issues related to the natural resources, disaster management, and urban areas are escaping the attention of the government. It may be noted that a group of citizens and professionals are already discussing and expressing their views on the above issues on their social media channels. It is high time that the government should make use of the information on the social media sites for better governance to their citizens (Flynn,2012). Research scholars can develop a prototype model on the basis of the information available on the social media channels. This model will be more useful to the government for making polices on the basis of the data available in their private cloud environment (Jeffrey A Hoffer, Ramesh V, & Heikki Todi,2013).

CONCLUSION

The concept of cloud computing along with the concepts of collaborative technology will facilitate a government in providing a good governance to their citizens. The four illustrations discussed in this chapter clearly explain the importance of the above concepts for the benefit of citizens in a country.

REFERENCES

Buyya & Sukumar. (2011). Platforms for Building and Developing Applications for Cloud Computing. *CSI Communications Journal, 35*(2), 6-11.

Chandra, A. H., & Ghosh, S. K. (2006). *Image Interpretation, Remote sensing and Geographical Information System*. New Delhi: Narosa Publishing House.

Chiras Daniel, D., & Reganold John, P. (2010). *Natural Resource Cononservation Management and Management for a Sustainable Future*. Prentice Hall.

Conroy & Paterson. (2013). *Decision Making Natural Resource Management: A Structured Adaptive Approach*. Wiley-Blackwell.

Flynn. (2012). *The Social Media Hand Book*. New Delhi: Wiley India Private Limited.

Glynn, H. J., & Heinke, G. W. (2004). *Environmental Science and Engineering*. Singapore: Private Limited.

Golden, B. (2012, June). How Cloud Computing can transform Business. *Harvard Business Review*.

Ho, V., & Wong, S. S. (2009). Knowing who knows what and who knows whom: Experise recognition, network recognition and individual performance. *Journal of Occupational and Organizational Psychology, 82*(1), 147–189. doi:10.1348/096317908X298585

Hoffer & HeikkiTodi. (2013). Modern Database Management (10th ed.). New Delhi: Pearson.

Kaushik, A., & Kaushik, C. P. (2006). *Environmental Studies-A Multidisciplinary Subject: Perspectives in Environmental Studies*. New Delhi: New Age International Publishers.

Kraak & Ormelling. (2004). *Cartographic Visualization of Geospatial Data; New Delhi: Pearson Education*. Singapore: Private Limited.

Krutz, R. L., & Vines, R. D. (2010). *Cloud Security*. New Delhi: Wiley India Private Limited.

Levin, S. (2013). *Cooperation and Sustainability in Guru Prasad Madhavan, Barbara Oakley, David Green, David Koon, and Penny Low*. New York: Springer.

Majumdar. (2011). Resource Management on Clouds: Handling Uncertainties in Parameters and Polices. *CSI Communications Journal, 35*(2), 16-17.

Pujari. (2004). Data mining Techniques. New Delhi: Universities Press (India) Private Limited.

Quazi, S. A. (2009). *Principles of Physical Geography*. New Delhi: APH Publishing Corporation.

Raja Rao, K. N. (2005). *An Overview of Space and Satellite: Fundamental of Satellite Communication*. New Delhi: Prentice Hall of India.

Sahoo, Mehfuz, & Rai (2013). Applications of Cloud Computing for Agriculture Sector. *CSI Communications Journal, 37*(8), 10-17.

Schulz, G. (2012). *Cloud and Virtual Data Storage Net Working, Your Journey to Efficient & Effective Information Services*. New York: Taylor & Francis Group.

Sharada, V. N. (2006). *Environment and Agriculture*. New Delhi: Malhotra Publishing House.

Thakur, I. S. (2006). *Introduction Environmental Biotechnology*. New Delhi: I.K. International.

Tiwari. (2010). *Infrastructure for Sustainable Rural Development*. New Delhi: Regal Publications.

Tiwari, A. K. (2011). *Infrastructure for Sustainable Rural Development*. New Delhi: Regal Publications.

KEY TERMS AND DEFINITIONS

Ecology: Study of interactions of living organisms with their biotic and abiotic environment.

Governance: Exercise of political, economic, and administrative authority in the management of country's affairs, including citizens articulation of their interests.

Green Computing: Green Computing refers to environmentally sustainable computing.

Landfill: Solid wastes are dumped in the low-lying areas.

Natural Disasters: Hazards that destroy or damage wildlife habitats, property, and human settlements.

Social Media: It uses web-based technology to quickly disseminate knowledge and information to a large number of users.

Social Networks: This allows people to build personal web pages and then connect with friends to share content and communicate.

Chapter 6
Providing Healthcare Services in the Virtual Environment

N. Raghavendra Rao
FINAIT Consultancy Services, India

ABSTRACT

The concept of cloud computing provides a good scope for making use of information for knowledge updating among the medical fraternity. Large data are generated and available for analysis. One should know how well the data can be used for analysis and taking care of the patients. Medical fraternity needs to update with the latest knowledge to provide good healthcare services to patients. Software tools along with the concepts of collaborative technology are required to make use of the data and information stored in the cloud computing environment by the healthcare service institutions. Medical research group and software professionals can form a team to develop business models useful to the healthcare sector. This chapter explains with case illustrations designing and developing business models under the cloud computing environment with the concepts of collaborative technology.

DOI: 10.4018/978-1-5225-3182-1.ch006

INTRODUCTION

Health has been a concern of major importance across the world. The kind and amount of resources available now are increasing day by day. Technology has become the most important new resource in the present century. Emergence of new tools and devices has been helping the medical profession. Further, it is enhancing the medical professionals to provide better service to their patients. Advancements in information and communication technology have been making medicine and medical information systems integrated (Sunitha C, Vasantha Kokilam K, and Meena Preeti B, 2013). Electronic health or e-health is the result of the above integration. Most of the hospitals in the world have reasonably good information systems to manage the internal administrative and clinical processes for their patients (Vijayrani S, 2013). Exchange of information in the above infrastructure is mostly confined to their hospital and the hospitals attached to them.

Now it has become a necessity to integrate geographically distributed and organizationally independent organizations for medical information system. This integration gives a scope for designing a knowledge based system for health care sector. The present information and communication technology provides several concepts that enable to develop a health care information system more effectively.

Cloud Computing, Pervasive computing, Virtual Reality and other collaborative technologies are among a number of other concepts provided by information and communication technology. There are two types of approaches prevalent in the health care sector. They are 'Conservative approach' and 'Adaptive Change Approach'. The elements in the latter approach are reasoning, knowledge based understanding and enlightened creative wisdom blended with professional values. Implementation of emerging concepts in information and communication technology along with the elements in the first approach is possible under the latter approach.

NEED FOR KNOWLEDGE BASED SYSTEM

Due to the change in the life style of the people across the Globe, the nuclear family has become the order of the day. There used to be a doctor for each family when the joint family was prevalent. Most of these doctors knew the entire medical history of all the members of the family. These doctors used to organize all the medical services through their professional contacts whenever the family needed their services. The family doctor was considered as a part of the family, philosopher, and guide. The concept of 'Family Doctor" has disappeared today. In the present scenario, hospitals are the most important element in the health care delivery system. Every time a patient or patient's relative approaches a hospital, he or she comes with an expectation. What happens next will form an experience. A good experience may increase one's confidence in the hospital and he/she recommends the same hospital to friends and relatives. But a bad experience may dissuade probable patients not to make use of the services provided by a particular hospital. Health problems and needs are increasing and becoming more complex. The demands and pressures on the hospitals are also increasing. Providing timely service and care is the primary responsibility of all the hospital authorities. The ability to recognize this process and to actively manage it, forms the basis for "Knowledge Based Health Care System".

Healthcare organizations have a large volume of data which is generated by the number of transactions that take place during the services rendered to patients. One of the greatest difficulties in health care organizations is not so much in gathering data, but deciding what needs to be gathered to provide the necessary information and making sure that it is distributed to the right people at the right time and in the right form. "Knowledge Based Health Care System" will be useful in taking care of the above requirements.

Innovative Approach

Globalization is forcing the health care sector to focus on the need for an innovative approach in designing and developing knowledge based health care system. The World is poised to take a huge leap at the rate innovation is gaining importance. This is the result of the use of enhanced sharing of information and collaborative possibilities provided by cloud computing. Cloud computing (RajKumar Buyya, Christian Vecchiola, and Thamarai Sevi S, 2013) provides infrastructure for the creation of virtual hospitals with knowledge based health care system. The following case illustration talks about a knowledge based health care information system developed by a hospital in India.

Case Illustration I

A team of four medical doctors started a medical consulting center a decade ago in Chennai in India. They have taken a small area in a big building on rent. The area taken on rent could accommodate two doctors and twenty patients at any point of time in a day. These doctors would provide their services in their areas of specialization. It was because of the constraint in the space they have agreed among themselves to the specific time allotted to each doctor for their consultancy. They had a tie up with the selected clinical laboratories and investigating medical equipments Centers. These doctors would refer their patients to these centers for tests and investigations. The medical consulting center had a standalone system with ready-made application software for health care information system. This ready-made application software would support some basic functions required by the doctors. Over a period of time much advancement has taken place in the area of information and communication technology. To take advantage of these advancements, they have changed to an integrated health care information system in a relation database under client server technology. The new system has been more useful to the doctors in their professional work.

"Diagnosis" is the essence of patient health management. The doctors at the medical consulting center have proved themselves to be good at the correct diagnosis and appropriate treatment. India has been becoming more popular as one of the best health care service providers in the globalization scenario. Consequent to this many patients across the globe started preferring India for their health care destination. Some of the patients have been keen to visit a medical consulting center at Chennai.

This has led the doctors at the medical consulting center to start a separate full-fledged hospital with the advanced infrastructure. Care plus Cure hospital limited has been established by them. Many more specialists have joined the hospital to serve. The hospital has acquired the latest medical equipment for investigations. The hospital has set up its own clinical laboratories for testing. The hospital has been particular to concentrate on the following areas besides providing the regular health care services. The areas are 1) Medical Research 2) Medical education to patients 3) Developing formulas for medicines with the collaboration with the reputed pharmaceutical companies 4) Information for acquiring medical equipments 5) Sharing medical knowledge with the students of medicine 6) Providing hospital management systems to the hospitals who want to make use of this service.

Core teams in the hospital consisting of medical doctors who have knowledge in information and communication technology and software professionals have designed, developed and have been managing the system.

Many young medical doctors in India are evincing interested to start medical centers in the rural areas. They are looking for medical information system to support in their ventures. Care plus Cure hospital limited has extended its service to the young medical doctors in their venture. It is interesting to note that cloud computing and the collaborative technologies are the main components for the creation of "Care plus Cure" integrated health care system. Figure-1 illustrates the integrated hospital management system at Care plus Cure Hospital Limited.

Figure 1. Integrated hospital management system

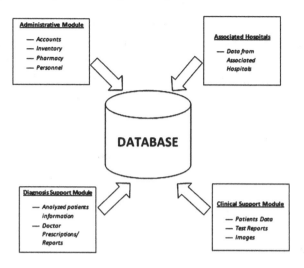

Goals of Care Plus Cure Hospital Limited

Every enterprise has a mission and vision goal of its enterprise. Care plus Cure Hospital Limited has realized the need for an integrated health care system under cloud computing environment. Their health care system is designed to support the following.

1. **Mission**: To provide health care and health care related services to their hospital and the needs of the other hospitals
2. **Strategy**: Designing integrating information health care system to support their mission
3. **Health Care Process Models**: Developing medical information process models to accomplish their strategy
4. **Hospital Functions**: To define the technology infrastructure needed for supporting the data and application in the health care system.
5. **Standards**: To document the required standards for hospitals.

Cloud Computing in Health Care Sector

Making use of cloud capabilities is more than the latest technology. It is moving from a traditional model to knowledge based model. Medical doctors, medical students, patients, and research scholars are the main participants in the latter model. It is much more important for the health care sector to understand the changing trends in the information and communication technology. The changing trends help health care sector also define the best strategy to leverage cloud computing. Basically cloud computing can divide the data center into application cloud, hardware, and computing cloud. Adoption of the cloud idea itself emphasizes that it is a mixture of centralized and distributed architecture.

Cloud Computing Provides Advantages

1. **Investment on Infrastructure**: Capital Investment optimizes the reduction of costs of hardware and software. This investment helps hospitals to make use of economies of scale and operational costs in information and communication technology.
2. **Innovative Approach**: Developing models under cloud computing environment facilitates to adopt innovative approach in health care information system.
3. **Electronic Devices:** Most of the electronic devices are connected to the internet. The internet is the main access in the cloud computing environment. Electronic Devices are more useful in a health care system.

Private Cloud Environment in Car Plus Cure Hospital Limited

There are four different models under the cloud computing concept with different characteristics. Care plus Cure hospital limited has chosen private cloud for their information system. A Private cloud (Chorafas, 2011) is considered to be suitable for maintaining sensitive data in health care systems. A Private cloud can be said to be a private data center and residing within the organization. This data center is exclusively for the use of their organization. This is shared and multi user environment built on highly efficient, automated and virtualized infrastructure. The advantage of Private cloud is setting up and managing the cloud services under the control of the enterprise who is owning it. The enterprise can take a better control of security and regulatory compliance issues. A private cloud is a better solution for health care organizations in leveraging the benefits of cloud computing within their firewall.

Virtual Environment

One of the big changes that is emerging in the present globalization scenario is virtual environment. This has given a scope for virtual medical conferences, virtual consultations and even virtual hospitals. The professional isolation that is experienced by so many professionals working away from distant places has become largely a thing of the past. Now they can take part in interactive exchanges and have access to online knowledge bases and expertise as anyone and anywhere in the World. The idea behind choosing private cloud by care plus cure hospital limited is to provide health care services under virtual environment.

Virtual Reality in Virtual Environment

Virtual reality is a way of creating a three-dimensional image of an object or scene. It is possible for the user to move through or around the image. Virtual reality imitates the way the real object or scene looks and changes. Information system helps to use information in databases to stimulate. The line dividing simulated tasks and their real-world counterparts is very thin. Virtual reality systems are designed to produce in the participant the cognitive effects of feeling immersed in the environment created by a computer system. The computer system uses sensory inputs such as vision, hearing, feeling and sensation of motion. The concept of multimedia is required in virtual reality process. The components of multimedia are tactile (Touch), Visual (Image) and auditory (Sound).

The concept of virtual reality is more useful for showing the advancements taking place in the health care sector especially in the area of surgery. Medical students will be benefited by upgrading their knowledge. Simulated tasks replicate the real medical tasks. Care plus Cure hospital Limited wants to make use of this concept in explaining the latest developments in surgery to medical students.

Research Activities in Health Care Sector

Certain diseases are peculiar to certain countries (Auewarkul, 2008). An independent research center or a center for a group of hospitals can be established to analyze the disease and its causes. Many samples of information are required for analysis. Generally, database in any hospital has the current information only to optimize the use of databases. The data from the database are transferred to historical database as backup.

Four types of hospital enterprises provide medical services in India (Dipti Govil and Neetu Purohit, 2011). They are 1) Corporate Hospitals 2) Government Hospitals 3) Hospitals managed by a group of trustees and 4) Nursing homes. Care plus Cure Hospitals Limited along with some of the above mentioned hospitals have agreed to have a joint research center. Care plus Cure Hospitals Limited is ready to store their data along with the data of other hospitals in their private cloud. It is mutually agreed that the data is to be used for research purpose only. Historical data and spatial data collected from several databases from different hospitals are stored in one database under a private cloud at Care plus Cure hospitals limited. Private cloud provides an extremely useful activity in the medical field for research. Figure-2 gives an overview of medical research base at Care plus Cure Hospital Limited.

The data warehouse concept is used by the above hospitals for their research work. The Data warehouse is a central store of data that is extracted either from the operational database or from historical data base. The data in data warehouses are subject oriented, non-volatile and of a historical nature. So data warehouse tends to contain extremely large data sets. It can be inferred that the purpose of a data ware house is 1) To slice and dice through data 2) To ensure that past data is stored accurately 3) To provide one version of data 4) To operate for analytical process and 5) To support the decision process.

Data Mining (Pujari, 2003) is a concept used in Data warehouse. Data Mining deals with discovering hidden data and unexpected patterns and rules in large database. The terms "Data Mining" and KDD (Knowledge Discovery in Databases)

Figure 2. Medical research base

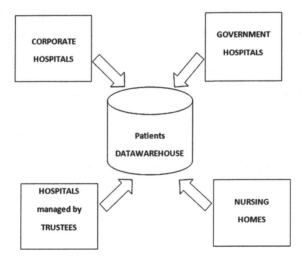

are considered as synonyms. At the first international conference on KDD in Montreal in the year 1995, it was proposed that the term "KDD" be employed to describe the whole process of extraction of knowledge from data. In this context knowledge means relationships and patterns between data and elements. It was proposed that the term "Data Mining" (Adriaans & Zatinge, 1999) should be used exclusively for the discovery stage of the KDD process. It is clear that KDD is not an activity that stands on its own. A good foundation in terms of a data warehouse is a necessary condition for effective implementation. Four types of knowledge can be identified in Data Mining. They are 1) Shallow Knowledge 2) Multidimensional Knowledge 3) Hidden Knowledge 4) Deep Knowledge

Shallow Knowledge

Information can be easily retrieved from databases using a query tool such as structured query language (SQL)

Multi-Dimensional Knowledge

Information can be analyzed using online analytical processing tools.

Hidden Knowledge

Data can be found relatively easily by using pattern recognition or machine learning algorithms.

Deep Knowledge

Information that is stored in the database can be located if one has a clue that tells the user where to look.

Information at a Hospital Level

The primary entity for a hospital is the patient. The information pertaining to patients, such as activities, habits, health problems, treatment and reactions to medicines may be available at a particular hospital where all the services needed are provided to patients. The information pertaining to the services rendered may be available in a same database or different databases and at different locations.

The required information transferred to a data warehouse in the private cloud at Care plus Cure Hospitals is limited for research. Combinations of data warehouse and data mining indicates an innovative approach to information management. Private cloud environment at Care plus Cure hospital limited has given a strategic source of opportunity to the doctors attached to the various hospitals to be a part of the research group for making use of their medical knowledge and experience in the area of research.

Case Illustration 2

The doctors have been highlighting some of the side effects of the drugs prescribed by them to their patients at the various medical conferences being held in India. It has been the practice among some of the pharmaceutical companies to send their executives in their R and D Departments to attend these conferences. On Call pharma Limited which has a base in India has felt it would be better to associate with a hospital to analyze the medical cases for improving and discovering a drug. On the basis of the proposal submitted by the above pharmaceutical company, Care plus Cure Hospitals Limited has accepted their proposal and is ready to share the data with them for discovering a drug. It has been mutually agreed that discovering a drug (Damayanti Bandopadhyay, 2013) should be on a rational approach. Further, it has been agreed to create a core team consisting of medical doctors, paramedical professionals, research executives and information technology professionals for this project. Members of the core team are from On Call Pharma Limited, Care plus Cure Hospital Limited and the professionals from the hospitals associated with Care plus Cure hospitals limited. The data in the private cloud at Care plus Cure hospital limited will be the base for research purpose.

Discovery of a Drug

A Drug is a molecule that interacts with target biological molecules in the body and through such interaction triggers a physiological effect. The target molecules are usually proteins. Drugs can be beneficial or harmful depending on their effect. The aim of discovering a drug is with specific beneficial effects to treat diseases in human beings.

Discovering a drug can be arrived by two methods (S., 2005). The methods are empirical and rational. Empirical method is a blind or loose method. It is also called black box method. Thousands of chemical compounds are tested on the disease without even knowing the target on which the drug acts and the mechanism of action. The rational method starts from the clear knowledge of the target as well as the mechanism by which it is to be attacked. Drugs act either to stimulate or block the activity of the target protein.

Role of Bio-Informatics in Drug Discovery

Bio Informatics is the storage, manipulation, and analysis of biological information by making use of information technology. Bio Informatics is an essential infrastructure under pinning biological research (Bryan Bergeron, 2003). Adoption of Bioinformatics based approach to drug discovery provides an important advantage in rational approach.

Biological Data

The properties that characterize a living organism (Species) are based on its fundamental set of genetic information. It is important to understand the fundamental terms of aspects such as DNA, RNA, Protein and their information in relation to Genome.

Different sequences of bases in DNA specify different sequences of bases in RNA. The sequence of bases in RNA specifies the sequences of amino acids in proteins. The central dogma states that DNA is transcribed into RNA, which is then translated later into protein (Attwood & Parry-Smith, 2005).

The main advantage in Bioinformatics discipline is biological data are available on the various websites (Krane & Raymer, 2005). The databases on these websites can be classified into two types such as generalized and specialized databases. The generalized databases contain information related to DNA, Protein or similar types. The generalized databases can again be further split into sequence databases and structured databases. Sequence databases hold the individual sequence records of either nucleotides or amino acids or proteins. Structured databases contain the individual sequence records of bio-chemically solved structures of macro-molecules.

Specialized databases are 1) EST (Expressed Sequence Tags) 2) GSS (Genome Survey Sequences) 3) SNP (Single Nucleotide Polymorphism) 4) STS (Sequence Tag Sites) 5) KABAT for Immunology Proteins and LIGAND for enzymes reaction legends. These databases can be further split into three types based on the complexity of the data stored.

1. **Primary Databases:** These databases contain data in its original form from the sequences.
2. **Secondary Databases**: These databases have value added data and derived information from the primary databases.
3. **Composite Databases**: Composite databases amalgamate a variety of different primary databases, structured into one. There are various software tools available to facilitate searching the above databases.

Developing or designing a drug is possible by making use of the information in the diverse chemical libraries along with the information pertaining to biological functions stored in the above databases before starting laboratory based experiments. It is always possible to generate as much information as possible about potential drug and target interaction from the above databases and chemical libraries.

Environmental Data in Health Care Management

Care plus Cure Hospital limited plans to emulate the UK experience in the environmental data in health care management. It is interesting to note a database containing environmental conditions and diagnosis at a patient's surroundings can be made use of in the health care system. This will facilitate in diagnosing and providing treatment for an individual patient. This was a pioneer health care system for diagnosing and monitoring asthma patients via the internet. This was introduced before Cloud computing came into existence.

Care plus Cure Hospitals Limited wants to collate data from different parts in India and monitor the patients, since they have the patient's data in the private cloud environment (Krishna Kumar L & Jimy Joy, 2013).

Middlesex University has created a central disease management system. Asthma patients and those with a chronic obstructive pulmonary disease would use a portable monitoring device to record breathing patterns up to four times a day in the comfort of their homes. The data were sent via modem and telephone lines to the central disease management system. It was processed and results were sent to the patient's doctor using the cable and wireless secure internet way. This system would record the date and time, temperature and humidity measures critical for analyzing the health of an asthma patient's surrounding such as air pollution and quality which would assist in providing the correct treatment and diagnosis for individual patients. Moreover, patients would record their symptoms and use of medication as well as their lung function data in central disease management, which would contain two parts of data in respect of asthma patients. One part of the data would be in respect of patient's data pertaining to date and time, temperature and humidity measure. The second part of the data would relate to environmental conditions, air pollution and quality.

Need for Self Learning Among Medical Students

Learning any subject and in depth understanding of it requires that learners actively construct their own personal meanings of the things they learn and integrate with their prior knowledge and skills. Medical students once they qualify themselves as professionals bear the responsibility for translating their in depth knowledge into practice. Their skills grow as learners can work towards enhancing themselves and improving both competence and confidence.

The knowledge based system developed at the Care plus Cure Hospitals limited provides the mechanism of interaction with their system. Patient Data Ware House in their system is useful for evidence based information resource. A medical student or a doctor makes use of the knowledge based system to get answers for the questions formulated on the basis of "Background" of a particular disorder/disease and "Fore Ground" of treatment of the patients concerned.

Case Illustration 3

Mr. X is an account executive in a private firm in India. He is 52 years old moderately obese with type 2 diabetes, diagnosed 11 years ago. He has been trying to quit his smoking habit of 25 years. No diabetic complications have been detected so far. His blood sugar is well controlled. But his blood pressure has been mildly elevated averaging 158/94 mm HG during the past three visits to the hospital. He has been unable to reduce his weight during the past two years despite his doctor's suggestion. He is also not keen to further medicate himself, preferring "Natural Remedies". However, he is open to taking medicines, if their efficacy proved in lowering his blood pressure and blood sugar. As an account executive, he wants to quantify the result of additional medication prescribed. The data related to the above patient is available in the patient data warehouse, at Care plus Cure Hospitals limited in the private cloud environment. Each patient information is stored under three groups. They are 1) History of the patient 2) History of the treatment prescribed, and 3) Summary of treatment given to the patients of similar complaints.

1.   The history of a patient consists of diagnosis, habits, tests conducted, test results, treatments, allergies, and reactions.
2.   History of the treatment prescribed covers drugs prescribed, composition of drugs, dosage, precautions, and likely reactions.
3.   The data related to the patients of similar complaints is available under the separate head in the patient's data warehouse.

A medical student or a doctor has to search from the basis of diseases and the treatments prescribed to similar patients. They can review the information downloaded from the patient data warehouse and can prepare an abstract. They can compare with the treatment perceived by the medical student or a doctor. This helps them to assess their knowledge in a particular case.

Analysis of the Approach of Care Plus Cure Hospital Ltd

Care plus Cure Hospital Limited has created a knowledge-based health care system. The idea behind creation of medical informatics system under the cloud computing environment is for easy accessibility by them and other hospitals associated with them. One more salient feature of the cloud computing is it enables the delivery of business models for IT services over the internet. Further most of the electronic devices are connected to the Internet. Care plus Cure Hospital Limited has felt that it is an advantage to make use of private cloud computing for their requirements. The core team at Care plus Cure Hospital Limited has made use of the collaborative technology in the private cloud computing environment to create a virtual hospital enterprise. Virtual hospital enterprise approach is to extend its services to the hospitals attached to them. Following paragraphs indicate the benefits derived from this approach.

Hospitals in Rural Areas

Medical fraternity who started the hospitals in the rural areas in India has taken advantage of the integrated hospital management system at Care+Cure hospital limited. Moreover, medical doctors are the part of the core team for designing and developing the system. The integrated hospital management system provides the benefits such as 1) Validation of data across the system 2) Parameterization in application software 3) Multilevel security 4) Multilevel authorization 5) Reduction in patients' waiting time 6) Elimination of wastage of stationery 7) Accuracy of Data 8) Educating Patients 9) Analysis of the reactions of medicines, and 10) Better coordination among different departments. Further their data is stored in the above system and is available to the broad group of users at different locations.

Drug Design

The purpose behind Care plus Cure Hospital Limited and hospitals associated with them is designing a drug with On Call Pharma Limited. They have actual data of medicines prescribed and the reactions on their patients. This data is most important for research in designing a drug. Private cloud provides the required space for storing and analysis. The rational method in designing a drug needs data from genial and the specialized databases in Bioinformatics.

The research team could make use of data related to the components of drugs prescribed and the relations on the patients for guidance for their research. This approach emphasizes the need for integrating health service research and designing research to reduce reactions on the patients. It is expected this approach will be better before laboratory tests take place in respect of new drugs produced. Figure 3 illustrates a rational approach for discovery and development of drugs.

Medical Research Activities

Any Research needs a large volume of data for research. There is not dearth of medical data in India. It is general practice in many hospitals in India for the sake of optimizing the use of databases their databases contain one-year data only. The earlier years' data are either transferred to another system as back up or deleted. The historical data are never made use of for any research purpose. The Care plus Cure Hospital Limited has initiated the process of the historical data of the patients of the hospitals associated with them for research. They could persuade corporate hospitals, Government hospitals, hospitals managed by trustees, and nursing homes to transfer the historical data of their patients to the patient data warehouse in their private cloud environment. Medical doctors who have researched bent of mind working in the above hospitals are associated with the research. The doctors at these hospitals need not move out of their hospitals for their research work. This has become possible because of private cloud environment and access through internet. They can conduct research with ease from their workplace by making use of data mining tool in the patient data ware house in the system.

Figure 3. Rational base approach for discovery and development of drugs

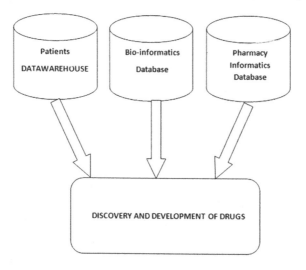

Virtual Reality Concept Under Private Cloud Environment

The inputs provided by the medical doctor who performed surgical operations by them is the latest methodology, the core team will develop a model. This model will consider the real medical world requirements. Parameters will be created on the basis of the requirements. A Simulated version of the human body is designed and the operation is carried out on the computer systems in the private cloud environment. Medical doctors in the core team have immersed themselves in every aspect of the design and testing. They have worked in front of a large screen of a computer, which has given a sense of surgical operation is taking place in the real medical world situation. The concept of virtual has helped them to look from the real medical world situation. The Private cloud environment has facilitated the above process with virtual reality.

Medical doctors working at the Care plus Cure Hospital Limited, the hospitals associated with them and medical students can take advantage of updating themselves the advancements made in the surgical operations. It is said visualization is more effective than giving a detailed description of an event (Epstein & Macvoy, 2011).

Emulating an Innovative Approach

Some years ago a telemedicine project was implemented in the United Kingdom. The participants of this project were telecommunication firm, Consortium of Industrial Academia, Clinical Partners across Europe, including, university, and college, London, Middlesex University, a German medical diagnostic business, The Whittington Hospital National Health Service Trust (North London) and Spains Hospital General.

The main essence of this project was the use of portable monitoring devices to record breathing patterns in the comfort of the patient's home. Modem and telephone lines were made use of sending data to central disease management system where it would be processed and results sent directly to the patient's consultant using the cable and wireless secure internet gateway.

The Core team at the Care plus Cure Hospital Limited has taken a lead from the above project. The team is evaluating the various portable medical devices on the similar type of project. Cloud computing has all the required features to support this type of project. In order to provide good health care to their patients in India and foreign Countries, the core team is working on this project. Once this model is developed and tested, there will be advantages to the patients. This model aims to save patient's time and travel expenses. Further, it reduces stress as they no longer have to visit the hospitals so frequently and do not have to keep paper records to monitor health. The core team wants to make use of their private cloud computing environment for developing this model with the various portable medical devices.

Evidence-Based Learning

Patient Data Ware House at Care plus Cure Hospital Limited is useful for evidence based learning. A medical student can make use of this data warehouse to get answers for the questions formulated on the basis of "Background" of a particular disorder/ disease and 'for ground' of treatment concerned. The Patient data warehouse contains the case history of the patients treated at various hospitals for learning purposes.

Three-dimensional visualization has the greatest potential in medical education and training. By making use of virtual reality concepts doctors and medical students can practice the surgical procedures. Pilots have been training on flight simulators for decades. The simulators are realistic that the trainee pilots before their first real flight can perform thousands of perfect takeoff and landing. The same way the medical students can learn the surgical skills before operating on the first patient. Figure 4 provides an idea of evidence-based learning.

Medical Information to Patients

Increasing number of people seeking information pertaining to disease/symptoms/ drugs/reactions are on the increase. One cannot be sure of the authenticity of the information available on the net.

Figure 4. Evidence-Based learning

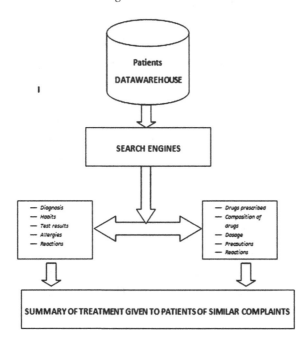

The Care plus Cure Hospital Limited has created an exclusive database in their system for their patients. This database provides the required information to dispel doubts arising in the minds of their patients. Access to this database is possible by their patients through the internet to a private cloud environment.

Device Management

The need for device management is obvious in a cloud computing environment. Heterogeneous devices, applications, and users' needs are to be administered. The important functionality of a pervasive device is to perform a task with high speed. For each application and type of device it has to support different kinds of user interfaces. The main requirement of device management is to take care of the operating system, structure, memory protection, security and multi tasking.

Health Care System Under Cloud Computing

Knowledge based health care system developed by Care plus Cure Hospital Limited proves that a useful system can be developed for the medical fraternity. The main significance in the system is making use of private cloud along with the collaborative technology. This system can increase the chances of successfully diffusing knowledge, technology and process. Advanced concepts in information and communication technology have drastically changed the medical informatics, providing new services and creating an interconnected medical fraternity.

Making Easy Access to Important Information

The management of the Care Plus Cure Hospital Limited felt the need for any more information useful to patients and doctors. There are many websites providing information required by doctors and patients. Some websites provide information related to diagnostic centers extending the services such as x-ray, scanning and clinical tests. Medical equipment manufacturers and pharmaceutical companies provide their product information, contact phone numbers are available on their respective websites. Information pertaining to health insurance service is available on the respective websites maintained by the various health insurance service providers. All the required information is scattered in the various web sites.

Doctors do not have time to browse the various websites for information. In the case of patients, many of them are not aware of the websites to be visited for their required information. Medical equipment manufacturers and pharmaceutical companies and health insurance service providers find it difficult to address their segments of their markets.

Case Illustration 4

The Care plus Cure Hospitals Limited has identified the marketing executives working in the different segments under the health care sector. Care plus Cure Hospitals Limited invited them for an interaction. At their meeting the Care plus Cure Hospitals Limited has expressed their desire to create a database under their private cloud environment, providing information exclusively to patients and doctors. The proposed database mainly covers the information pertaining to different medical equipments, various drugs, and the health insurance providers. Further, they have explained the need for this kind of database. This database is more like a directory, useful to doctors and patients only.

At the meeting the marketing executives have agreed to share their knowledge and experience in their line business activities. They suggested that they would form as a team and provide salient features of their products/services require the attention of the doctors and patients. Some of the marketing executives expressed that they would also provide information pertaining to service apartments situated near to the hospitals associated with the Care plus Cure Hospitals Limited. This information will be useful to the relatives and friends who accompany the patients for surgery. They can stay in any one of the apartments nearer to the hospital where the patient is admitted for the surgery/treatment. It will be possible for them to visit the patient at frequent intervals on rotation. The marketing executives have also suggested to include the information pertaining to travel agent services for organizing to book train and air tickets for patients and their relatives/friends. This kind of service will be useful for people who need to go to a hospital located far away from the place they are staying (Reur J, Arino J, & Olk P, 2011) . Care plus Cure Hospital Limited has expressed that they would identify software professionals in their organization to interact with the marketing executives. On the basis of the information provided by the marketing executives, the software professionals would start designing the database under their private cloud computing environment.

Observation

This is a unique way of thinking about creation of an information database. This approach can be said as an open innovation approach in providing information as a guide for those people who require the information without any hassle. One may say this type of information is already available in google. An effort is required by an individual to browse the various websites for the required information. This information guide can be considered as a one stop solution to doctors and patients. The private cloud environment at Care plus Cure Hospital Limited has facilitated them to design a date base as a one stop solution to doctors and patients (Bandopadhyay D, 2013).

Sharing of Knowledge Among Medical Students

Case Illustration 5

Care plus Cure Hospital Limited is already having a patient data warehouse under their private cloud environment for evidence base learning. The patient data warehouse contains the case history of the each patient treated at the various hospitals with them for learning purposes. Medical students can make use the patient data warehouse to know the treatment provided to a particular disorder/disease. This approach facilitates to update their knowledge in the context of the treatment in respect of a particular disease/disorder.

A group of medical students has decided to form as a "Knowledge Sharing Team" for discussion on medically related subjects and topics. They have requested Care plus Cure Hospital Limited to make use of their patient data warehouse of knowledge sharing purpose. Care plus Cure Hospital Limited has agreed to their request and stipulated that it should be exclusively for their academic discussion only.

A few members among "Knowledge Sharing Team" have been identified to prepare a case study on the basis of the data related to diseases/disorders treated at the Care plus Cure Hospital Limited and the hospitals attached to them and stored in the patient data warehouse. The actual treatment given to to the patients is not mentioned in the case study. Each member of the group is expected to go through each case study. After studying the case study each member suggests a treatment on the basis of the member's knowledge. Two or three medical students can together suggest a treatment. Later all their suggested treatments are stored in the patient data warehouse. Then discussion takes place on the suggested treatments. After their discussion, they will compare with the actual treatment given to the patient. This method facilitates them to update their knowledge. Further, it sharpens their professional thinking.

Observation

It may be noted that the medical students who live in different locations can take part in the academic discussion by the "Knowledge Sharing Team". The Care plus Cure Hospital Limited is able to provide the opportunity to the medical students in their private cloud computing environment for sharing their knowledge. The management of the Care plus Cure Hospital Limited strongly believes the knowledge is for sharing.

Case Illustration 6

Guidance for Social Workers

A group of social workers in South India visit the various rural parts of their social work. During their visits, they make it a point to explain to the rural people the importance of hygiene and the good health habits to be followed by them. During their talk, they use various charts and diagrams related to basic health education. They use to interact with them after their talk. During their interaction, they felt that there is not good impact of their health related tips mentioned in their talk of the rural people. They felt there was a need to change the method of presenting their health related tips to rural people. They have met the management of Care plus Cure Hospital Limited for getting their guidance in conducting the basic health related talk.

The management of the Care plus Cure Hospital Limited has agreed to help them and considered it as a corporate responsibility to the society (Aye K, 2016). The Care plus Cure Hospital Limited has decided to create a "General Health Data Warehouse" under their private cloud computing environment.

This database mainly talks about the salient features in health care information to be explained to the rural people. A simulated version of the human body is created and stored in the data warehouse. The function each part of the body is explained in the recorded voice. Mainly ten different languages are spoken in the rural parts of the South India. The explanation in respect of the functions human body is explained in the ten different languages. An option is given to the social workers for choosing the language spoken in the place where they give their talk. Orientation sessions are organized by the Care plus Cure Hospital Limited for the benefit of social workers. This orientation session helped them to understand in using the "General Health Data Warehouse. The orientation session has helped them to talk with confidence and to explain the salient features related to health information.

The internet facility is available in the rural parts of South India. The social workers make use of their laptops along with the other supporting devices to conduct their sessions at the various rural locations. The social workers are happy that they are able to make an impact on the rural people with the new approach.

Observation

It is interesting to note that the Care plus Cure Hospital Limited is able to help the social workers to carry out their work with "Genral Health Data Warehouse" developed by them. The basic requirement is to get access to the above data warehouse in the private cloud environment is the internet. The internet is already available in the places wherever the social workers are conducting health awareness programs.

Artificial Intelligence in Healthcare Sector

The management of the Care plus Cure Hospital Limited has decided to make use of the concept of artificial intelligence in their health activities. The Care plus Cure Hospital Limited is already having a large volume of data in, its data warehouse pertaining to the patient's history, diseases/disorders and the treatment given the patients. The data pertaining to clinical and images are stored in the data warehouse. The data in the data warehouse are also from the hospitals associated with them. Application of the concept of artificial intelligence will be more useful in analyzing and interpreting from the high volume of data. Artificial intelligence will facilitate to predict the possibility of a disease developing in an individual. This will help to indicate the requirement of more intensive treatment than another with a similar condition. It can also suggest a treatment that would suit better for a particular patient.

Analyzing Patterns

The most common usage now is to employ algorithm to detect patterns which would in turn help in predicting a possible a possible outcome. Some research findings have indicated that it would be possible to identify patients whose condition was likely to deteriorate which the doctors could prevent by taking extra care. It can also help to finalize a treatment protocol by factoring in the age, lifestyle, family history and other related details (Khon M S & Skaulis, 2012).

Visual Diagnosis

The concept of Artificial Intelligence can help the doctors to look at thousands of pieces of past data to analyze and find out anomalies much better than the human eye (Deepa S N & Aruna Devi B, 2011). The visual pattern recognition software is already considered superior to the human eye in interpreting results from radiology, pathology, ophthalmology, and dermatology.

Diagnosis

This is different than the other two. As this has an additional element often known as intuition. Beyond information and learning, this is a matter of approach which is not easy for a machine to learn. Efforts are being made by research scholars to learn from the experts for including the intuitive feature in the artificial intelligence (Neill D B, 2012).

The research team at Care plus Cure Hospital Limited has studied the various applications of artificial intelligence techniques in the health care area. Some of the following applications stress the importance of the role of artificial intelligence in the health care sector.

Fuzzy Expert Systems in Medicine

Fuzzy logic is used in the data handling methodology. This method permits ambiguity and hence is particularly suited to medical applications. It captures and uses the concept of fuzziness in computationally effective manner. This is most useful in medical diagnostics and to a lesser extent in the description of biological systems.

Evolutionary Computation in Medicine

Evolutionary computation is the general term for several computational techniques based on natural evolution process that imitates the mechanism of natural selection and survival of the fittest in solving real world problems. The most widely used forms of evolutionary computation for medical applications are "Genetic Algorithms". The principles genetic algorithms have been used to predict outcome in critically ill patients. MRI segmentation of tumors and analysis of mammographic micro calcification is done through evolutionary computation.

Medical Image Classification

Artificial intelligence techniques are used for diagnostic sciences in Biomedical image classification. Model based analysis and decision support tools are important for diagnosis and evaluation. This facilitates radiologists to express their opinions.

Artificial Intelligence for Patient Care

Recent advances in machine learning and predictive models facilitate to make realtime inferences from large patient data. Data from outpatient settings such as preventive care and management of chronic disease is required to be considered while making use of artificial intelligence in patient care model in a health care system. This facilitates to improve many aspects of the patient care process.

FUTURE TRENDS

Integrating of knowledge and experience of medical professionals with the support of software professionals facilitate to develop new and innovative medical healthcare information systems (Ilkka Kunna Mo, 2015). Cloud computing is providing a scope for radical changes in designing healthcare models. Artificial intelligence is gaining importance in the healthcare sector. Generally, data in the healthcare sector are available as disperse elements. The concept of artificial intelligence helps to compile these elements into meaningful patterns. There is a good scope for research scholars to develop innovative healthcare information models under the concept of artificial intelligence in the cloud computing environment(Nagafeeson Madison, 2014).

CONCLUSION

The term "Virtual" is now appearing in many forms. Knowledge based health care systems developed at Care plus Cure Hospital Limited explains the need for adopting innovative approach in involving medical fraternity and software professionals applying the concept of "Mind Invoking". Hospitals will find that private cloud is a better solution for them in leveraging the benefits of cloud computing. Care plus Cure Hospital Limited has proved the importance of virtual hospitals under the cloud computing environment. Sharing the common resources for computing power, accessing data and sharing of knowledge are possible under cloud computing environment. The above aspects are clearly discussed with the case illustrations.

REFERENCES

Adriaans & Zantinge. (1999). *Data Mining*. Addison Wesley Longman.

Attwood, T. K., & Parry-Smith, D. J. (2005). *Introduction to Bioinformatics; New Delhi: Pearson Education*. Singapore: Private Limited.

Bandopadhyay. (2013). A Technology Lead Business Model for Pharma – Collaborative Patient Care. *CSI Communications Journal, 37*(9), 12-13, 26.

Bergeron, B. (2003). *Bioinformatics Computing; New Delhi: Pearson Education*. Singapore: Private Limited.

Buyya, Vecchiola, & Selvi. (2013). *Mastering Cloud Computing*. New Delhi: McGraw Hill Education (India) Private Limited.

Chorafas, D. N. (2011). *Cloud Computing Strategies*. Boca Raton, FL: CRC Press Taylor & Francis Group.

Deepa & Aruna. (2011). A Survey on Artificial Intelligence Approaches for Medical Image Classifications. *Indian Journal of Science and Technology, 4*(11).

Epstein, R. A., & Macvoy, S. P. (2011). Making A Scene in the Brain. In L. R. Harris & M. R. M. Jenkin (Eds.), *Vision in 3D Environments* (pp. 270–273). Cambridge, UK: Cambridge University Press. doi:10.1017/CBO9780511736261.012

Govil & Purohit. (2011). Health Care Systems in India. In Health Care Systems – A Global Survey (pp. 576-612). New Delhi: New Century Publications.

Ignacimuthu, S. (2005). *Basic Informatics*. New Delhi: Narosa Publishing House.

Khon & Skarulis. (2012). IBM Watson Delivers New Insights for Treatment and Diagnosis. *Digital Health Conference*.

Kok, A. (2016). *Cultural, Behavioral and Social Considerations in Electronic Collaboration USA*. IGI Global. doi:10.4018/978-1-4666-9556-6

Krane, D. E., & Raymer, M. L. (2005). *Fundamental Concepts of Bioinformatics; New Delhi: Pearson Education*. Singapore: Private Limited.

Krishna & Jimy. (2013). Application of Zigbee Wireless Frequency for Patient Monitoring System. *CSI Communications Journal, 37*(9), 17-18.

Madison, N. (2014). *Health Information Systems, Opportunities and Challenges*. Retrieved from http//commons.nmu.edu/facwork_book chapters/14

Mo. (2015). How to Build an Ideal Health Care Information System. In The World Book of Family Medicine European Edition 2015. Academic Press.

Neill, D. B. (2012). Fast Subsect Scan for Spatial Pattern Detection. *Journal of the Royal Statistical Society. Series B, Statistical Methodology, 74*(2), 2012. doi:10.1111/j.1467-9868.2011.01014.x

PrasertAuewarkul. (2008). The Past and Present Threat of Avian Influenza in Thailand. In E. M. Yichenlu & B. Roberts (Eds.), *Emerging Infections in Asia* (pp. 31–34). New York, NY: Springer. doi:10.1007/978-0-387-75722-3_2

Pujari. (2003). Data Mining Techniques. Hyderabad: Universities Press (India) Private Limited.

Reur, J., Arino, J., & Olk, P. (2011). *Entrepreneural Alliances (Vol. 1)*. Boston: Pearson Higher Education.

Sunitha, C., VasanthaKokilam, K., & MeenaPreethi, B. (2013). Medical Informatics-Perk up Health Care through Information. *CSI Communications Journal, 37*(9), 7-8.

Vijayrani, S. (2013). Economic Health Records- An Overview. *CSI Communications Journal, 37*(9), 9-11.

KEY TERMS AND DEFINITIONS

Artificial Intelligence: Artificial intelligence is an area of computer science that emphasizes creation of intelligent machines that work and react like humans.

Collaborative Technology: This refers to various concepts in information and communication technology that facilitate joint work.

Evidence-Based Learning: This refers to any concept or strategy that is derived from or informed by objective evidence.

Fuzzy Logic: Fuzzy logic is a method of reasoning and resembles human reasoning.

Knowledge Sharing: Knowledge sharing is an activity through which knowledge is exchanged among professionals and communities.

Mind Invoking: Making an earnest effort in an innovative approach.

One Stop Solution: A one stop source is a business or office where multiple services are offered.

Chapter 7
BIG Data:
An Enabler in Developing Business Models in Cloud Computing Environments

K. Hariharanath
SSN School of Management, India

ABSTRACT

The basic functions such as production, marketing, and finance continue to be the same from an agricultural economy to an industrial economy. Business processes, procedures, methods, strategy, management thinking, and approach related to basic functions have been changed due to global market competition. Consequent to global competition, business activities have become more complex. Due to this complexity, the type and quantum of information required by the business enterprises are increasing. It is interesting to note that information and communication technology is providing many new concepts to handle and manage the complex information to remain competitive in the global market. The concepts such as big data and cloud computing along with other collaborative technology facilitate creating conceptual business models for facing realities in the global market. This chapter mainly explains with two case illustrations of the importance of the above concepts for developing business models for textile and retail sectors.

DOI: 10.4018/978-1-5225-3182-1.ch007

INTRODUCTION

Globalization, which was initially viewed with fear and distrust has opened up huge new markets for many business enterprises across the globe. This has been focusing on the need for an innovative approach in conducting business by enterprises. It is apt to recall the observation of Peter Ducker on innovation. "A Business enterprise has two and only two basic functions, marketing and innovation. Marketing and innovation produce results. All the other departments are cost centers. The dividing factors in the market are niche markets and unique products or services. Innovative approach is needed to achieve the above factors in the present competitive market. Strategic thinking is required for any innovative approach. Strategic thinking decisions are based on the following:

1. An understanding of the current and emerging needs
2. An understanding of the organizations current and anticipated future core competences such as special skills or knowledge resources and culture and
3. A future view of the industry sector and marketplace.

Even the most stable industries and the strongest brands can be blown to bits by the emerging concepts in information and communication technologies. Technology is forcing to rethink its business models and organizational designs as it contributes to the re-balancing of power in the market place. It is no longer guaranteed to those organizations that have the financial resources and size on their side. Smaller organizations that are fast and flexible can now outmaneuver the traditional large enterprises by employing new technology that enables them to deliver goods and services to their customers at a faster pace and lower cost (Kumar & Kumar, 2013).

NEED FOR A BUSINESS MODEL

The problem arises when the organizations are spending too much time tinkering with the existing business models of their organizations instead of re allying their teams around the potential doing something extraordinary in the market place. Tinkering is like painting a Car when the engine is weak. The challenge today is to develop sustainable business that is compatible with the current economic reality. In the present global market scenario an enterprise remaining competitive in the market depends on its ability to focus on core business and adapting to changes quickly. Now it has become imperative for every business enterprise to innovate a process that will help them to remain competitive in the market. Innovative process is nothing but identifying what is relevant to the emerging technologies and develop a business model suitable for their business enterprise.

DESIGNING A BUSINESS MODEL

One of the most interesting opportunities in the present scenario is the dynamic nature of the information and communication technology capabilities available in almost every sector that one could imagine. Business enterprises need to know how to make use of the capabilities of information and communication technology and their relevance and context to their business requirements. Business process, technological applications, practices, past business performances, market potential and target market are the factors to be considered in designing a business model. A case study of a textile mill in India is discussed in this chapter and how they developed a business model on the basis of the above factors transforming their business process and market share.

CASE ILLUSTRATION

3G Textile Mill is one of leading textile mills in India. This Textile mill has been in the business over five decades. The unique aspect of this mill is that it is managed by a management team consisting of a President, Senior Vice President and Vice President who belong to three different generations. Their approach and decisions are based on their experiences, business insight and education.

3G Textile Mill products range from western and Indian cloth materials for ladies, suiting and shirting materials and ready-made garments for ladies and gents. Each management team member has taken the responsibility to be in charge of one of their product range. Their responsibility covers all the activities related from production to marketing of the product. The major financial activities such as purchase of capital items and investment activities will be the responsibility of the Management Team. The product design, production schedule, purchase of raw materials and other materials will be purchased by the concerned team member of the product he is associated with. The cost of common support services such as finance, human resource and administrative are borne by the product divisions. Activity based costing method is followed in allocating the cost of common support services.

Selection of cotton and mix of various varieties of cotton for the production of different "count of yarn" is the main activity in any textile mill in India It is interesting to note the method followed for the selection of cotton and mix of cotton varies among the management team.

The President of 3G Textile Mill who is looking after the activity related to the production of ladies cloth materials and ladies garments has three decades of rich experience in all the aspects related to the textile field. Though he has no formal education, he updates himself in information technology, textile technology and marketing aspects of textile products. Further he is aware of Indian and Global economy. The method he follows is the method of testing the strength of the cotton manually. He interacts with the vendors who bring the cotton sample. In his interaction with them, he gets the information such as the year of crop, place and country of origin of cotton. He mentally calculates the costing for the mix of two varieties of cotton. He also recalls the economic conditions, weather conditions, currency exchange rates and other relevant information pertaining to the year of crop and preceding years on the basis of these factors. He fixes the purchase price for imported cotton and the cotton produced in India. He also further visualizes the design of the end market for a particular market segment.

The senior vice president who is looking after the activities related to "shirting" material has a degree in textile technology and fifteen years of experience in the Textile Industry. He has formal business interaction with the cotton vendors. Then he selects few samples of cotton and sends them to quality department for testing and analysis of the cotton. He works out the costing for the mix of cotton for the production of yarn on the basis of the report given by the quality department. He uses the calculator to arrive at the cost of "Mix of Cotton". He negotiates with vendors for the purchase price.

The Vice President who is in charge of the activities related to "Pant Material" has a master's degree in textile technology and a Masters Degree in Business Management from a world renowned University. He never meets any cotton vendor. Vendors are expected to hand over the samples of cotton to the group of purchasing executives identified for this type of assignment. It is the responsibility of this group to send the samples to the quality department for testing. They arrive at the cost of the cotton mix on the basis of the report given by the quality department. Costing for the different mix of cotton is arrived at by using a software developed for this purpose. The report generated from the computer system is sent along with the report given by the quality department to the Vice President. He decides the purchase of the cotton on the basis of the reports received by him.

The 3G textiles mills have been making profits, even though the three management team members follow their own methods. They also never claim that their methods are best. Every team member has his own information system for his product related activities such as production, design, purchases and marketing. The information pertaining to finance is only integrated for all the activities related to all the products manufactured by 3G textiles, the 3G textile mill has been in the market over a period of three decades. Their business models worked well. Their products are well received in the market. Their market has been encouraging. Though the overall profit and the market share of the company is fluctuating, overall performance of 3G textiles is not affected. It is because one product's dip in profit is offset by the other products profits of the company. The management team has felt this trend is not encouraging a healthy sign. The President of the company has analyzed the situation and came to the conclusion that the linear process in their business models that is research through design, development and marketing is not conductive to the present globalization scenario. It is also due to global market being open to many players across the globe.

SERVICES OF A CONSULTANCY FIRM

3G Textile Mills hired the services of a consultancy firm who have experience in textile domain, information and communication technology and global market scenario. The assignment given to them is to study the present working of the mills. On the basis of their study, they are expected to suggest a business process. A New business process needs to be discussed with the management before developing a business model.

The study conducted by the Consultant indicated that 3G Textile Mills has cost advantage over the competitors in the areas of process technology and size of business enterprise. They do not have an edge over the competitors in the areas of distribution networking, product technology and brands in the global market. The company has barriers to entry due to brands and retaliatory capability. But the company has vertical bargaining power due to sound financial resources. Information systems in the company are isolated and not integrated. Further the company has not made use of the emerging concepts in the areas of information and communication technologies.

BUSINESS MODEL FOR 3G TEXTILE MILLS

The consultants have designed a business model for 3G Textile Mills with cloud computing as a base component with the concepts of virtual reality, data warehouse and big data (Adam Jorgensen, James Rowland-Jones, John Welch, Dan Clark, Christopher Price & Brain Mitchell, 2014).

The information pertaining to all the products produced by the three divisions is to be integrated and stored in a centralized system. Purchase of cotton for the production of cloth material is to be centralized. Marketing information and its activities are to be centralized. Domain experts with rich experience across the globe in the area of textile sector need to be hired. The domain experts can operate with their team members from their respective countries. Their role is to design the textile material (cloth) and ready-made garments for men and women. Domain experts are expected to design as per the tastes of the people of their country. Domain experts would guide the technical personnel of the 3G Textile Mills in India for implementing the design developed by them. Types of cotton and mix of cotton information will be provided for their design. The color of dyes and combination and the required quantities are to be provided by the domain experts. Vendors who will supply cotton, dyes and other materials as per the ISO standards, they will be given access to the bills of material module in the system for knowing the quantity of cotton and dyes, date of supply. The domain experts are expected to suggest marketing strategies that would work in their countries. The approach suggested by the domain experts is based on virtual organizations.

CLOUD COMPUTING FOR VIRTUAL ORGANIZATION

The essence of Virtual Organization is a collaboration of participants who are both geographically and organizationally distributed. Cloud Computing helps to implement virtualization in information and communication technologies. Advancements in the internet has facilitated that there is no need to limit group collaboration in a single enterprise network environment. Use from multiple locations within their and other organizations can have access to the systems through internet. Cloud computing helps the users to create a centralized pool of virtual servers, storage and networking equipment (Tim Mather, Subra Kumaraswamy &Shahed Latif, 2010).

Application virtualization allows for an application to run from a remote server rather than on the user's system. Each application is bundled with its own configuration set and the user can execute it on demand.

VIRTUAL REALITY

Virtual reality refers to the presentation of computer generated data made available in such a way that those who use it can perceive the information at their disposal. The ability to get real world perception inter activity through computers, explains interest associated with 3-D Graphics Virtual Reality. One can master the concept of virtual reality through simulation. The way business model is being developed provides scope for the study of complex real world situations. It also helps to develop steps for simulation and studying complex business concepts.

DATA MANAGEMENT

The data formats are most important aspect in any integrated database. The data may be put into the particular resource and the results from the resource on the execution of a specific task if the database is not designed properly. The data movement in geographically distributed systems can cause scalability problems. Data movement in any cloud computing environment requires absolutely secure data transfers both to and from the respective resources.

MOBILE COMPUTING

The concept of mobile computing is to facilitate end users to have access to data, Information or logical objects through a device in any network while one is on the move. It also enables the users to perform a task from anywhere using a computer device which has features or mobile computing. Generally, mobile computing is used in different contexts with different names. The most common names are 1. Mobile computing, 2. Anywhere, anytime information 3. Virtual home environment 4. Nomadic Computing 5. Pervasive Computing 6. Ubiquitous Computing, 7. Global service portability, and 8. Wearable Computers.

DEVICES

The convergence of information and communication technology is responsible for the production of new generation devices working on wireless technology. These devices can make the concept of cloud computing a workable solution in a virtual organization scenario. Even though many mobile and wireless devices are available there will be many more in the future. There is no precise classification of such devices by size, shape, weight or computing power. Currently the mobile device range is sensors, mobile phones, pocket computer, notebook, laptop, tablet and I pads.

BIG DATA

The term "Big Data" it suggests "Bigness" in data (Bill Franks, 2014). It indicates the volume of data is only the major factor. Industry analyst firm Gartner defines it as: Big data are high volume, high velocity and high variety information assets that demand cost-effective, innovative forms information processing for enhanced insight and decision making.

A major driving force behind this big data growth is ubiquitous connectivity through rapidly growing mobile devices constantly connected to the networks (Bill Schmarzo, 2014). It is remarkable to note that only a small portion of the digital universe is visible, in the form of videos, pictures, documents and tweets. A vast amount of data is being created about humans by the digital universe. Data will be analyzed by the enterprise such as internet service providers and Cloud Service providers of different varieties of services. They are infrastructure-as-a-service, platform-as-a-service and software-as-a-service.

Social data, websites, machine generated data and traditional enterprise data are the main elements of big data. Social data on social media sites cover Facebook, Twitter,and LinkedIn. Sensor reading and satellite communication form a part of machine generated data. Data on websites, blogs and portals provide specific information. Traditional enterprise data are confined to products, purchase, sales, customer and financial information. Figure 1 shows the elements in big data.

PROCESSING OF DATA IN BIG DATA

Technology provides access to a vast amount of usable information in big data. The users in enterprises need to master integrating that information and those technology capabilities to create relevant context. The relevance and content would come out of what would actually help in transforming their business.

The following steps are required to be considered while making use of big data.

1. **Search Engines:** Search engines are available to analyze large unstructured data.

Figure 1. The elements of big data

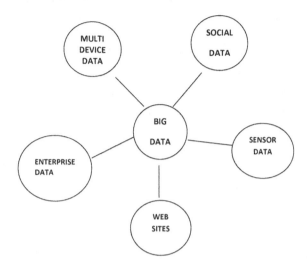

2. **Business Intelligence Tools:** Analytics tools are used to get new and create visualizations to intuitively depict the meaning of data.
3. **Storage of Data:** Private and public cloud are made use of the required infrastructure to store the big data.
4. **Cloud Computing:** Software-as-a –service in cloud environment will be useful to run the required software for processing the big data.
5. **Predictive Analytics:** This will be more effective for analyzing data from multiple dimensions.

Enterprises in the present business scenario need more data for analysis. Till recently it was possible only to store selected important data in the systems of business enterprises. This was due to cost effective way of storing data for business decision. Business analysts feel for the need for the huge volume of data for analysis and designing of business models. Mathematical and statistic tools are required to be used for designing these business models. These models facilitate to solve complex business problems. In the present business context big data is considered to be a better solution for storing data for business analysis. Velocity, variety and volume are the three main elements in big data. Generally it is known as 3rd of big data.

The term "BIG DATA" can be pretty nebulous in the same way that the term "CLOUD" covers diverse technologies. Input data to big data systems could be from social networks, web server logs, traffic flow sensors, satellite imagery, broadcast audio systems, and content of web pages, GPS trails and market data. This list indicates the basis for 3 elements in big data. The three elements volume, velocity and variety can be referred as a lens to view and understand the data and the software platforms for making use of them. Volume refers to the said data in terms of petabytes or xetabytes. Velocity talks about the rate at which the data is growing. Variety indicates structured, semi structured and unstructured another three features which play an important role in creating a database, they are consistency, availability and platform tolerance. Consistency means even if current updates are happening, users will get updated data irrespective of the place from where they are accessing the data, available to the users 24 x 7 irrespective of the load on the server. Platform tolerance means even in the case of partial failures in the system should be functional.

WHY BIG DATA?

Big data are considered for exceeding the processing capacity of conventional database systems. Big data are required wherever the data is too big and does not fit the structures of the conventional database architectures. Big data is an alternative way to process the data. It facilitates to gain value from this data. Big data have become viable as a cost effective approach. Earlier information was hidden because of the amount of work required to extract them.

The value of big data to an enterprise falls into two categories. One is for analytical use and another is for enabling new products. Big data analytics can reveal insights hidden previously by data too costly to process (Minelli, Chambers & Dhiraj, 2014). Big data help to reveal peer influence among customers by analyzing shoppers' transactions, social and geographical data. It enables to process every item of data in reasonable time. It removes the need for sampling and promotes an investigative approach to data. It facilitates to avoid the static nature of generating predetermined reports. The past decades successful web startups are important examples of big data used as an enabler for introducing new products and services.

Facebook has been to make use of highly personalized user experience and create a new kind of advertising business. It is no coincidence that the major share of ideas and tools in big data have emerged from Google, Yahoo, Amazon and Facebook. The emergence of big data in the business enterprises has made the experiment and explore for the business purposes. The business purposes can be for the creation of new products or looking for ways to gain competitive advantage.

VOLUME, VELOCITY AND VARIETY

Many business innovators are excited about the potential use in creating new design and developing a wide range of new products and services based on big data concept. Volume, Velocity and Variety need to be understood clearly by them.

VOLUME

The benefit gained from the ability to process large amounts of data is the main attraction for big data analytics. More data for analysis helps to create better models. Any complex mathematics formulas will appear more simple and effective in big data as many factors as 500 factors can be considered for forecasting to know demand pattern. This volume presents a challenge to conventional information technology structures. Then it calls for scalable storage and a distributed approach to querying. Many companies have large amounts of achieved data. They may not have required capacity to process it.

Data warehouse needs predetermined schemas suiting a regular dataset. Apache Hadoop on the other hand places no conditions on the structure of the data it can process. Hadoop is a platform for distributing computing problems across a number of servers. First developed and released as an open source by Yahoo. It implements the map reduce approach pioneered by Google in compiling its search indexes. Hadoop's map reduces involves distributing data set among multiple servers and operating on the data at map stage. The partial results are then recombined at the reduction stage.

To store data, Hadoop utilized its own distributed file systems. HEFS makes data available to multiple computing nodes. A typical Hadoop usage pattern involves three stages. They are (1) Loading data into HDFS (2) Map reduces operation and (3) Retrieving results from HDFS. This process is by nature a batch operation suited for analytical purpose or non interactive computing tasks. It can be considered as an adjunct to a data base.

VELOCITY

The increasing rate at which data flows into an enterprise is increasing. Data's velocity problems similar to volume previously restricted to certain segments of industry are now presenting themselves in a much broader setting. The internet and mobile era is making velocity more complex. Online retailers are able to compile large histories of customers every click and interaction not just the final sales. Retailers will gain a competitive advantage by making use of the information for recommending additional purchases. The Smart Phone is also increasing the rate of data inflow. Consumers who carry these devices will have a stream source of Geo Located Imagery and audio data.

Streaming data or complex event processing is the terms used in enterprises. The term complex event processing was used more in product categories before the term streaming processing data gained more widespread relevance. There are two main reasons to consider streaming processing. The first is when the input data are too fast to store in their entirety. In order to keep storage requirements practical, some level of analysis must occur as the data streams in. The second reason is where the application requires immediate response to the data.

VARIETY

A common theme in big data systems that source data is diverse and does not fall into a neat rational structure. Data can be from social networks, image data, and data from sensor source. None of this comes ready for integration into application. A common use of big data processing is to take unstructured data and convert it into meaningful data or structured input for an application.

CLOUD SERVICES FOR BIG DATA

The majority if big data solutions are now provided in three methods. They are (1) Software only (2) An Application and (3) Cloud –Based. Selection of a method depends on many factors. Some of the factors are location of Data, Privacy, Regulations, Human Resources and Project Requirements. Generally Enterprises prefer hybrid computing. They make use of the resources of private cloud along with public cloud. A cloud environment is preferred for processing because the nature of data being big (Reese, 2010). Another aspect is required to be considered besides information technology infrastructure cleaning the data. It is apt to recall the Pete wardens observation in his big data glossary. "I probably spend more time turning messy source data into some timing usable than I do the rest of the data analysis process combined".

DATA SCIENCE

Data science is a discipline that combines Mathematics, Statistics and software programming. Big data have also similar features of Data science. Business analytics that make use of big data concepts need to have the qualities such as experience, curiosity, storytelling and innovation.

EXPERTISE

Expertise is required in one of the areas such as mathematics or statistics or software programming with good knowledge of either mathematics or statistics.

CURIOSITY

A desire is required to go deep into the data for analysis and creating a set of hypotheses for testing.

STORY TELLING

One should have the ability to use data to tell a story.

INNOVATION

Ability is needed to look at a problem differently and suggest an innovative solution (Hameed M A, Counsell S, &Swift S, 2012).

ETHICS OF BIG DATA

Big Data is persistent. It is persistent in a way that business and society have never experienced before persistence of data influences the very important concepts such as privacy, ownership and identity for both individuals and enterprises, as information is aggregated and correlated by not only the originating entity, but also by those who may seek to further innovate products and services using the original information. It is very difficult to have a control over the information used once it is out of one's hands (Davis & Patterson, 2012).

Big data is mostly about people and their characteristics, and behavior. The potential use of this acquired data extends in a great many directions. The concerns about the consequences of having personal data captured, aggregated and linked to other data are slowly realized now. These risks are not just limited to individuals. It is equally applicable to enterprises. Enterprises are not in the business of misusing the information of their customers. Hospitals generally do not disclose the patient's confidentiality. Yet there is a risk of using big data technology.

Organizations must explicitly and transparently evaluate the ethical impacts of the data they collect from their customers. Ethical evaluation must indicate the utilization of customers' data. It must clearly describe the historical actions, characteristics, data handed practices and the value system followed by the organization, organizations work more effectively once their value is shared across their organization.

PRIVACY

Digital data can be used by any one. It does not differentiate the users.It is inevitable that Governments change, laws change, social mores change, but data once collected and placed on a global distributed network, such as the internet, is for all practical purposes permanent. The laws are required to regulate the usage of data collected. If the regulations are strict in saying that no data should be collected without user consent, then only there will be hope for privacy in data (Craig & Ludloff, 2013).

SOFTWARE TOOLS

There has been an innovative approach in the development of data /software tools. The innovative approach has become possible due to the trends in information and communication technology discipline. These trends can be classified under three areas (1) Techniques originally developed by website for scaling issues are being extended to other domains. (2) Google has proven that research techniques from computer science can be effective at solving problems and creating value in many real world situations. (3) Presently the machines with a decent amount of processing power can be hired for large scale date processing tasks. Open source has become an alternative for high priced data software.

These trends have led to an explosion of new software tools, and systems for big data. They cover databases, storage systems, and servers, processing tools, machine learning systems, acquisition tools, data visualization tools and serialization (Singh & Kumar, 2014).

DATA MANAGEMENT IN CLOUD ENVIRONMENT

Data movement is an important factor, especially in the development of a hybrid solution. Generally the requirement is moving data to and from the cloud environment. An effective software tool is needed to move data to either populate a solution in the cloud with the data or to bring the data from the cloud to the enterprise computing environment. It would be better to integrate big data solutions to the analytics and business intelligence infrastructure of the enterprises. This will facilitate many executives in the enterprise to gain insights in the solutions (Warden, 2012).

EVALUATION OF BIG DATA STRATEGY

The following points need to be considered for evolving a big data strategy for an enterprise.

BUSINESS UNITS INVOLVEMENT

It must be remembered that bigdata is not an isolated activity. Enterprises can leverage huge volumes of data to learn more about customers, process and events with big data. Proper implementation of big data strategy can have a broad impact on the effectiveness of business strategy.

CLOUD COMPUTING FOR DATA

Big data have petabytes of data. Cloud computing environment, infrastructure has the facility to store and manage petabytes of data.

BIG DATA AND DATA WARE HOUSE

It is a common opinion among the many enterprises that traditional data warehouse is no longer required. It is because of big data analytics are providing the required results for them. This is not correct. Enterprises have to make use of the results of big data analytics in conjunction with their data warehouse. The data warehouse. The data warehouse includes the information about the enterprise operate. It is advisable to compare the big data results against the benchmarks of the core data for decision making.

CONSISTENT META DATA

Enterprises have to be careful while taking data from customer service sites and social media environment. Generally the data from these sources is not cleansed. Enterprises have to make sure that they are dealing with a consistent set of mata data for analysis.

HANDLING DATA

A Proper tool has to be selected for managing volume, velocity and variety of data.

BIG DATA ANALYTICS

A lot of important technologies are available for big data analysis. They are text analytics, predictive analytics, streaming data environments and spatial data analysis. Evaluation of each technology is required for the job to be accomplished.

Suggestion

It is advisable that enterprises start with pilot projects to gain experience. Enterprises need to take the expert advice to avoid, mistakes in inference and decision making.

INTEGRATION OF DATA

Many better technologies in the market are focused on making it easier to integrate the results of big data analytics with other data sources.

MANAGEMENT OF DATA

Big data demonstrate that enterprises can make use of more data than before at a faster rate of speed than before (O'Reilly Media Inc, 2013). Enterprises are benefited by this capability. If the data are not managed in an effective way, it will create problems for the enterprises. Enterprises need a road map for managing data under big data (Bhandarkar, 2013).

SECURITY

Security is a part of the big data life cycle. Enterprises should be aware of the third party data licenses and government regulations.

BIG DATA IN THE MARKETING PERSPECTIVE

Traditionally the major source of data has been from expanding CRM application. In the present business scenario the complexity of data sources is increasing. The data sources which contribute to the complexity are (1) Primary Research, (2) Secondary Research, (3) Internet data (4) Device Data, (5) Image Data, and (6) Supply Chain Data.

Figure 2. Business model for 3G textile mills

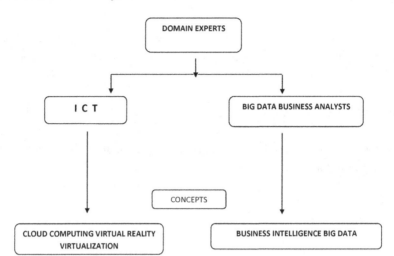

(1). Primary Research provides data related to surveys, experiments, and observations. (2). Secondary Data is based on business data, industries reports, market place and competitive date (3). The source for internet data is click stream, social media, and social networking (4). The data from the devices such as mobile phones, sensors, RF devices and telemetry add to the complexity of data. (5). Image data play an important role in Big Data and (6). Vendor data and pricing from supply chain data are considered as another important source. The data from the above sources become the part of volume, velocity and variety in the data storage of big data (Judith Hurwitz, Alan Nugent, Fern Halper & Marica Kaufman, 2014).

NEW SCHOOL OF MARKETING UNDER BIG DATA

It is apt to quote the observation of DAN SPRINGER CEO of responses on new school of marketing "To days consumers have changed. They have put down the newspaper, they fast forward through TV commercials, and they junk unsolicited email. Why? They have new options that best fit their digital lifestyle. They can choose which marketing messages they receive, when, where, and from whom. They prefer marketers who talk with them, not at them. New school marketers will deliver what today's consumers want: relevant, interactive communication across the digital power channels: email, mobile, social, display and the web".

Cross channel life cycle marketing approach is gaining importance. This approach only talks about a conversation, stickiness, win back and permission.

CLOUD AND BIG DATA

Most of the data in big data are unstructured. Cloud is an ideal computing environment to store big data sets. Big data is known in its volume, variety and velocity. These 3V's can be managed without much difficulty in the cloud computing environment. Market economics are forcing enterprises to consider new business models (Miller, 2009).

BUSINESS ANALYTICS

Analytics are generally defined as the scientific approach of transforming data into insight for making better decisions. Business analytical professionals require special skills, and they are to be familiar with technologies, business applications and practices for continuous, interactive exploration and analyzing of past business performance to gain insight and prepare business planning.

BIG DATA ANALYTICS

Big data analytics need new skills such as fairly good knowledge in mathematics and information technology. They should be adept at visualizing large data and discerning between signal and noise. They need to be in position to weave together data that has traditionally not been woven together. The skill required in this product or organization on is the Facebook with the contents made recently about the product or organization on Twitter. Once all data is woven together, the quality of the prediction gets better and better

PRIVATE CLOUD ENVIRONMENT

Infrastructure in private cloud environment is owned or leased by a single enterprise and is operated solely for that organization. The advantage being in private cloud environment is highly secure, flexible, visible, traceable and manageable (Michael Miller, 2009).

CONCEPTS AND PRACTICES

Concepts and practice are generally divergent. The challenge of developing an effective business model by a global virtual team is substantially greater than identifying relevant concepts in management and information and communication technology. The consultants have indicated that in order to grow in the global market, it is not just enough to be competitive. The products produced by 3G Textile Mills should be acceptable in the global market, so also domain experts in the areas of design, production and marketing of the products manufactured by the 3G Textile Mills. The Domain experts are based in Paris (Europe), Sydney (Australia), Singapore and Hong Kong. The global virtual team is familiar with the global development team frame. They are also aware that 3G Textile Mills business has become highly competitive and dominated by a set of aggressive global players.

Figure 2 gives an overview of the concepts made use of in the business models developed by the domain experts in the respective countries.

The Business Model for 3G Textile Mills focuses on the three main areas.

1. Designing cloth materials and Ready-made garments
2. Materials required for manufacturing products of the above in bill of materials module and
3. Analyzing the global market scenario with the company's performance.

MACRO LEVEL DESIGN

The Figure 3 indicates the use of resources such as hardware and software made by the domain experts from their respective countries.

Figure 3.

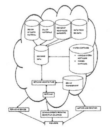

CLOTH MATERIAL

Cloth material is designed by the domain experts from their experience based on the needs of the consumer requirements. Color combination of dyes with the cotton mix will be suggested by them. The concept of Virtual reality is made use of in designing the cloth material.

READYMADE GARMENTS

The domain experts design and create ready-made garments on the basis of real-world requirements. Simulated version of ready-made garments is carried out on computer systems in the cloud computing environment. The concept of virtual reality helped them to look from the real world situation. Resources in cloud computing have made it possible for the domain experts make use of virtual reality concepts.

3G TEXTILE MILLS IN INDIA

The management team along with their technical executives of 3G Textile Mills in India is able to view the designs of cloth and design of ready-made garments. On their system from India they can also suggest changes if required.

MARKETING WING

The proposed design of ready-made garments is uploaded in company's portal and Facebook by the marketing executives for feedback from their prospective customers. After evaluating the feedback from the prospective customers, production and marketing plan will be prepared for the different countries' requirements.

VENDORS

Vendors of 3G Textile Mills are given an access to the information needed for the supply of materials from them. Bill of materials will provide details of the quality, variety of cotton, dyes and other material to the Vendors.

DEVICE MANAGEMENT

The need for device management is required in a cloud computing environment. Heterogeneous devices, applications and users needed to be managed. The core functionality of a private device is to perform tasks with high speed. The main requirement of device management is to take care of the operating system, structure, memory protection, security and multi-tasking.

DEVELOPMENT OF A NEW PRODUCT IN 3G TEXTILE MILLS

The domain experts have proved that a new product can be jointly designed by the experts in a global virtual team through a process of continuous exchange of ideas between members dispersed across the globe. This process helps in generating alternative ideas by taking inputs from different sources and structuring through virtual reality application. This model provides an idea for the creation of the global innovation model. Further, it helps to structure the work flow by visualizing the various phases of the development of a product. Customers' tastes are becoming more homogeneous around the globe. Consequently, 3G Textile Mills can provide a better product through the economies of scale with a common design. The 3G Textile Mills model can increase the chances of successfully diffusing knowledge, technology and process. Advanced tele-communication technologies have drastically changed the business operation, providing new services and creating an interconnected world-wide community.

SUMMARY OF THE DEVELOPMENT OF 3G TEXTILE MILLS

Till recently the standard model of innovation has been a linear process from research through design, development and then manufacturing. In the case of 3G Textile Mills model many of these processes are carried out concurrently and collaborating through the concepts of information technology in the private cloud deployment model. In the management team of 3G Textile Mills could hire the services of the domain experts from the respective countries. The employees of 3G Textile Mills and Domain experts with their team members have formed a virtual team to develop 3G

Textile Mills model. It is because of cloud computing, they could develop 3G Textile Mills models by making use of the virtual reality concept and the features in Big Data. At the same time the bill of materials required for ready-made garments and designing of cloth material to be produced is made available in the 3G Textile Mills model.

CASE ILLUSTRATION 2

ROA FCCD Limited has a registered office at Coimbatore in India. This company has business interests in the products related to dairy, agricultural, consumer, and consumer durable items. The company has been in the business for the past two decades in producing and marketing the above products. The company was started by the four professionals from the four different disciplines. All the four professionals have equal financial stakes in the company. The management team consists of agricultural scientist, dairy farm specialist, mechanical and electrical engineers. The company owns their own farmland. The company grows fruits and vegetables in their farmland. The agricultural scientist looks after from the cultivation to the marketing of the above products. Similarly the diary farm specialist takes care of the production to marketing of milk, butter, cheese, curd, and ghee.

The company owns cows and buffaloes for the production of the milk. The company has two separate divisions. One division is for the production and marketing of consumer products. The other division is for the production and marketing of their consumable products. The above two divisions are managed by the mechanical and electrical engineers who are the part of the management team. Their range of consumer products are toothpaste, shaving cream, talcum powder, tooth brushes, and shaving brushes. Their consumer durable products are rice and vegetable pressure cookers, coffee makers, and grinders. These products are suitable to Indian home requirements.

Initially the company had separate stand-alone information systems for each of their business activities. They meet weekly once to review their business activities in respect of their products related to production and marketing. They exchange information among themselves with the print outs

Generated from their information systems. As their business has started growing they have switched over to an integrated Enterprise Resource Planning system for all their products. It has become easy for each division head to browse all the information pertaining to all the divisions of their company. This has facilitated them to discuss and exchange views on production and sales of all their products. Their discussions have helped them to take to take decisions without waiting for formal business meetings. This approach has increased the demand for their products in the market. To meet the market demand they have started some units for their products at different locations in South India. The expansion of their units has forced them to move their ERP system to a private cloud environment. They acquired the required infrastructure to maintain their systems in the private cloud environment.

The competition for their products in the market has increased due to globalization policy followed by India. It has become necessary for them to hire the services of an analyst who has experience in applying the concepts of business analytics. The business analyst hired by them has studied their requirements. The business analyst applied the three analytics approach to their marketing problems. They are descriptive, predictive, and perspective.

Descriptive Analytics

The concepts such business intelligence and data mining are applied to the data of the previous years. This will help them to take strategic decisions for their business.

Predictive Analytics

The company has a large volume of the transaction data and unstructured data in their database. Source for this data is from social media content, shopping experiences, and survey reports. Enterprises can make use of this data for predicting their likely future prospects for their products in the market scenario.

Perspective Analytics

The above two methods will enterprises to understand the outcome of their analysis pertaining to their business and market prospects for their products.

This will facilitate them to take corrective action on their analysis and decisions.

Interpretation of Business Data

Data pours from the multiple systems, channels, and regions around the clock. The challenge is how to consolidate, organize, and interpret business meaning from the data from the various sources.

Business analytics provides the keys to the business analyst. These keys help the business analysts to unlock the mysteries hidden deep within the enterprise's data. This facilitates them to identify the trends and to discover the underlying causes and issues. The analysis of data has helped ROA FCCD Limited many aspects related to their products such as adding new features, venturing into new market areas, and new ways of promoting their products.

Farm Products

Analysis of the market in respect of the farm products has made them realize the need for changing the cultivation of vegetables and fruits in the organic method.

Dairy Products

Till recently they have concentrated on the products such as milk, curds, and ghee. From their analysis they have felt the need for adding the new products such as ice cream, milkshake, and buttermilk. They offered the new products with the different flavors. Different sizes in packing of these products are made available depending on the tastes of the consumers.

Consumer Products

They have come to know that the toothbrush for children is not manufactured. Toothpaste and shaving cream are not available in an economy package. Their products are mainly for everyone in a family. They have introduced a family pack containing all their products.

Consumer Durable Products

The existing features in the home appliances are redesigned to the needs of the Indian customers. Many new features are also added to the home appliances.

Action Plan

1. Demonstration of the home appliances is arranged at frequent intervals at their own sales outlets. Similar types of demonstrations for their home appliances are conducted at the other department stores and at the meetings of the various ladies clubs.
2. Cookery classes are conducted at their sales outlets. The importance of the consuming of vegetables in the daily diet is explained. The Indian way of preparing pickles is also explained. The process of making home made fruit juices is demonstrated. Their farm products are made use of while preparing pickles and fruit juices. Their home appliances are used while preparing pickles and fruit juices.
3. The promotional offers for their home appliances are highlighted at their cookery and demonstration sessions
4. Preparation of selected Indian sweets with the dairy products is explained.

Their dairy products are used while preparing the sweets.

Other Business Alliances

1. In some locations it is not viable to have their own sales outlets. They have entered into franchise agreements for their products with the department stores who have required infrastructure as a sales outlets.
2. They conduct orientation courses for their own sales force sales force of the franchise outlets.
3. They have an agreement with the selected leading hotels to manufacture soaps, toothpaste, and shaving creams in the name of the hotel. These hotels take providing these products as complementary items to the guests who are staying in their hotels.

Diversification

Their analysis with the tools of business analytics has helped them to improve their market share for their products. Their financial results are also encouraging. They realized that the due to the globalization, it is required to venture into manufacturing other related products to the existing products. They have started food processing units such as various types of vegetable sauces and soup mix products. They have also started to make ready mix food items for the domestic consumers. They included the production of talcum powder under their consumer products. They have added electronic cookers and kettles under their consumer durable products. They have taken care of the type of features needed in their domestic appliances as per the international standard. This has facilitated them to compete in the global market. They have organized road shows in the various countries. They have taken part in having stalls in the exhibitions held in the different countries.

Seeds, fertilizers and other necessary farming inputs such as pesticides and technical-how are mare available to farmers in a time bound manner. These facilitates to grow cereal, wheat, sugarcane, potato, and paddy. Technical know how is provided to farmers on the subject like agriculture, horticulture, animal husbandry and fisheries at the Farmers Continous Learing School. Topics such as Bio fencing and cluster farming are also taught at this school.

Free cattle health fairs are organized for health check up and vaccination for cattle herds.

New sugar mills are established near sugar cane farms. Distillery unit has also been planned to be established.

Most of the distributors for their products are associated with them over a long period marketing their products. The company has maintained a good relationship with their distributors. With the support of the distributors the company's market share has been increasing. Due to globalization, many new players have entered the market. This has resulted the company's market has started fluctuating. The management RAO FCCD Limited has realized that it is not advisable to depend on their distributors alone marketing their products. They have decided to open their own showrooms at the various locations in South India. They have employed their marketing team to sell all their products. The company has created an exclusive social media channel for knowing the suggestions, opinions, and feedback from their customers.

FUTURE TRENDS

Practices in the management of knowledge and information have changed significantly in space and time. There are many changes taking place in managing information and knowledge in business enterprises. Till recent knowledge has been generated and managed by individuals. In the present business scenario, group dynamics dominate.

The concepts such as Big Data, Cloud Computing, Virtual Reality and Data warehouse are driving force to facilitate in designing and developing business models in the present scenario. There is a good scope for research scholars to involve themselves in making use of the above concepts in designing the conceptual business models.

CONCLUSION

Globalization has created many business opportunities. These opportunities have led to creating virtual enterprises. Information and communication technology has increased virtualization in business activities and ways of working. Virtualization overcomes time and distance. Virtualization facilitates the business enterprises to think differently and follow a new approach for achieving their business goals. The critical business needs to decide the type of information required for developing the conceptual business model. In recent times innovation initiative is gaining importance for the strategic management purposes. Cloud Computing, Big Data, and Virtualization are providing a good scope for adopting innovative approach in developing business models for the benefit of the business enterprises (Semolic & Baisya, 2013). The two case illustrations discussed in this chapter give a clear idea about the virtualization in the enterprises' business activities and ways of working.

REFERENCES

Anahory, S., & Hurray, D. (2011). *Data Ware Housing in the Real World*. New Delhi: Pearson.

Bhandarkar. (2013). Big Data Systems: Past, Present & (Possibly) Future. *CSI Communications Journal, 37*(1), 7-8, 16.

Craig, T., & Ludloff, M. E. (2013). *Privacy and Big Data*. Mumbai: Shroff Publishers & Distributors Private Limited.

Davis & Patterson. (2012). *Ethics of Big Data*. Mumbai: Shroff Publishers & Distributors Private Limited.

Franks, B. (2014). *Taming the Big Data Tidal Wave*. New Delhi: Wiley India Private Limited.

Hameed, M. A., Counsell, S., & Swift, S. (2012). A conceptual Model for the process of IT, Innovation Adoption in Organizations. *Journal of Engineering and Technology Management, 29*(3), 358–390. doi:10.1016/j.jengtecman.2012.03.007

Hurwitz, J., Nugent, A., Halper, F., & Kaufman, M. (2014). *Big Data for Dummies*. New Delhi: Wiley India Private Limited.

Jorgensen, A., Rowland-Jones, J., Welch, J., Clark, D., Price, C., & Mitchell, B. (2014). *Microsoft Big Data Solutions*. New Delhi: Wiley India Private Limited.

Kumar. (2013). Big Data- A Big game changer. *CSI Communications Journal, 37*(1), 9-10.

Mather, Kumaraswamy, & Latif. (2010). *Cloud Security and Privacy*. Mumbai: Shroff Publishers & Distributors Private Limited.

Miller, M. (2009). *Cloud Computing*. Private Limited.

Minelli, M., Chambers, M., & Dhiraj, A. (2014). *Big Data Analytics*. New Delhi: Wiley India Private Limited.

O'Reilly Media Inc. (2013). *Big Data Now Current Perspectives from O'Reilly Media*. Mumbai: Shroff Publishers & Distributors Private Limited.

Pandey, U. S. (2012). *Varinder Kumar*. Computer Applications in Business.

Reese, G. (2010). *Cloud Application Architecture*. Mumbai: Shorff Publishers & Distributors Private Limited.

Schmarzo, B. (2014). *Big Data Understanding How Data Powers Big Business*. New Delhi: Wiley India Private Limited.

Schulz, G. (2012). *Cloud and Virtual Data Storage, Networking*. New York: Taylor & Francis Group.

Semolic & Baisya. (2013). *Globalization and Innovative Business Models*. New Delhi: Ane Books Private Limited.

Singh & Kumar. (2014). Big Data Visualization using Cassandra and R. *CSI Communications Journal, 38*(8), 15, 21.

Warden, P. (2012). *Big Data Glossary*. Mumbai: Shroff Publishers & Distributors Private Limited.

KEY TERMS AND DEFINITIONS

Big Data: The capability to manage a huge volume of disparate data, at the right speed and within the right time frame, to allow real time analysis and reaction.

Business Analytics: Business analytics is the combination of skills, technologies, applications, and processes used by organizations to gain insight into their business-based data and statistics to drive business planning.

Cloud Computing: A computing model that makes information technology resources such as servers, middleware, and applications available over the internet as services to business organizations in a self-service manner.

Conceptual Model: A conceptual model is a representation of a system made of the composition of concepts which are used to help people know, understand, or simulate a subject the model requirements.

Data Cleansing: Software used to identify potential data quality problems.

Data Science: Data science is an interdisciplinary field that uses scientific methods, processes, algorithms, and systems to extract knowledge and insights from data in various forms, both structured and unstructured similar to data mining.

Data Warehouse: A large data store containing the organization's historical data, which is used primarily for data analysis and data mining.

Predictive Analytics: A statistical or data mining solution consisting of algorithms and techniques that can be used for both structured and unstructured data to determine future outcomes.

Private Cloud: A private cloud is a set of computing resources within the organization that serves only the organization.

Streaming Data: An analytic computing platform that is used to speed.

Unstructured Data: Data that does not follow a specific data format.

Variability: Along with the velocity the data flows can be highly inconsistent with periodic peaks.

Variety: In the present business scenario data comes in all types of forms.

Velocity: This means how fast the data is being produced and how fast the data needs to be processed to meet the demand.

Volume: Many factors contribute towards increasing volume streaming data and data collected from sensors.

Section 4
Service Models in the Manufacturing Sector

Chapter 8
Cloud–Based Design and Manufacturing

Sudarsanam S. K.
Vellore Institute of Technology Chennai, India

Umasankar V.
Vellore Institute of Technology Chennai, India

ABSTRACT

Cloud-based manufacturing is a computing and service-oriented model developed from existing advanced manufacturing models and enterprise technologies with the support of cloud computing, IOT, and virtualization. In this chapter, various definitions of cloud manufacturing are discussed. New service models other than the existing cloud computing service models are being discussed elaborately. Cloud-based design manufacturing is also being discussed. A comparison of cloud manufacturing and cloud-based design manufacturing is elaborately discussed. Key technologies and challenges in cloud manufacturing are highlighted.

DOI: 10.4018/978-1-5225-3182-1.ch008

INTRODUCTION

The National Institute of Standards and Technology (NIST) offers the following definition of Cloud Computing (Mell, P. & Grance, T., 2011). According to them, Cloud computing is a model for enabling ubiquitous, convenient, on-demand network access to a shared pool of configurable computing resources (e.g., networks, servers, storage, applications, and services) that can be rapidly provisioned and released with minimal management effort or service provider interaction.

Many authors proposed definitions of Cloud Manufacturing. Li, B.H., Zhang, L.,...&Jiang, X.D., 2010 proposed a first definition of Cloud Manufacturing. According to them, Cloud manufacturing is a computing and service-oriented manufacturing model developed from existing advanced manufacturing models (e.g. ASP, AM, NM, MGrid) and enterprise information technologies under the support of cloud computing, IoT, virtualization and service-oriented technologies, and advanced computing technologies. It transforms manufacturing resources and manufacturing capabilities into manufacturing services, which can be managed and operated in an intelligent and unified way to enable the full sharing and circulating of manufacturing resources and manufacturing capabilities. CM can provide safe and reliable, high quality, cheap and on-demand manufacturing services for the whole lifecycle of manufacturing. The concept of manufacturing here refers to big manufacturing that includes the whole lifecycle of a product (e.g. design, simulation, production, test, maintenance). Cloud manufacturing is a type of parallel, networked, and distributed system consisting of an integrated and inter-connected virtualized service pool (manufacturing cloud) of manufacturing resources and capabilities as well as capabilities of intelligent management and on-demand use of services to provide solutions for all kinds of users involved in the whole lifecycle of manufacturing.

Xu, X., 2011 defines Cloud Manufacturing as a set of distributed resources which are encapsulated into cloud services and managed in a centralized way. Clients can use cloud services according to their requirements. Cloud users can request services ranging from product design, manufacturing, testing, management, and all other stages of a product life cycle.

Giriraj, S. & Muthu, S., 2012 investigated the guaranteeing assembly process information flow in real time, enterprise wide, from assembly station sensors directly to the industry policy making offices, is the true solution for improving productivity competence, reducing loses and greater than ever profits. In fact, the ideal production lies on the real machine or assembly capabilities of working non-stop at maximum speed, lacking downtimes or inactivity and assembled goods reject threats. Assembly lines will be prone to standstills and will produce defective pieces if the machines are unable to working to their full capability or demands made of them. This is often the case of misinformed factory management on real time factory floor performances. Even though equipped with original equipment manufacturer indicator knowledge about their systems, they still can' t get that efficiency so needed to improve yield. Transformation is necessary to ride the expected tide of change in the today's manufacturing environment, particularly in the information technology and automation landscape. A multinational company strives to reduce computing costs, to improve plant floor visibility and to achieve more efficient energy and surroundings use of their IT hardware and software investments. Cloud computing infrastructure accelerates and promotes these objectives by providing unparalleled flexible and dynamic IT resource collection, virtualization, floor visibility and high accessibility.

Wu, D., Thames, L., Rosen, D. & Shaefer, D.(2012) propose the following definition of CBDM. According to them, Cloud-Based Design and Manufacturing refers to a product realization model that enables collective open innovation and rapid product development with minimum costs through a social networking and negotiation platform between service providers and consumers. It is a type of parallel and distributed system consisting of a collection of inter-connected physical and virtualized service pools of design and manufacturing resources (e.g., parts, assemblies, CAD/CAM tools) as well as intelligent search capabilities for design and manufacturing solutions.

CLOUD BASED MANUFACTURING

CMfg is proposed by Tao F, Zhang L, Venkatesh VC, Luo Y, Cheng Y (2011) after cloud computing, and cloud computing is a core enabling technology for CMfg. The resources involved in cloud computing primarily are computational resources (e.g. server, storage, network, software), and they are provided as services for the user in the following three models.

1. Infrastructure as a service (IaaS). The storage and compute capabilities are provided as a service; examples are Amazon's S3 storage service, Rackspace Cloud Servers, and EC2 computing platform.
2. Platform as a service (PaaS). The platform is provided as a service, which can enable the development and deployment of applications without the cost and

complexity of buying and managing the underlying hardware and software layers; examples are Microsoft's Azure Services Platform, Google App Engine, Amazon's Relational Database Services.

3. Software as a service (SaaS). The application and software are offered as a service, in which the application runs on the cloud, the need to install and run the application on the client computer are eliminated;

In CMfg, in addition to the information technology (IT) resources, all manufacturing resources and abilities involved in the whole life cycle of manufacturing are to be provided for the user. To achieve this objective, the following service models are proposed.

1. Design as a service (DaaS) – the design resource and ability are provided as a service;

Cloud-based design and manufacturing (CBDM) refers to a service-oriented networked product development model in which service consumers are able to configure products or services and reconfigure manufacturing systems through Infrastructure-as-a-Service (IaaS), Platform-as-a-Service (PaaS), Hardware-as-a-Service (HaaS), and Software-as-a-Service (SaaS) (Wu, D., Schaefer, D., & Rosen, D.W. (2013).

Cloud-Based Design (CBD) refers to a networked design model that leverages cloud computing, service-oriented architecture (SOA), Web 2.0 (e.g., social network sites), and semantic web technologies to support cloud-based engineering design services in distributed and collaborative environments.

2. Manufacturing as a service (MFGaaS) – the manufacturing resource and ability are offered as a service;

Cloud-Based Manufacturing (CBM) refers to a networked manufacturing model that exploits on-demand access to a shared collection of diversified and distributed manufacturing resources to form temporary, reconfigurable production lines which enhance efficiency, reduce product lifecycle costs, and allow for optimal resource allocation in response to variable-demand customer generated tasking. (Wu, D., Greer, M.J., Rosen, D.W., & Schaefer, D. (2013).

3. Experimentation as a service (EaaS) – the experimentation resource and ability are provided as a service;

The validation of research results in large-scale, real life experimental infrastructures is essential for the design and deployment of products, applications and services on the Future Internet. Manufacturing Organizations needs access to an integrated Experimental Infrastructure as part of cloud computing infrastructure. This would help them perform experiments of any size, complexity, or networking technology. Experimenters need to run experiments under controlled and replicable conditions, according to specific requirements by accessing real or virtual equipment, services, systems and tools on demand, seamlessly and regardless of their geographical location. A dynamic and promising segment of experimenters, in particular small and medium-size organizations cannot afford testbeds or testing equipment of their own and need to be provided easy and affordable access to said capacities. Real-world prototyping and experimenting environments are needed for innovation creation.

4. Simulation as a service (SIMaaS) – the simulation resource and ability are provided as a service;

Simulation software imitates physical phenomena with a set of mathematical formulas (Assuncao, Costanzo, and Buyya, 2009). Increasingly, simulations executed using high-performance computing (HPC) are providing efficiencies to industry. General Motors uses HPC to simulate crash testing of automobiles and reported that it can reduce the number of full-size crash vehicle tests by more than 85 per cent, at a cost savings of $500,000 per test (Gould, 2011). Unfortunately, realizing the benefits of HPC simulations requires an investment in hardware, software and expertise that is beyond the means of many small and medium businesses.

5. Management as a service (MaaS) – the management resource and ability are provided as service;

Cloud Management as a Service (CMaaS) helps customers integrate the disparate management tools deployed in their environments through an enterprise command center approach that gives a singular view into physical, virtual, and public cloud workloads.

6. Maintain as a service (MAaaS) – the maintainance resource and ability are provided as a service;

Offering maintenance services in the cloud hinges on the integration of multi-sensor data within a cloud computing infrastructure. This is already a trend in the Industrial Internet-of-Things (IIoT), as measurements from sensors and wireless sensor networks are increasingly integrated and processed in the cloud.

These integrations provide a number of distinct benefits including:

- Capacity: The cloud provides the means for storing very large volumes of data. This is important given the large datasets that need to be processed as part of maintenance processes, including the processing of historic information.
- Scalability: Cloud computing provides cost-effective scalability, which is key when dealing with the rapid and continually-growing amount of maintenance datasets, including data from sensors and business information systems.
- Elasticity: A key characteristic of cloud services is their ability to optimize the use of computing resources, by allocating more storage and processing capacity during times of peak demands. This optimization takes place in an automated and elastic manner and does not rely on human intervention for provisioning or deprovisioning computing resources.
- Reliability: Cloud infrastructures provide high redundancy and reliability. This is critical to ensure the continuity and graceful execution of maintenance and asset management applications.
- Quality of Service: The cloud provides access to the required amount of computing resources, which guarantees low latency in data processing. Overall, it provides a high quality of service.
- Pay-as-you-go and pay-as-you-grow: The integration of maintenance data in the cloud removes the need for costly upfront investments (i.e. capital expenses) in computing infrastructures. Rather, the cloud enables plant owners, plant operators and equipment vendors to convert capital expenses to monthly bills (i.e. operational expenses).

In a cloud context, users pay for what they use. Likewise, they are provided with ways to start a maintenance service with low investments in computing infrastructure. They can gradually pay more as they scale up cloud-based maintenance deployment, including the addition of machines, devices and datasets.

Beyond these benefits, the integration and processing of datasets in the cloud enable the support of entirely new services for industrial maintenance, based on novel business models that emphasize access to these services from remote and in a pay-per-use fashion.

This is the most important benefit of using cloud services for industrial maintenance, since it holds the promise to disrupt the way maintenance services are deployed from equipment vendors and offered to their customers.

7. Integration as a service (INTaaS) – the integrated resource and ability, information system, and platform are provided as a service.
8. Fault detection as a Service: As part of this service, plant owners and operators are provided with detailed information about the status of their assets, including predictions about anticipated failures based on parameters such as EOF (End of Life) and MTBF (Mean Time Between Failures).
9. Training-as-a-Service: Using data available in the cloud, equipment providers can offer a rich portfolio of cloud-based training services, including services based on Virtual Reality (VR) and/or Augmented Reality (AR).
    ○ **Cloud Manufacturing Architecture**: Lv (2012) proposed an architecture for Cloud Manufacturing consisting of five layers:
    ○ **Physical Resource Layer**: Includes all the manufacturing resources and manufacturing capabilities, and links those resources and capabilities to the global network by using technologies such as Internet of Things.
    ○ **Virtual Resource Layer:** Prepare the manufacturing resources and manufacturing capabilities for the cloud environment by virtually encapsulating physical resources, and publishing them into the core service layer.
    ○ **Core Service Layer**: Manages the cloud services of the encapsulation of manufacturing resources and manufacturing capabilities for the users (provider, operator, and consumer), hence: cloud services include registration, service booking, charge, and search.
    ○ **Application Interface Layer**: Provide integration between the existing manufacturing application system and the cloud service in order to deliver a manufacturing application system according to user demands. Application layer: Provides access for users to request a Cloud Manufacturing service from any device (PC, laptop, smart phone), from anyware (company, home, aboard).

CLASSIFICATION OF CLOUD MANUFACTURING SERVICE PLATFORM

For the consideration of security and safety, and utilization scope, there are primarily four kinds of CMfg service platform, namely:

1. A public CMfg service platform;
2. A private CMfg service platform;
3. A community CMfg service platform;
4. A hybrid CMfg service platform.

A public CMfg service platform is characterized as being available from a third-party service provider and demander, and is used to realize the sharing and optimal allocation of the entire manufacturing resources and abilities distributed in and owned by different enterprises and organizations, especially for small and medium-sized enterprises (SMEs).

A private CMfg service platform offers many of the benefits and services of a public CMfg service platform environment, but is managed within an organization or enterprise. It provides greater control over its resource and service, and is usually established and used to realize the sharing and optimal allocation of a group enterprise's in-house manufacturing resources and abilities distributed in its branch companies or subsidiary companies, research centres, different departments, etc., so as to promote utilization and reduce the cost.

A community CMfg service platform is controlled and used by a group of organizations that have shared interests, such as specific security requirements or a common mission.

An hybrid CMfg service platform is a combination of a public and a private CMfg service platform. Noncritical services or information are outsourced to the public CMfg service platform, whereas business critical services and data are kept within the control of the organization.

CLOUD BASED DESIGN AND MANUFACTURING

Cloud-based design manufacturing (CBDM) refers to a service-oriented networked product development model in which service consumers are enabled to configure, select, and utilize customized product realization resources and services ranging from computer-aided engineering software to reconfigurable manufacturing systems. The key characteristics of CBDM include ubiquitous access to distributed large datasets, high-performance computing and computing scalability, on-demand self-services, cloud-based social collaboration, rapid manufacturing scalability, and pay-per-use. Based on these key characteristics, a future CBDM system should provide the following functional features: a cloud based social collaboration platform, a cloud-based distributed file system, an open-source programming framework for cloud computing, a multi-tenancy architecture, a ubiquitous sensor network, an intelligent semantic search engine, and a real-time quoting engine. CBDM differs from traditional distributed and collaborative design and manufacturing from a number of perspectives, including computing architectures, design communication and collaboration sourcing processes, ICT infrastructures, programming models, data and file systems and business models.

One of the most important benefits of the afore mentioned cloud-based CAE tools is that they allow for computing capacity scalability through the creation of a virtual machine that acts like a real computer with an operating system, also referred to as virtualization. Cloud-based CAE software executed on virtual machines is separated from hardware. Virtualization enables enterprises to separate engineering software packages, computing resources, and data storage from physical computing hardware, thereby supporting time and resource sharing.

Communication and Collaboration in Engineering Design

One of major challenges in engineering design is to enhance design communication and collaboration, especially in geographically dispersed settings. The major purposes of design communication include articulating an issue, asking for clarification, eliciting requirements, generating concepts or principles, reverse engineering, requesting information, comparing solutions, and making decisions. Capturing the purposes of design communications can significantly improve the effectiveness and efficiency of design communication by ensuring that engineers know what expected inputs and outputs should be from a communication. With respect to the content or artefacts that are exchanged or shared among individuals or teams, almost all design communications revolve around artefacts including sketches, engineering drawings, computer-aided design files, simulation, finite element analysis files, physical product, calculation, assembly, prototype, and report.

COMPARISON OF CLOUD BASED MANUFACTURING AND CLOUD BASED DESIGN AND MANUFACTURING

Cloud-Based Manufacturing (CBM) refers to a networked manufacturing model that exploits on-demand access to a shared collection of diversified and distributed manufacturing resources to form temporary, reconfigurable, and scalable production lines which enhance efficiency, reduce product lifecycle costs, and allow for optimal resource allocation in response to variable demand customer generated tasking.

In the context of CBM, rapid manufacturing scalability is accomplished through cloud-based sourcing processes. Manufacturing capacity is a metric that indicates how many objects such as parts or products can be produced per day by a manufacturing system.

Manufacturing capacity needs to be adjusted in response to fluctuations in market demand. Capacity scalability refers to the adjustability of manufacturing capacity to adapt throughputs to changing market demand. For example, as market demand increases and exceeds the designed manufacturing capacity, manufacturing capacity needs to be increased to fulfil more orders and make more profits. On the other hand, as market demand decreases and is less than the designed manufacturing capacity, manufacturing capacity needs to decrease to reduce maintenance costs or avoid waste of resources. Addressing the capacity scalability problem is essentially to determine when, where, and by how much the capacity of a manufacturing system should be scaled.

In traditional manufacturing systems, if market demand grows, the cost of capacity expansion is justified by the economy of scale of the expanded capacity and the reduction of the shortage cost. Typically, manufacturing capacity expansion can be achieved in two ways: by scaling the capacity of an individual manufacturing resource and by adding manufacturing resources to existing in-house manufacturing systems. However, in case of unexpected and rapidly changing market demand, the expanded manufacturing capacity may later on actually become excess capacity if market demand weakens. Thus, capacity utilization will slacken. Because the capacity utilization rate is a key indicator of how efficient a manufacturing system is, the lower capacity utilization – the increasing amount of excess capacity – the less efficient a manufacturing system is.

CBM has the potential to achieve both capacity expansion and reduction in small- and medium-volume production cost effectively through the HaaS model. For instance, in the context of CBM, manufacturing companies may opt to crowdsource part of their manufacturing tasks that are beyond the existing in-house manufacturing capacity to third-party CBM service providers by renting their manufacturing equipment instead of purchasing more machines. To rapidly scale up and down manufacturing capacity in CBM, it is challenging to design a manufacturing network that allows for rapid and cost-effective manufacturing scalability.

Therefore, the specific research issue pertaining to CBM is to develop a new approach that helps identify potential manufacturing bottlenecks that determine manufacturing scalability prior to the implementation and deployment of CBM systems.

Considering the costs of ownership, operations, and maintenance, manufacturers in small- and medium volume production can benefit more from HaaS by temporarily renting manufacturing resources or sourcing manufacturing tasks to third-party service providers without purchasing and owning manufacturing equipment than those in large-volume production. Moreover, small- and medium volume production is fairly common in industry, including the personalization industry, the rapid prototyping industry, the maintenance and repair industry, the medical device industry, the industrial electronics industry, and so on.

In contrast, in large-volume production (approximately more than 15,000 units per year), including mass customization and mass production, the relative growth rate in market demand is generally small in comparison to large production volumes. Manufacturers in large-volume production may not significantly increase their ROI by satisfying relatively small market demand growth. As a result, manufacturers in large-volume production may not benefit as much from CBDM through the HaaS model. However, it does not mean that manufacturers in large-volume production cannot benefit from CBDM at all. Note that CBDM delivers design and manufacturing services through four major service models: IaaS, PaaS, HaaS, and SaaS. Although manufacturers in large-volume production probably do not benefit as much from implementing HaaS, they can still benefit from implementing IaaS, PaaS, and SaaS. For instance, as stated previously, manufacturers in the aerospace and automotive industries such as Boeing, BMW, and GE benefit from CBDM by implementing IaaS, PaaS, and SaaS.

It is also assumed that a CBDM service consumer can almost always find qualified service providers whose manufacturing capacity is not fully utilized using cloud-based global sourcing platforms as stated before. This assumption seems strong; however, considering the entire life cycle of a manufacturing system, the time when a manufacturing system utilized at maximum capacity is usually short, although a manufacturing system is optimally designed. Moreover, even if a manufacturing service provider is operating at full capacity, in order to make more profits or receive larger orders, this service provider may still prioritize manufacturing tasks and reallocate their manufacturing capacity to accommodate more profitable business opportunities.

In addition, it is assumed that the most prevalent pay-per-use pricing model, which is based on constant price per service unit, is generally a desirable characteristic of CBDM. In addition to the pay-per-use pricing model, another common pricing model is subscription in which users subscribe based on constant price per service unit and a longer period of time. More flexible pricing models are also available, including assured volume of service units plus per-unit price rate, per-unit rate with a ceiling, and so on.

Although the pay-per-use pricing model is widely implemented, it is certainly not always the most desirable pricing model. For instance, in the SaaS model, it may be more cost-effective to utilize CAD and CAE application software in a pay-per-use fashion without an up-front investment or long-term commitment in situations where the software is occasionally utilized. However, pay-per-use can lead to unexpected high expenses in situations where the software will be constantly utilized for a long period of time. Similarly, in the HaaS model, it may be more cost-effective to rent manufacturing equipment in situations where manufacturing capacity needs to be temporarily scaled up to adapt to relatively small market demand increase.

The key benefits of CBDM across sectors over short term and long term has been highlighted in **Figure 1.**

Figure 1. Benefits of CBDM across sectors over time

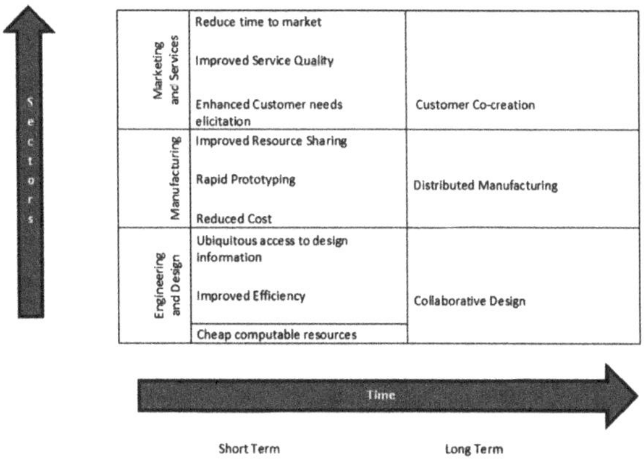

In the marketing and services sector, in the short term, CBDM has the potential to accelerate product time-to-market, enhance quality of service (QoS), and improve the elicitation of customer needs and requirement analysis. In the long term, a CBDM system enables the implementation of customer co-creation, mass collaboration, and social product development. With respect to engineering design, in the short term, CBDM allows designers to have ubiquitous access to massive amount of datasets related to design, streamline design processes, and improve performance in computationally expensive design tasks. In the long term, cloud-based social collaboration platforms will significantly improve collaborative design in geographically dispersed environments. With respect to manufacturing, in the short term, CBDM has the potential to improve manufacturing resource sharing, rapid prototyping, and reduce costs of ownership, operations, maintenance. In the long term, CBDM will significantly improve responsiveness to rapidly changing market demand and unexpected disturbances from internal and external manufacturing environments and enhance remote diagnosis, prognosis, and maintenance in distributed manufacturing.

In the fourth generation manufacturing viz. Industry 4.0 essential features are communication and data exchange. Expected enablers in Cloud based manufacturing are dynamic decentralized planning and execution, adaptive processes interfaces for communication ensuring adaptability and flexibility of systems. This also provides smart human machine interaction through smart sensors. Basically the platform has virtualization and interoperability platform framework, manufacturing process and optimization framework and collaboration and stakeholder interaction framework. The detailed tool kit platform for Provider view, Customer view and Operator view has been given in **Figure 2**

A public cloud manufacturing set for a typical small and medium enterprises is provided in detail in **Figure 3.**

Figure 2. Cloud based manufacturing tool kit platform

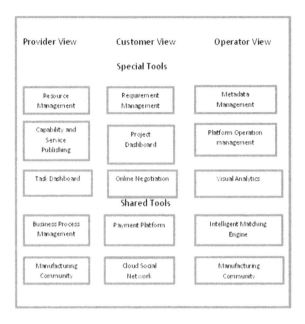

KEY TECHNOLOGIES OF CLOUD MANUFACTURING

The following are the key technologies of Cloud Manufacturing. This encompasses architecture, models, standards, physical manufacturing resources including software and hardware, virtualization and virtual resourcing, cloud service models, deployment, cloud service management, task management, service platform management and safety and security technologies.

- Architecture, models, standards, and criteria for CMfg;
- Intelligent perception, connection technologies, and equipment for various physical manufacturing resource and ability, including hardware and software resource;
- Knowledge-based resource virtualization and virtual resource management technologies;
- Cloud service encapsulation technologies of manufacturing resource and ability, including cloud service modelling, description, deployment, and so forth;
- Cloud service comprehensive management technologies, such as aggregation and classification, cost management, QoS (quality of service) management,

Figure 3. A public cloud manufacturing for SMEs

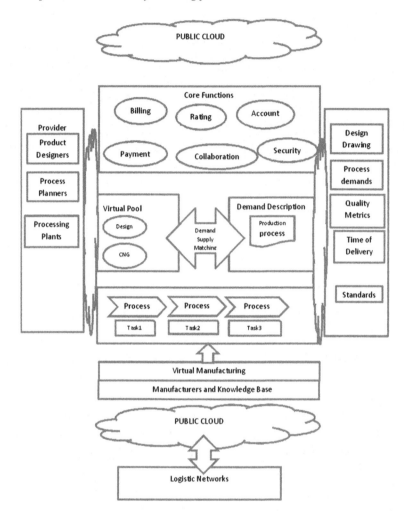

integrated evaluation, composition, trust and reliability management, scheduling and optimal allocation of cloud service;

- CMfg task management, such as task definition, description, decomposition, evaluation, and scheduling;
- Manufacturing ability and cloud service transaction process management;
- CMfg user business management and ubiquitous interface development;
- CMfg service platform development and management;
- CMfg safety and security technologies

TAXONOMY FOR CLOUD MANUFACTURING

Capturing requirements for Cloud Manufacturing and its types, characteristics and attributes in the form of taxonomy allows enterprises to understand and choose a suitable Cloud Manufacturing system. Taxonomy of Cloud Manufacturing is presented in **Figure 4.**

This taxonomy provides a classification of Cloud Manufacturing into five main areas, where the distinguishing attributes are listed under each main area.

Figure 4. Cloud manufacturing taxonomy

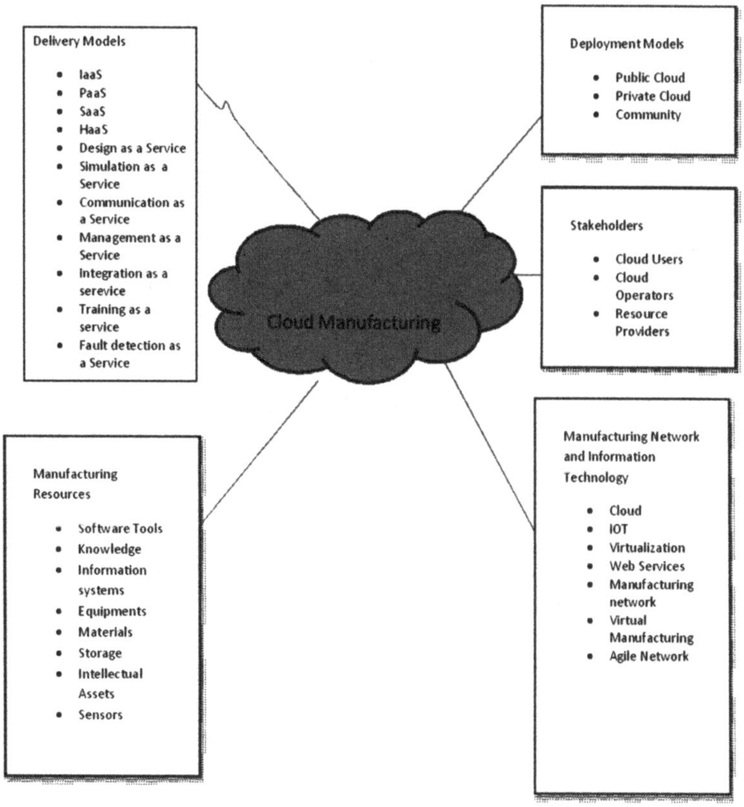

KEY ADVANTAGES OF CLOUD MANUFACTURING

1. It can reduce resource idle capacity and increase utilization. In conventional manufacturing models, manufacturing resource utilization is low, e.g. estimated at 15–20 per cent for IT resources, while the estimates for other manufacturing resources are lower. In contrast, a CMfg platform can increase the utilization across many customers, e.g. the IT resource utilization attains at least 40 per cent.

2. It can reduce the up-front investments and lower the cost of entry for SMEs trying to benefit from high-value manufacturing resources and specific manufacturing abilities that were hitherto available only to the larger corporations. These manufacturing resources or abilities involve large amounts of investment for a relatively short period of time. CMfg makes such dynamic provisioning of resources possible, and provides an almost immediate access to these resources and abilities without up-front capital investments (Tao, F., Hu, Y. F., and Zhang, L, 2010).

3. It can lead to reduced infrastructure and administrative cost, energy saving, and reduced upgrades and maintenance cost (Tao, F., Zhang, L., Venkatesh, V.C., Luo, Y. and Cheng, Y., 2011).

4. CMfg makes it easier for manufacturing enterprises (both smaller and larger) to scale their production and business according to client demand. As the resources and services can be easily obtained, so they can be invoked and assembled very quickly as new requirements arise for an enterprise.

5. CMfg also can generate new types and classes of manufacturing/business model or process and deliver manufacturing services that were not previously possible, such as mfg.com (see www .mfg.com) and Local-Motors.com (www. localmotors.com)

6. It can optimize industrial distribution and speed up the transformation from a distributed and high-energy-consumption manufacturing model to a centralized, resource-and environment friendly manufacturing model, and from production-oriented manufacturing to service-oriented manufacturing.

Furthermore, it can promote the specialization division of manufacturing, because under a CMfg environment, an enterprise does not need to carry out all activities involved in the whole life cycle of manufacturing, they only need to execute their core business and service, even if it is a very small part.

CLOUD MANUFACTURING CHALLENGES

Many enterprises, which implemented or trying to use Cloud Computing Technology, have major consideration about this technology. Today, most of enterprises which use Cloud Computing Technology have fears of putting their critical data and application in the Cloud due to trust issue. To host of all data and applications in the Cloud environment will be impossible for any enterprise. They will use Cloud Technology for hosting some servers and utilize their existing servers for critical business functions.

Most important challenge in Cloud Manufacturing is security, where many issues such as privacy, data deliver, data control, and hackers are the major issues of security in the Cloud environment, and many enterprises do not want adopt this technology for the above mentioned issues. Also, the complexity of Cloud Manufacturing can create suitable environment for security breaches and losing control of data and applications that are critical for the enterprise. Because of the complexity of Cloud Manufacturing system which involves many advanced technologies and networks that need to be integrated efficiently, many technical challenges exist in the cloud.

Among these challenges, transform manufacturing resources and capabilities into cloud, network outage and system failures (availability), the ability to work together with different information systems, more than one cloud, and different software applications (interoperability), and easily grow of information system due to increase demand for cloud services (scalability). Both of manufacturing resources and manufacturing capabilities are core of Cloud Manufacturing system, and it need many technologies such as Internet of Things and wireless sensors to coordinate between Cloud Manufacturing system and manufacturing process. But the amount of data collected from different equipments and tools lead to overload in network and make it very slow for exchange data in Manufacturing Cloud system. Also, need more storage space into the cloud due to data collection of real-time manufacturing resources, and need more process resource from cloud to handle this data. All those issues can result in Cloud Manufacturing system failure.

Although, cloud providers invests a lot in their systems to guarantee availability of the cloud systems, but there are many incidents, such as Gmail outage for 100 minutes in 2009, can create doubts about the cloud capabilities for delivering critical data and application for enterprises. The cloud providers guarantee deliver cloud services to customers under any circumstances, but sometimes enterprises cannot access their data and cloud resources due to network outage and system failures. The outage may be permanent as provider company gone out of business or temporary as failure in provider company systems. Either way, fail to provide data and cloud resources can be disaster on enterprise, where the enterprise can not function without their data and cloud resources.

The aim of Cloud Manufacturing is to share the resources and capabilities between different parties (manufacturing units, suppliers, other enterprises, and customers). But to manage different information systems and different manufacturing systems under Cloud Manufacturing umbrella can be a difficult task for both enterprises and cloud providers. For example, legacy systems are substantially irreplaceable in many enterprises, and it is costly and time consuming to put it into the cloud. Moreover, many cloud systems are architecture designed as closed systems, which prohibit interaction with other cloud systems. Also, different cloud providers can create a vendor lock-in situation, where each cloud provider has its own way to run the cloud different from other providers. This limits the choices for enterprises to choose between other cloud providers in the market. Its too risky for organizations to depend on one cloud service provider for all their services. The interoperability between the cloud service providers is not that smooth.

Availability, performance, and quality are the major concerns when enterprises using cloud services. The relationship between cloud provides and their customers need to be more efficient and effective by using standards, agreements, and regulations to know the responsibilities and duties of each party in Cloud Manufacturing system.

Lacking control of the data and its location in the cloud may create conflict with regulations and laws in the enterprise's country. As an example for this dilemma, European Union and American countries have laws that prohibit moving certain data types outside the enterprise's country. The cloud provides need to educate their customers about their services by using Service Level Agreement (SLA) which covers all these issues in detail.

A standard need to be setup for Cloud Computing technology in Manufacturing which will ensure uniformity across cloud service providers.

From the economic perspective, the purpose of using Cloud Manufacturing is to reduce the cost of investment in IT. Cloud Technology allows enterprises, especially SMEs, to use computing resources and capabilities at low cost. A research indicates that the implementation of cloud technology in enterprise has financial benefits reach to nearly 37%. However, the implementation of Cloud Manufacturing can raise the cost of using network communication (bandwidth) to send and receive data from the cloud. Moreover, Using Cloud Manufacturing for large enterprises can be costly due to need of more Cloud resources for their large projects. Also, possibility of switching Cloud providers because of dissatisfaction of Cloud provider service is not that smooth as it involves switching costs and other costs.

CONCLUSION

A computing and service-oriented manufacturing model called CMfg using the support of cloud computing, IoT, advanced computing, virtualization and service-oriented technologies has been discussed. Also, Cloud Based Design and Manufacturing model with the potential areas of implementation has been discussed. Also this chapter briefly discusses the Cloud based design and manufacturing a service oriented model. The key features, tools and benefits of Cloud based Design and Manufacturing have also been discussed. A comparison of traditional and cloud based manufacturing has been highlighted. The cloud based service models applicable in manufacturing industry have been described and discussed elaborately. Key technologies, advantages and challenges in Cloud Manufacturing are discussed.

FUTURE RESEARCH TRENDS

Future research can be focused on (Liu, Y., Wang, L. and Wang, X.V, 2018) Standardisation of Cloud Manufacturing, Big Data analytics of the data generated through the usage of cloud computing resources and servers in Manufacturing, Security of enterprise data, intellectual properties, Software, CAD designs and equipments used in Cloud Manufacturing and Scheduling as an on demand services model in cloud manufacturing. The current meta-heuristics-based, centralized approaches for scheduling in cloud manufacturing need to be revised to include critical factors and ingredients of cloud manufacturing such as involvement of larger-scale resources, autonomy of participants, higher dynamics, dynamic task arrivals, involvement of wide-area logistics, multi-granularity and multi-level resources/services.

Figure 5. Research trends in cloud manufacturing

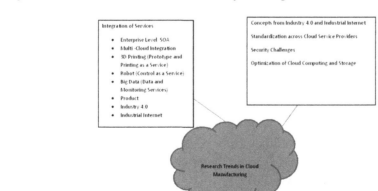

The key research trends in Cloud Manufacturing are highlighted in **Figure 5.**

Future research could also be focused on developing a sematic search engine to allow enterprises to search for qualified service providers. Currently, most search engines in design and manufacturing systems are based on keywords. None of the existing search engines is capable of searching for design concepts, 2D and 3D sketches, and manufacturing processes. It is very worthwhile to provide a scientific answer to the questions of what metrics should be defined to measure the performance of a design and manufacturing search engine, how to crawl and index design and manufacturing solutions and produce more satisfying search results.

REFERENCES

Giriraj, S., & Muthu, S. (2012). From Cloud Computing to Cloud Manufacturing Execution Assembly System. *International Conference on Intelligent Robotics, Automation, and Manufacturing IRAM 2012: Trends in Intelligent Robotics, Automation, and Manufacturing*, 303-312.

Guo, H., Tao, F., Zhang, L., Su, S., & Si, N. (2010). Correlation-aware web services composition and QoS computation model in virtual enterprise. *International Journal of Advanced Manufacturing Technology*, *51*(5), 817–827. doi:10.100700170-010-2648-9

Howe, J. (2009). *Why the power of the crowd is driving the future of business* (1st ed.). Beijing: CITIC Press.

Laili, Y., Tao, F., Zhang, L., & Sarker, B. R. (2012). A study of optimal allocation of comput-ing resources in cloud manufacturing systems. *International Journal of Advanced Manufacturing Technology*, *63*(5), 671–690. doi:10.100700170-012-3939-0

Li, B. H., Zhang, L., Wang, S. L., Tao, F., Cao, J. W., Jiang, X. D., & ... . (2010). Cloud manufacturing: A new service-oriented networked manufacturing model. *Jisuanji Jicheng Zhizao Xitong*, *16*(1), 1–7.

Liu, Y., Wang, L., & Wang, X. V. (2018). Cloud Manufacturing: Latest Advancements and Future trends. *Procedia Manufacturing*, *25*, 62–73. doi:10.1016/j.promfg.2018.06.058

Lv, B. (2012). A Multi-view Model Study for the Architecture of Cloud Manufacturing. *2012 Third International Conference on Digital Manufacturing and Automation (ICDMA)*, 93-97. 10.1109/ICDMA.2012.22

Mai, J., Zhang, L., Tao, F., & Ren, L. (2012). Architecture of hybrid cloud for manufacturing enterprise. *Asia Simulation Conference (AsiaSim'2012) & the International Conference on System Simulation and Scientific Computing (ICSC'2012),* 365-372.

Marston, S., Li, Z., Bandyopadhyay, S., Zhang, J., & Ghalsasi, A. (2011). Cloud computing – the business perspective. *Decision Support Systems, 51*(1), 176–189. doi:10.1016/j.dss.2010.12.006

Mell, P., & Grance, T. (2011). *The NIST definition of cloud computing.* National Institute of Standards and Technology, U.S. Department of Commerce. Retrieved from http://csrc.nist.gov/publications/nistpubs/800-145/SP800-145.pdf, 2011.

Rosenthal, M., Mork, P., Li, M. H., Stanford, J., Koester, D., & Reynolds, P. (2009). Cloud computing: A new business paradigm for biomedical information sharing. *Journal of Biomedical Informatics, 43*(2), 342–353. doi:10.1016/j.jbi.2009.08.014 PMID:19715773

Tao, F. (2012). FC-PACO-RM: A parallel method for service com-position optimal-selection in cloud manufacturing system. *IEEE Transactions on Industrial Informatics,* doi:10.1109/TII.2012.2232936

Tao, F., Cheng, Y., Zhang, L., & Zhao, D. (2012). Utility modelling, equilibrium, and coordina-tion of resource service transaction in service-oriented manufacturing system. *Proceedings of the Institution of Mechanical Engineers. Part B, Journal of Engineering Manufacture, 226*(6), 1099–1117. doi:10.1177/0954405412438011

Tao, F., Guo, H., Zhang, L., & Cheng, Y. (2012). Modeling of combinable relationship-basedcomposition service network and the theoretical proof of its scale-free characteristics. *Enterprise Information Systems, 6*(4), 373–404. doi:10. 1080/17517575.2011.621981

Tao, F., Hu, Y. F., & Zhou, Z. D. (2008). Study on manufacturing grid & its resource service optimal-selection system. *International Journal of Advanced Manufacturing Technology, 37*(9), 1022–1041. doi:10.100700170-007-1033-9

Tao, F., Hu, Y. F., & Zhou, Z. D. (2009). Application and modeling of resource service trust – QoS evaluation in manufacturing grid system. *International Journal of Production Research, 47*(6), 1521–1550. doi:10.1080/00207540701551927

Tao, F., Zhang, L., Venkatesh, V. C., Luo, Y., & Cheng, Y. (2011). Cloud manufacturing: A computing and service oriented manufacturing model. *Proceedings of the Institution of Mechanical Engineers. Part B, Journal of Engineering Manufacture, 225*(10), 1969–1976. doi:10.1177/0954405411405575

Tao, F., Zhao, D., Yefa, H., & Zhou, Z. (2010). Correlation-aware resource service compositionand optimal-selection in manufacturing grid. *European Journal of Operational Research, 201*(1), 129–143. doi:10.1016/j.ejor.2009.02.025

Wang, X. V. (2012). *Development of an Interoperable Cloud-based Manufacturing System* (PhD thesis). Mechanical Engineering, University of Auckland.

Wu, D., Greer, M. J., Rosen, D. W., & Schaefer, D. (2013). Cloud Manufacturing: Drivers, Current Status, and Future Trends. *Proceedings of the ASME 2013 International Manufacturing Science and Engineering Conference (MSEC13), Paper Number: MSEC2013-1106, Madison, Wisconsin, U.S.* 10.1115/MSEC2013-1106

Wu, D., Schaefer, D., & Rosen, D. W. (2013). Cloud-Based Design and Manufacturing Systems: A Social Network Analysis. *International Conference on Engineering Design (ICED13)*, Seoul, Korea.

Wu, D., Thames, J. L., Rosen, D. W., & Shaefer, D. (2012). Towards a cloud-based design and manufacturing paradigm: looking backward, looking forward. *ASME 2012 International Design Engineering Technical Conferences & Computers and Information in Engineering Conference (IDETC 2012) IDETC/CIE.*

Xu, X. (2012). From cloud computing to cloud manufacturing. *Robotics and Computer-integrated Manufacturing, 28*(1), 75–86. doi:10.1016/j.rcim.2011.07.002

Yadekar, Y., Shehab, E., & Mehnen, J. (2013). Challenges of Cloud Technology in Manufacturing Environment. *Proceedings of the 11th International Conference on Manufacturing Research*, 177-182.

Zhang, L., Luo, Y., Tao, F., Li, B. H., Ren, L., & Zhang, X. (2012). Cloud manufacturing: A newmanufacturing paradigm. *Enterprise Information Systems*, 1–21.

ADDITIONAL READING

Atzori, L., Iera, A., & Morabito, G. (2010). The Internet of Things: A survey. *Computer Networks, 54*(5), 2787–2805. doi:10.1016/j.comnet.2010.05.010

Bremer, C. F., & Eversheim, W. (2000). From an opportunity identification to its manufacturing: A references model for virtual manufacturing. *CIRP Ann. Mfg Technol., 49*(1), 325–329.

Cai, M., Zhang, W., Chen, G., Zhang, K., & Li, S. (2009). SWMRD: A semantic web-basedmanufacturing resource discovery system for cross-enterprise collaboration. *International Journal of Production Research, 48*(12), 3445–3460. doi:10.1080/00207540902814330

Cai, M., Zhang, W., & Zhang, K. (2011). Manuhub: A semantic web system for ontology-based service management in distributed manufacturing environments. *IEEE Transactions on Systems, Man, and Cybernetics. Part A, Systems and Humans, 41*(3), 574–582. doi:10.1109/TSMCA.2010.2076395

Chryssolouris, G., Mavrikios, D., Papakostas, N., Mourtzis, D., Michalos, G., & Georgoulias, K. (2009). Digital manufacturing: history, perspectives, and outlook. *Proc. IMechE, Part B: J. Engineering Manufacture, 223*(5), 451–462. doi:10.1243/09544054JEM1241

Ding, B., Tu, X. Y., & Sun, L. J. (2012). A cloud-based collaborative manufacturing resource sharing services. *Information Technology Journal, 11*(9), 1258–1264. doi:10.3923/itj.2012.1258.1264

Dong, B., Qi, G., Gu, X., & Wei, X. (2011). Web service-oriented manufacturing resource applications for networked product development. *Advanced Engineering Informatics*, 282–295.

Edstrom, D. (2010). Cloud computing in manufacturing. *Production Machining, 10*, 28–31.

Erkes, J. W., Kenny, K. B., Lewis, J. W., Sarachan, B. D., Sobolewski, M. W., & Sum, R. N. Jr. (1996). Implementing shared manufacturing services on the World-Wide Web. *Communications of the ACM, 39*(2), 34–45. doi:10.1145/230798.230802

Gao, X., Yang, M., Liu, Y., & Hou, X. (2013). Conceptual model of multi-agent business collaboration based on cloud workflow. *Journal of Theoretical and Applied Information Technology, 48*(1), 108–112.

Goldhar, J. D., & Jelinok, M. (1990). Manufacturing as a Service Business: CIM in the 21stCentury. *Computers in Industry, 14*(1-3), 225–245. doi:10.1016/0166-3615(90)90126-A

Hao, Q., Shen, W., & Wang, L. (2005). Towards a cooperative distributed manufacturing management framework. *Computers in Industry, 56*(1), 71–84. doi:10.1016/j.compind.2004.08.010

Kara, S., Manmek, S., & Herrmann, C. (2010). Global manufacturing and the embodied energy of products. *CIRP Ann. Mfg Technol., 59*(1), 29–32.

Katzel, J. (2011). Power of the cloud. *Control Engineering, 58,* 16–21.

Kshetri, N. (2013). Privacy and security issues in cloud computing: The role of institutions and institutional evolution. *Telecommunications Policy, 37*(4), 372–386. doi:10.1016/j.telpol.2012.04.011

Liu, L. L., Yu, T., Shi, Z. B., & Fang, M. L. (2003). Self-organization manufacturing grid and its task scheduling algorithm. *Computer Integrated Manufacturing System (China), 9*(6), 449–455.

Marston, S., Li, Z., Bandyopadhyay, S., Zhang, J., & Ghalsasi, A. (2011). Cloud computing-The business perspective. *Decision Support Systems, 51*(1), 176–189. doi:10.1016/j.dss.2010.12.006

Meier, H., Roy, R., & Seliger, G. (2010). Industrial Product-Service Systems – IPS2. *CIRP Ann. Mfg Technol., 59*(2), 607–627.

Meier, M., Seidelmann, J., & Mezgár, I. (2010). ManuCloud: The next-generation manufacturing as a service environment. *European Research Consortium for Informatics and Mathematics News, 83,* 33–34.

Mitsuishi, M., & Nagao, T. (1999). Networked manufacturing with reality sensation for technology transfer. *CIRP Ann. Mfg Technol., 48*(1), 409–412.

Panchal, J. H., & Schaefer, D. (2007). Towards achieving agility in web-based virtualenterprises: A decision-centric approach. *International Journal of Internet Manufacturing and Services, 1*(1), 51–74. doi:10.1504/IJIMS.2007.014483

Parker, N. (2007). Intellectual property issues in joint ventures and collaborations. *Journal of Intellectual Property Law and Practice, 2*(11), 729–741. doi:10.1093/jiplp/jpm167

Putnik, G. (2012). Advanced manufacturing systems and enterprises: Cloud and ubiqui-tous manufacturing and an architecture. *Journal of Applied Engineering Science, 10*(3), 127–134. doi:10.5937/jaes10-2511

Sako, M. (2012). Technology strategy and management: Business models for strategy and innovation. *Communications of the ACM, 55*(7), 22–24. doi:10.1145/2209249.2209259

Schultz, B. (2011). Cloud Storage a STEEP CLIMB. *Computerworld, 45*(6).

Sharifi, H., Colquhoun, G., Barclay, I., & Dann, Z. (2001). Agile manufacturing: a management and operational framework. *Proc. IMechE, Part B: J. Engineering Manufacture, 215*(6), 857–869. doi:10.1243/0954405011518647

Shi, S., Mo, R., Yang, H., Chang, Z., & Chen, Z. (2011). An implementation of modeling resource in a manufacturing grid for resource sharing. *International Journal of Computer Integrated Manufacturing, 20*(2-3), 169–177. doi:10.1080/09511920601020805

Suh, S. H., Cho, J. H., & Hong, H. D. (2002). On the architecture of intelligent STEP-compliant CNC. *International Journal of Computer Integrated Manufacturing, 15*(2), 168–177. doi:10.1080/09511920110056541

Symonds, M. (2012). Cloud ERP meets manufacturing, quality magazine. *BNP Media, 51*, 40–43.

Tao, F., Hu, Y. F., & Zhou, Z. D. (2009). Zu De Zhou. Application and modeling of resource service trust-QoS evaluation in manufacturing grid system. *International Journal of Production Research, 47*(6), 1521–1550. doi:10.1080/00207540701551927

Tao, F., Zhang, L., & Nee, A. Y. C. (2011). A review of the application of grid technology in manufacturing. *International Journal of Production Research, 49*(13), 4119–4155. doi:10.1080/00207541003801234

Tao, F., Zhang, L., Venkatesh, V. C., Luo, Y., & Cheng, Y. (2011). Cloud manufacturing: A com-puting and service oriented manufacturing model. *Proceedings of the Institution of Mechanical Engineers. Part B, Journal of Engineering Manufacture, 225*(10), 1969–1976. doi:10.1177/0954405411405575

Tao, F., Zhang, L., Venkatesh, V. C., Luo, Y., & Cheng, Y. (2011). Cloud manufacturing: A computing and service-oriented manufacturing model. *Proceedings of the Institution of Mechanical Engineers. Part B, Journal of Engineering Manufacture, 225*(10), 1969–1976. doi:10.1177/0954405411405575

Tao, F., Zhao, D., Hu, Y. F., & Zhou, Z. D. (2008). Resource service composition and its optimal-selection based on particle swarm optimization in manufacturing grid system. *IEEE Transactions on Industrial Informatics*, 4(4), 315–327. doi:10.1109/TII.2008.2009533

Torrisi, N. M., & de Oliveira, J. F. G. (2012). Remote monitoring for high-speed CNC processes over public IP networks using Cyber OPC. *International Journal of Advanced Manufacturing Technology*, 60(1), 191–200. doi:10.100700170-011-3580-3

Wagner, S. M., Eggert, A., & Lindemann, E. (2010). Creating and appropriating value in collaborative relationships. *Journal of Business Research*, 63(8), 840–848. doi:10.1016/j.jbusres.2010.01.004

Xu, X. W., & He, Q. (2004). Striving for a total integration of CAD, CAPP, CAM and CNC. *Robotics and Computer-integrated Manufacturing*, 20(2), 101–109. doi:10.1016/j.rcim.2003.08.003

Xu, X. W., Wang, H., Mao, J., Newman, S. T., Kramer, T. R., Proctor, F. M., & Michaloski, J. L. (2005). STEP-compliant NC research: The search for intelligent CAD/CAPP/CAM/CNC integration. *International Journal of Production Research*, 43(17), 3703–3743. doi:10.1080/00207540500137530

Zhang, W., Zhang, S., Cai, M., & Liu, Y. (2012). A reputation-based peer-to-peer architecture for semantic service discovery in distributed manufacturing environments. *Concurrent Engineering, Research and Applications*, 20(3), 237–253. doi:10.1177/1063293X12457402

KEY TERMS AND DEFINITIONS

AR: Augmented reality systems may also be considered a form of VR that layers virtual information over a live camera feed into a headset or through a smartphone or tablet device giving the user the ability to view three-dimensional images.

CAD: Computer-aided design (CAD) is the use of computer systems (or workstations) to aid in the creation, modification, analysis, or optimization of a design.

CBDM: Cloud-based design and manufacturing – a service-oriented networked product development model in which service consumers are enabled to configure, select, and utilize customized product realization resources and services ranging from computer-aided engineering software to reconfigurable manufacturing systems.

CBM: Cloud-based manufacturing.

Cloud Carrier: An intermediary that provides connectivity and transport of cloud services from cloud providers to cloud consumers.

Cloud Consumer: A person or organization that maintains a business relationship with, and uses service from, cloud providers.

Cloud Provider: A person, organization, or entity responsible for making a service available to interested parties.

CMfg: Cloud manufacturing.

Grid Computing: Grid computing is a computer network in which each computer's resources are shared with every other computer in the system. Processing power, memory, and data storage are all community resources that authorized users can tap into and leverage for specific tasks.

HaaS: Hardware as a service refers to managed services or grid computing, where computing power is leased from a central provider.

Hybrid Cloud: Hybrid cloud is a cloud computing environment that uses a mix of on-premises, private cloud, and third-party, public cloud services with orchestration between the two platforms.

IaaS: The storage and compute capabilities are provided as a service.

IoT: The internet of things is the network of physical devices, vehicles, home appliances, and other items embedded with electronics, software, sensors, actuators, and connectivity which enables these things to connect, collect, and exchange data, creating opportunities for more direct integration of the physical world into computer-based systems, resulting in efficiency improvements, economic benefits, and reduced human exertion.

PaaS: The platform is provided as a service, which can enable the development and deployment of applications without the cost and complexity of buying and managing the underlying hardware and software layers.

Private Cloud: Private cloud refers to a model of cloud computing where IT services are provisioned over private IT infrastructure for the dedicated use of a single organization.

Public Cloud: The public cloud is defined as computing services offered by third-party providers over the public Internet, making them available to anyone who wants to use or purchase them. They may be free or sold on-demand, allowing customers to pay only per usage for the CPU cycles, storage, or bandwidth they consume.

SaaS: Software as a service (SaaS) is a software distribution model in which a third-party provider hosts applications and makes them available to customers over the internet.

SME: Small and medium enterprises.

Virtualization: Virtualization is a technique how to separate a service from the underlying physical delivery of that service. It is the process of creating a virtual version of something like computer hardware.

VR: Virtual reality is an interactive computer-generated experience taking place within a simulated environment that incorporates mainly auditory and visual but also other types of sensory feedback. This immersive environment can be similar to the real world or it can be fantastical, creating an experience that is not possible in ordinary physical reality.

Compilation of References

10 . jobs that didn't exist 10 years ago. (2016, June 7). Retrieved August 8, 2018, from https://www.weforum.org/agenda/2016/06/10-jobs-that-didn-t-exist-10-years-ago/

Abolfazli, S., Sanaei, Z., Sanaei, M. H., Shojafar, M., & Gani, A. (2016). Mobile Cloud Computing. In S. Murugesan & I. Bojanova (Eds.), *Encyclopedia of Cloud Computing* (pp. 29–40). Chichester, UK: John Wiley & Sons, Ltd. doi:10.1002/9781118821930.ch3

Adriaans & Zantinge. (1999). *Data Mining*. Addison Wesley Longman.

Agosti, M., Ferro, N., & Silvello, G. (2016). Digital library interoperability at high level of abstraction. *Future Generation Computer Systems*, *55*, 129–146. doi:10.1016/j.future.2015.09.020

Agostinho, C., Ducq, Y., Zacharewicz, G., Sarraipa, J., Lampathaki, F., Poler, R., & Jardim-Goncalves, R. (2016). Towards a sustainable interoperability in networked enterprise information systems: Trends of knowledge and model-driven technology. *Computers in Industry*, *79*, 64–76. doi:10.1016/j.compind.2015.07.001

Akande, A., April, N., & Belle, J. (2013). Management Issues with Cloud Computing. In *Proceedings of the Innovative Computing and Cloud Computing*. Wuhan, China: The Association of Computing Machinery.

Al-Aqrabi, H., Liu, L., Hill, R., & Antonopoulos, N. (2015). Cloud BI: Future of Business Intelligence in the Cloud. *Journal of Computer and System Sciences*, *81*(1), 85–96. doi:10.1016/j.jcss.2014.06.013

Alcaraz, J., Calero, J., Edwards, N., Kirschnick, J., & Wilcock, L. (2010). Toward an architecture for the automated provisioning of cloud services. *Communications Magazine, IEEE*, *48*(12), 124–131. doi:10.1109/MCOM.2010.5673082

Alenezi, M., & Magel, K. (2014). Empirical evaluation of a new coupling metric: Combining structural and semantic coupling. *International Journal of Computers and Applications*, *36*(1). doi:10.2316/Journal.202.2014.1.202-3902

Al-Fuqaha, A., Guizani, M., Mohammadi, M., Aledhari, M., & Ayyash, M. (2015). Internet of things: A survey on enabling technologies, protocols, and applications. *IEEE Communications Surveys and Tutorials, 17*(4), 2347–2376. doi:10.1109/COMST.2015.2444095

Anahory, S., & Hurray, D. (2011). *Data Ware Housing in the Real World*. New Delhi: Pearson.

Anam, S., Kim, Y., Kang, B., & Liu, Q. (2016). Adapting a knowledge-based schema matching system for ontology mapping. In *Proceedings of the Australasian Computer Science Week Multiconference* (p. 27). New York, NY: ACM Press. 10.1145/2843043.2843048

Andersen, A., Brunoe, T., & Nielsen, K. (2015). Reconfigurable Manufacturing on Multiple Levels: Literature Review and Research Directions. In S. Umeda, M. Nakano, H. Mizuyama, N. Hibino, D. Kiritsis, & G. von Cieminski (Eds.), *Advances in Production Management Systems: Innovative Production Management Towards Sustainable Growth* (pp. 266–273). Cham, Switzerland: Springer International Publishing.

Andres, C. (1999). *Great Web Architecture*. Foster City, CA: IDG Books World Wide.

Anschuetz, L., Keirnan, T., & Rosenbaum, S. (2002). Combining Usability Research with Documentation Development for Improved User Support. In *Proceedings of the SIGDOC*. Toronto, Canada: The Association of Computing Machinery.

Armbrust, A., Fox, A., Griffith, R., Joseph, A., Katz, R., Konwinski, A., ... Zaharia, M. (2010). Above the Clouds: A View of Cloud Computing. *Communications of the ACM, 53*(4), 50. doi:10.1145/1721654.1721672

Attwood, T. K., & Parry-Smith, D. J. (2005). *Introduction to Bioinformatics; New Delhi: Pearson Education*. Singapore: Private Limited.

Babat, M., & Chauhan, M. (2011). A Tale of Migration to Cloud Computing for Sharing Experiences and Observations. In *Workshop on Software Engineering for. Cloud Computing*. Honolulu, HI: IEEE.

Babu, D., & Darsi, M. (2013). A Survey on Service Oriented Architecture and Metrics to Measure Coupling. *International Journal on Computer Science and Engineering, 5*(8), 726–733.

Bandopadhyay. (2013). A Technology Lead Business Model for Pharma – Collaborative Patient Care. *CSI Communications Journal, 37*(9), 12-13, 26.

Banerjee, B. (2010). *Fundamental of Financial Management*. New Delhi: PHI Learning Private Limited.

Bange, C., & Eckerson, E. (2017). *BI and Data Management in the Cloud: Issues and Trends*. Retrieved April 9, 2018 from https://www.eckerson.com/articles/bi-and-data-management-in-the-cloud-issues-and-trends

BARC. (2017). *BI and Data Management in the Cloud: Issues and Trends*. Retrieved June 23, 2018 from https://s3.amazonaws.com/eckerson/content_assets/assets/000/000/115/original/BARC_Research_Study_BI_and_Data_Management_in_the_Cloud_EN.pdf?1487101351

Bassett, L. (2015). *Introduction to JavaScript Object Notation: A to-the-point Guide to JSON*. Sebastopol, CA: O'Reilly Media, Inc.

Beall, A. (2018, February 16). What are quantum computers and how do they work? WIRED explains. *Wired UK*. Retrieved from https://www.wired.co.uk/article/quantum-computing-explained

Becker, S., & Mottay, F. (2001). A global perspective on website usability. *IEEE Software*, *18*(1), 61–54. doi:10.1109/52.903167

Behrendt, M., & Breiter, G. (2009). Life Cycle Characteristics of Services in the World of Cloud Computing. *IBM Journal of Research and Development*, *53*(4), 527–534.

Bergeron, B. (2003). *Bioinformatics Computing; New Delhi: Pearson Education*. Singapore: Private Limited.

Berman, N. (2018). The Current State of Cloud Business Intelligence. *Money INC*. Retrieved June 22, 2018 from https://moneyinc.com/the-current-state-of-cloud-business-intelligence/

Bhandarkar. (2013). Big Data Systems: Past, Present & (Possibly) Future. *CSI Communications Journal, 37*(1), 7-8, 16.

Bidve, V. S., & Sarasu, P. (2016). Tool for measuring coupling in object-oriented java software. *IACSIT International Journal of Engineering and Technology*, *8*(2), 812–820.

Bi-survey. (2018). *The Real BI Trends in 2018*. Retrieved May 21, 2018 from https://bi-survey.com/top-business-intelligence-trends

Botta, A., de Donato, W., Persico, V., & Pescapé, A. (2016). Integration of cloud computing and internet of things: A survey. *Future Generation Computer Systems*, *56*, 684–700. doi:10.1016/j.future.2015.09.021

Brandt, C., & Hermann, F. (2013). Conformance analysis of organizational models: A new enterprise modeling framework using algebraic graph transformation. *International Journal of Information System Modeling and Design*, *4*(1), 42–78. doi:10.4018/jismd.2013010103

Bratanis, K., Braun, S., Paraskakis, I., Rossini, A., Simons, A., & Verginadis, Y. (2014). Advanced Service Brokerage Capabilities as the Catalyst for Future Cloud Service Ecosystems. In *Proceedings of the Cross Cloud Brokers*. Bordeaux, France: The Association of Computing Machinery.

Butrico, M., Silva, D., & Youseff, L. (2008). Toward a unified ontology of cloud computing. In *Grid Computing Environments Workshop*. Austin, TX: IEEE.

Buyya & Sukumar. (2011). Platforms for Building and Developing Applications for Cloud Computing. *CSI Communications Journal, 35*(2), 6-11.

Buyya, Vecchiola, & Selvi. (2013). *Mastering Cloud Computing*. New Delhi: McGraw Hill Education (India) Private Limited.

Candela, I., Bavota, G., Russo, B., & Oliveto, R. (2016). Using cohesion and coupling for software remodularization: Is it enough? *ACM Transactions on Software Engineering and Methodology, 25*(3), 24. doi:10.1145/2928268

Capel, M., & Mendoza, L. (2014). Choreography Modeling Compliance for Timed Business Models. In *Proceedings of the Workshop on Enterprise and Organizational Modeling and Simulation* (pp. 202-218). Berlin, Germany: Springer. 10.1007/978-3-662-44860-1_12

Chaka. (2013). *Virtualization and Cloud Computing Business Model in the Virual Cloud*. Hershey, PA: IGI Global

Chandra, A. H., & Ghosh, S. K. (2006). *Image Interpretation, Remote sensing and Geographical Information System*. New Delhi: Narosa Publishing House.

Chen, H., & Li, S. (2010). SRC: A Service Registry on Cloud Providing Behavior-aware and QoS-aware service discovery. In *International Conference on Service-Oriented Computing and Applications*. Perth, Australia: IEEE.

Chen, Y. (2015). A RDF-based approach to metadata crosswalk for semantic interoperability at the data element level. *Library Hi Tech, 33*(2), 175–194. doi:10.1108/LHT-08-2014-0078

Chiras Daniel, D., & Reganold John, P. (2010). *Natural Resource Cononservation Management and Management for a Sustainable Future*. Prentice Hall.

Chorafas, D. N. (2011). *Cloud Computing Strategies*. Boca Raton, FL: CRC Press Taylor & Francis Group.

Choudary, S. P. (2015). *Platform Scale: How an emerging business model helps startups build large empires with minimum investment* (1st ed.). Platform Thinking Labs.

Christensen, C. M. (1997). *The Innovator's Dilemma: The Revolutionary Book that Will Change the Way You Do Business*. Collins Business Essentials.

Cisco. (2011). *The Need for Service Catalog Design in Cloud Services Development*. Corporate White Paper.

Clutter Buck, D. (2012). *The Talent Wave*. London: Kogan Press.

Columbus, L. (2018). The State of Business Intelligence. *Forbes*. Retrieved June 08, 2018 from https://www.forbes.com/sites/louiscolumbus/2018/06/08/the-state-of-business-intelligence-2018/#86ec7d278289

CompTIA. (2018, March). 2018 Tech Industry Job Market & Salary Trends Analysis. *Cyberstates by CompTIA*. Retrieved August 9, 2018, from https://www.cyberstates.org/index.html#keyfindings

Conroy & Paterson. (2013). *Decision Making Natural Resource Management: A Structured Adaptive Approach*. Wiley-Blackwell.

Craig, T., & Ludloff, M. E. (2013). *Privacy and Big Data*. Mumbai: Shroff Publishers & Distributors Private Limited.

Danneels, E. (2004). Disruptive technology reconsidered: A critique and research agenda. *Journal of Product Innovation Management, 21*(4), 246–258. doi:10.1111/j.0737-6782.2004.00076.x

Davis & Patterson. (2012). *Ethics of Big Data*. Mumbai: Shroff Publishers & Distributors Private Limited.

Dediu, H. (2012, April 11). *When will smartphones reach saturation in the US?* Retrieved August 1, 2018, from http://www.asymco.com/2012/04/11/when-will-smartphones-reach-saturation-in-the-us/

Deepa & Aruna. (2011). A Survey on Artificial Intelligence Approaches for Medical Image Classifications. *Indian Journal of Science and Technology, 4*(11).

Dharanipragada, J. (2016). *Grid and Cloud Computing. New Delhi: McGraw Hill Education.* India: Private Limited.

Dooley, J., Spanoudakis, G., & Zisman, A. (2008). Proactive Runtime Service Discovery. In *Proceedings of IEEE 2008 International Service Computing Conference*. Honolulu, HI: IEEE.

Dudharejia, M. (2018). Four major challenges of adopting cloud business intelligence – and how to overcome them. *Cloudtech*. Retrieved June 20, 2018 from https://www.cloudcomputing-news.net/news/2018/jun/11/four-major-challenges-adopting-cloud-business-intelligence-and-how-overcome-them/

Durugbo, C. (2016). Collaborative networks: A systematic review and multi-level framework. *International Journal of Production Research, 54*(12), 3749–3776. doi:10.1080/00207543.2015.1122249

Dzida, W., Herda, S., & Itzfelt, W. (1978). User-perceived quality of interactive systems. *IEEE Transactions on Software Engineering, SE-4*(4), 270–276. doi:10.1109/TSE.1978.231511

Ebrahimifard, A., Amiri, M., Arani, M., & Parsa, S. (2016). Mapping BPMN 2.0 Choreography to WS-CDL: A Systematic Method. *Journal of E-Technology, 7*, 1–23.

Edgerton, D. (2011). *Shock of the old: Technology and global history since 1900*. Profile books.

Elshwimy, F., Algergawy, A., Sarhan, A., & Sallam, E. (2014). Aggregation of similarity measures in schema matching based on generalized mean. In *Proceedings of the IEEE International Conference on Data Engineering Workshops* (pp. 74-79). Piscataway, NJ: IEEE Computer Society Press. 10.1109/ICDEW.2014.6818306

Enabling Technology. (n.d.). In *BusinessDictionary.com*. Retrieved from http://www.businessdictionary.com/definition/enabling-technology.html

Epstein, R. A., & Macvoy, S. P. (2011). Making A Scene in the Brain. In L. R. Harris & M. R. M. Jenkin (Eds.), *Vision in 3D Environments* (pp. 270–273). Cambridge, UK: Cambridge University Press. doi:10.1017/CBO9780511736261.012

Erl, T., Merson, P., & Stoffers, R. (2017). *Service-oriented Architecture: Analysis and Design for Services and Microservices*. Upper Saddle River, NJ: Prentice Hall PTR.

Esposito & Evangalista. (2014). Investigating Virtual Enterprises Models. *International Journal of Production Economics*.

Esposito, E., & Evangelista, P. (2014). Investigating virtual enterprise models: Literature review and empirical findings. *International Journal of Production Economics*, *148*, 145–157. doi:10.1016/j.ijpe.2013.10.003

Evelson, B., & Nicolson, N. (2008). Topic Overview: Business Intelligence—An Information Workplace Report. *Forrester*. Retrieved June 08, 2018 from www.forrester.com/report/Topic+Overview+Business+Intelligence/-/E-RES39218

Farid, A. (2017). Measures of reconfigurability and its key characteristics in intelligent manufacturing systems. *Journal of Intelligent Manufacturing*, *28*(2), 353–369. doi:10.100710845-014-0983-7

Fawcett, J., Ayers, D., & Quin, L. (2012). *Beginning XML*. Indianapolis, IN: John Wiley & Sons.

Fielding, R., Taylor, R., Erenkrantz, J., Gorlick, M., Whitehead, J., Khare, R., & Oreizy, P. (2017). Reflections on the REST architectural style and principled design of the modern web architecture. In *Proceedings of the 2017 11th Joint Meeting on Foundations of Software Engineering* (pp. 4-14). New York, NY: ACM Press. 10.1145/3106237.3121282

Flynn. (2012). *The Social Media Hand Book*. New Delhi: Wiley India Private Limited.

Folmer, E., Gurp, J., & Bosch, J. (2004). Software Architecture Analysis of Usability. *The 9th IFIP Working Conference on Engineering for Human-Computer Interaction*.

Franks, B. (2014). *Taming the Big Data Tidal Wave*. New Delhi: Wiley India Private Limited.

Freeman, C., & Louca, F. (2001). *As Time Goes by: The Information Revolution and the Industrial Revolutions in Historical Perspective*. New York, NY: Oxford University Press, Inc.

Frey, C. B., & Osborne, M. A. (2017). The future of employment: How susceptible are jobs to computerisation? *Technological Forecasting and Social Change, 114*, 254–280. doi:10.1016/j.techfore.2016.08.019

Gartner. (2018). Reviews for Analytics and Business Intelligence Platform. *Gartner Peer Insights.* Retrieved June 23, 2018 from https://www.gartner.com/reviews/market/business-intelligence-analytics-platforms

Geetika, R., & Singh, P. (2014). Dynamic coupling metrics for object oriented software systems: A survey. *Software Engineering Notes, 39*(2), 1–8. doi:10.1145/2579281.2579296

Ghobakhloo, M., Tang, S., Sabouri, M., & Zulkifli, N. (2014). The impact of information system-enabled supply chain process integration on business performance: A resource-based analysis. *International Journal of Information Technology & Decision Making, 13*(05), 1075–1113. doi:10.1142/S0219622014500163

Giriraj, S., & Muthu, S. (2012). From Cloud Computing to Cloud Manufacturing Execution Assembly System. *International Conference on Intelligent Robotics, Automation, and Manufacturing IRAM 2012: Trends in Intelligent Robotics, Automation, and Manufacturing*, 303-312.

Glynn, H. J., & Heinke, G. W. (2004). *Environmental Science and Engineering.* Singapore: Private Limited.

Golden, B. (2012, June). How Cloud Computing can transform Business. *Harvard Business Review.*

Gosh, P. (2018). Business Intelligence and Analytics Trends in 2018. *Datavaresity.* Retrieved June 02, 2018 from http://www.dataversity.net/business-intelligence-analytics-trends-2018/

Govil & Purohit. (2011). Health Care Systems in India. In Health Care Systems – A Global Survey (pp. 576-612). New Delhi: New Century Publications.

Graydon, P., Habli, I., Hawkins, R., Kelly, T., & Knight, J. (2012). Arguing Conformance. *IEEE Software, 29*(3), 50–57. doi:10.1109/MS.2012.26

Grefen, P., Mehandjiev, N., Kouvas, G., Weichhart, G., & Eshuis, R. (2009). Dynamic business network process management in instant virtual enterprises. *Computers in Industry, 60*(2), 86–103. doi:10.1016/j.compind.2008.06.006

Guo, H., Tao, F., Zhang, L., Su, S., & Si, N. (2010). Correlation-aware web services composition and QoS computation model in virtual enterprise. *International Journal of Advanced Manufacturing Technology, 51*(5), 817–827. doi:10.100700170-010-2648-9

Hameed, M. A., Counsell, S., & Swift, S. (2012). A conceptual Model for the process of IT, Innovation Adoption in Organizations. *Journal of Engineering and Technology Management, 29*(3), 358–390. doi:10.1016/j.jengtecman.2012.03.007

Hameed, M. A., Counsell, S., & Swift, S. (2012). A Conceptual Model for the process of IT. *Innovation Adoption in Organizations. Journal of Engineering and Technology Management.*

Hendricksen, D. (2014). *12 More Essential Skills for Software Architects.* Upper Saddle River, NJ: Addison-Wesley Professional.

He, W., & Da Xu, L. (2014). Integration of distributed enterprise applications: A survey. *IEEE Transactions on Industrial Informatics, 10*(1), 35–42. doi:10.1109/TII.2012.2189221

Hoffer & HeikkiTodi. (2013). Modern Database Management (10th ed.). New Delhi: Pearson.

Hoffer , & Tudi, . (2013). *Modern Database Management.* New Delhi: Pearson.

Ho, V., & Wong, S. S. (2009). Knowing who knows what and who knows whom: Experise recognition, network recognition and individual performance. *Journal of Occupational and Organizational Psychology, 82*(1), 147–189. doi:10.1348/096317908X298585

Howe, J. (2009). *Why the power of the crowd is driving the future of business* (1st ed.). Beijing: CITIC Press.

Hurwitz, J., Nugent, A., Halper, F., & Kaufman, M. (2014). *Big Data for Dummies.* New Delhi: Wiley India Private Limited.

Hussain, T., Mehmood, R., Haq, A., Alnafjan, K., & Alghamdi, A. (2014). Designing framework for the interoperability of C4I systems. In *International Conference on Computational Science and Computational Intelligence* (102–106). Piscataway, NJ: IEEE Computer Society Press. 10.1109/CSCI.2014.102

Ignacimuthu, S. (2005). *Basic Informatics.* New Delhi: Narosa Publishing House.

Ilieva, G., Yankova, T., & Klisarova, S. (2015). Cloud Business Intelligence: Contemporary Learning Opportunities in MIS training. *Proceedings of the 2015 Balkan Conference on Informatics: Advances in ICT.*

Imache, R., Izza, S., & Ahmed-Nacer, M. (2012). An enterprise information system agility assessment model. *Computer Science and Information Systems, 9*(1), 107–133. doi:10.2298/CSIS101110041I

ISO. (2006). *Enterprise integration -- Framework for enterprise modelling. ISO/CEN Standard 19439:2006.* Geneva, Switzerland: International Organization for Standardization.

ISO. (2010). *Systems and software engineering – Vocabulary. ISO/IEC/IEEE 24765:2010(E) International Standard* (p. 186). Geneva, Switzerland: International Organization for Standardization.

Iyengar, S., & Brooks, R. (Eds.). (2016). *Distributed sensor networks: sensor networking and applications.* Boca Raton, FL: CRC Press.

Janecek, P. (2007). Faceted classification in web information architecture: A framework for using semantic web tools. *The Electronic Library*, *25*(2), 219–233. doi:10.1108/02640470710741340

Jeng, J. (2005). Usability assessment of academic digital libraries: Effectiveness, efficiency, satisfaction, and learnability. Libri. *International Journal of Libraries and Information Services*, *55*(2/3), 96–121.

Job Openings and Labor Turnover Summary. (2018, August 7). Retrieved August 13, 2018, from https://www.bls.gov/news.release/jolts.nr0.htm

Jorgensen, A., Rowland-Jones, J., Welch, J., Clark, D., Price, C., & Mitchell, B. (2014). *Microsoft Big Data Solutions*. New Delhi: Wiley India Private Limited.

Jovanovic, B., & Rousseau, P. L. (2005). General purpose technologies. In *Handbook of economic growth* (Vol. 1, pp. 1181–1224). Elsevier.

Juric, M., & Weerasiri, D. (2014). *WS-BPEL 2.0 beginner's guide*. Birmingham, UK: Packt Publishing Ltd.

Karat, J. (1997). User-centered software evaluation methodologies. In M. Helander, T. K. Landauer, & P. Prabhu (Eds.), *Handbook of Human-Computer Interaction* (pp. 689–704). New York: Elsevier Press. doi:10.1016/B978-044481862-1.50094-7

Karvonen, K. (2000). The beauty of simplicity. In *Proceedings of the ACM Conference on Universal Usability*. Arlington, VA: The Association of Computing Machinery.

Kaushik, A., & Kaushik, C. P. (2006). *Environmental Studies-A Multidisciplinary Subject: Perspectives in Environmental Studies*. New Delhi: New Age International Publishers.

Khalfallah, M., Figay, N., Barhamgi, M., & Ghodous, P. (2014). Model driven conformance testing for standardized services. In *IEEE International Conference on Services Computing* (pp. 400–407). Piscataway, NJ: IEEE Computer Society Press. 10.1109/SCC.2014.60

Khon & Skarulis. (2012). IBM Watson Delivers New Insights for Treatment and Diagnosis. *Digital Health Conference*.

Knoke, B., Missikoff, M., & Thoben, K. D. (2017). Collaborative open innovation management in virtual manufacturing enterprises. *International Journal of Computer Integrated Manufacturing*, *30*(1), 158–166.

Knot. (2017). *How Innovation Really Works*. Chennai: McGraw Hill Education (India) Private Limited.

Kok, A. (2016). *Cultural, Behavioral and Social Considerations in Electronic Collaboration USA*. IGI Global. doi:10.4018/978-1-4666-9556-6

Kostoska, M., Gusev, M., & Ristov, S. (2016). An overview of cloud interoperability. In *Federated Conference on Computer Science and Information Systems* (pp. 873-876). Piscataway, NJ: IEEE Computer Society Press. 10.15439/2016F463

Kovács, G., & Kot, S. (2017). Economic and social effects of novel supply chain concepts and virtual enterprises. *Journal of International Studies, 10*(1), 237–254. doi:10.14254/2071-8330.2017/10-1/17

Kraak & Ormelling. (2004). *Cartographic Visualization of Geospatial Data; New Delhi: Pearson Education.* Singapore: Private Limited.

Krane, D. E., & Raymer, M. L. (2005). *Fundamental Concepts of Bioinformatics; New Delhi: Pearson Education.* Singapore: Private Limited.

Krishna & Jimy. (2013). Application of Zigbee Wireless Frequency for Patient Monitoring System. *CSI Communications Journal, 37*(9), 17-18.

Krug, S. (2000). *Don't Make Me Think.* Indianapolis, IN: New Riders Publishing.

Krutz, R. L., & Vines, R. D. (2010). *Cloud Security.* New Delhi: Wiley India Private Limited.

Kumar. (2013). Big Data- A Big game changer. *CSI Communications Journal, 37*(1), 9-10.

Laili, Y., Tao, F., Zhang, L., & Sarker, B. R. (2012). A study of optimal allocation of comput-ing resources in cloud manufacturing systems. *International Journal of Advanced Manufacturing Technology, 63*(5), 671–690. doi:10.100700170-012-3939-0

Lecerof, A., & Paterno, F. (1998). Automatic Support for Usability Evaluation. *IEEE Transactions on Software Engineering, 24*(10), 863–888. doi:10.1109/32.729686

Levin, S. (2013). *Cooperation and Sustainability in Guru Prasad Madhavan, Barbara Oakley, David Green, David Koon, and Penny Low.* New York: Springer.

Liao, Y., Deschamps, F., Loures, E., & Ramos, L. (2017). Past, present and future of Industry 4.0 - a systematic literature review and research agenda proposal. *International Journal of Production Research, 55*(12), 3609–3629. doi:10.1080/00207543.2017.1308576

Li, B. H., Zhang, L., Wang, S. L., Tao, F., Cao, J. W., Jiang, X. D., & ... . (2010). Cloud manufacturing: A new service-oriented networked manufacturing model. *Jisuanji Jicheng Zhizao Xitong, 16*(1), 1–7.

Li, G., & Wei, M. (2014). Everything-as-a-service platform for on-demand virtual enterprises. *Information Systems Frontiers, 16*(3), 435–452. doi:10.100710796-012-9351-3

Lipsey, R. G., Carlaw, K. I., & Bekar, C. T. (2005). *Economic transformations: general purpose technologies and long-term economic growth.* OUP Oxford.

Liu, Y., Wang, L., & Wang, X. V. (2018). Cloud Manufacturing: Latest Advancements and Future trends. *Procedia Manufacturing*, *25*, 62–73. doi:10.1016/j.promfg.2018.06.058

Louis, C. (2018). The state of business intelligence, 2018. *Forbes*. Retrieved from https://www.forbes.com/sites/louiscolumbus/2018/06/08/the-state-of-business-intelligence-2018/#65e863247828

Lv, B. (2012). A Multi-view Model Study for the Architecture of Cloud Manufacturing. *2012 Third International Conference on Digital Manufacturing and Automation (ICDMA)*, 93-97. 10.1109/ICDMA.2012.22

Madison, N. (2014). *Health Information Systems, Opportunities and Challenges*. Retrieved from http//commons.nmu.edu/facwork_book chapters/14

Mai, J., Zhang, L., Tao, F., & Ren, L. (2012). Architecture of hybrid cloud for manufacturing enterprise. *Asia Simulation Conference (AsiaSim'2012) & the International Conference on System Simulation and Scientific Computing (ICSC'2012)*, 365-372.

Majumdar. (2011). Resource Management on Clouds: Handling Uncertainties in Parameters and Polices. *CSI Communications Journal, 35*(2), 16-17.

Market Research Future. (2018). *Business Intelligence Market Research Report – Global Forecast to 2022*. Retrieved May 22, 2018 from https://www.marketresearchfuture.com/reports/business-intelligence-market-2299

Marston, S., Li, Z., Bandyopadhyay, S., Zhang, J., & Ghalsasi, A. (2011). Cloud computing – the business perspective. *Decision Support Systems*, *51*(1), 176–189. doi:10.1016/j.dss.2010.12.006

Marz, N., & Warren, J. (2015). *Big Data: Principles and best practices of scalable realtime data systems*. Greenwich, CT: Manning Publications Co.

Matentzoglu, N., Parsia, B., & Sattler, U. (2017). OWL Reasoning: Subsumption Test Hardness and Modularity. *Journal of Automated Reasoning*, 1–35. PMID:30069069

Mather, Kumaraswamy, & Latif. (2010). *Cloud Security and Privacy*. Mumbai: Shroff Publishers & Distributors Private Limited.

Mathur, H. P., Singh, S. K., & Mohan, A. (2013). Creating Value through Innovation. New Delhi: Shree Publishers & Distributors.

McLay, A. (2014). Re-reengineering the dream: Agility as competitive adaptability. *International Journal of Agile Systems and Management*, *7*(2), 101–115. doi:10.1504/IJASM.2014.061430

Mell, P., & Grance, T. (2011). *The NIST definition of cloud computing*. National Institute of Standards and Technology, U.S. Department of Commerce. Retrieved from http://csrc.nist.gov/publications/nistpubs/800-145/SP800-145.pdf, 2011.

Mentes, A. & Turan, A. (2012). Adressing the Usability Of University Websites: An Empirical Study On Namik Kemal University. *Tojet, 11*(3).

Mezgár, I., & Rauschecker, U. (2014). The challenge of networked enterprises for cloud computing interoperability. *Computers in Industry, 65*(4), 657–674. doi:10.1016/j.compind.2014.01.017

Miller, M. (2009). *Cloud Computing*. Private Limited.

Minelli, M., Chambers, M., & Dhiraj, A. (2014). *Big Data Analytics*. New Delhi: Wiley India Private Limited.

Mo. (2015). How to Build an Ideal Health Care Information System. In The World Book of Family Medicine European Edition 2015. Academic Press.

Muchahari, M., & Sinha, S. (2012). A New Trust Management Architecture for Cloud Computing Environment. *2012 International Symposium on Cloud and Services Computing (ISCOS)*, 136-140 10.1109/ISCOS.2012.30

Myers, J. (2015). *Analytics in the Cloud. An EMA End Users Research Report*. Retrieved May 14, 2018 from https://www.tableau.com/sites/default/files/media/ema_analytics_in_the_cloud_research_report_2015.pdf

Neill, D. B. (2012). Fast Subsect Scan for Spatial Pattern Detection. *Journal of the Royal Statistical Society. Series B, Statistical Methodology, 74*(2), 2012. doi:10.1111/j.1467-9868.2011.01014.x

Nielsen, J. (1998). Introduction to web design. In *Proceedings of the SIGCHI on Human Factors in Computing Systems*. Los Angeles, CA: The Association of Computing Machinery.

Nielsen, J. (2000). *Designing Web Usability. Indianapolis, IN: New Riders Publishing. Nielsen, J. & Tahir, M. (2002). Homepage Usability: 50 Websites Deconstructed*. Indianapolis, IN: New Riders Publishing.

O'Reilly Media Inc. (2013). *Big Data Now Current Perspectives from O'Reilly Media*. Mumbai: Shroff Publishers & Distributors Private Limited.

OECD. (2016). Getting Skills Right: Assessing and Anticipating Changing Skill Needs. *READ online*. Retrieved from https://read.oecd-ilibrary.org/employment/getting-skills-right-assessing-and-anticipating-changing-skill-needs_9789264252073-en

Pandey & Kumar. (2012). *Computer Applications in Business*. New Delhi: Variety Book Publishers and Distribution.

Pandey, U. S. (2012). *Varinder Kumar*. Computer Applications in Business.

Panetto, H., & Whitman, L. (2016). Knowledge engineering for enterprise integration, interoperability and networking: Theory and applications. *Data & Knowledge Engineering, 105*, 1–4. doi:10.1016/j.datak.2016.05.001

Patrignani, N., & Kavathatzopoulos, I. (2016). Cloud computing: The ultimate step towards the virtual enterprise? *ACM SIGCAS Computers and Society*, *45*(3), 68–72. doi:10.1145/2874239.2874249

Pautasso, C. (2014). RESTful web services: principles, patterns, emerging technologies. In A. Bouguettaya, Q. Sheng, & F. Daniel (Eds.), Web Services Foundations (pp. 31-51). New York, NY: Springer.

Pearrow, M. (2000). *Web Site Usability Handbook*. Independence, KY: Charles River Media.

Perez, C. (2002). *Technological revolutions and financial capital: The dynamics of bubbles and golden ages*. Edward Elgar Publishing. doi:10.4337/9781781005323

Platform as a Service (PaaS). (2018). Retrieved August 6, 2018, from https://www.statista.com/study/31311/platform-as-a-service-statista-dossier/

Popplewell, K. (2014). Enterprise interoperability science base structure. In K. Mertins, F. Bénaben, R. Poler, & J. Bourrières (Eds.), *Enterprise Interoperability VI: Interoperability for Agility, Resilience and Plasticity of Collaborations* (pp. 417–427). Cham, Switzerland: Springer International Publishing. doi:10.1007/978-3-319-04948-9_35

PrasertAuewarkul. (2008). The Past and Present Threat of Avian Influenza in Thailand. In E. M. Yichenlu & B. Roberts (Eds.), *Emerging Infections in Asia* (pp. 31–34). New York, NY: Springer. doi:10.1007/978-0-387-75722-3_2

Prashant, C. (2012). *The Unlimited Business Opportunities on the Internet*. Indore: Xcess Infostore Private Limited.

Preidel, C., & Borrmann, A. (2016). Towards code compliance checking on the basis of a visual programming language. *Journal of Information Technology in Construction*, *21*(25), 402–421.

Pujari. (2003). Data Mining Techniques. Hyderabad: Universities Press (India) Private Limited.

Pujari. (2004). Data mining Techniques. New Delhi: Universities Press (India) Private Limited.

Quazi, S. A. (2009). *Principles of Physical Geography*. New Delhi: APH Publishing Corporation.

Raja Rao, K. N. (2005). *An Overview of Space and Satellite: Fundamental of Satellite Communication*. New Delhi: Prentice Hall of India.

Reese, G. (2010). *Cloud Application Architecture*. Mumbai: Shorff Publishers & Distributors Private Limited.

Reur, J., Arino, J., & Olk, P. (2011). *Entrepreneural Alliances (Vol. 1)*. Boston: Pearson Higher Education.

Rezaei, R., Chiew, T., & Lee, S. (2014). A review on E-business interoperability frameworks. *Journal of Systems and Software*, *93*, 199–216. doi:10.1016/j.jss.2014.02.004

Ritter, D., May, N., & Rinderle-Ma, S. (2017). Patterns for emerging application integration scenarios: A survey. *Information Systems*, *67*, 36–57. doi:10.1016/j.is.2017.03.003

Robkin, M., Weininger, S., Preciado, B., & Goldman, J. (2015). Levels of conceptual interoperability model for healthcare framework for safe medical device interoperability. In *Symposium on Product Compliance Engineering* (pp. 1–8). Piscataway, NJ: IEEE Computer Society Press. 10.1109/ISPCE.2015.7138703

Rosenthal, M., Mork, P., Li, M. H., Stanford, J., Koester, D., & Reynolds, P. (2009). Cloud computing: A new business paradigm for biomedical information sharing. *Journal of Biomedical Informatics*, *43*(2), 342–353. doi:10.1016/j.jbi.2009.08.014 PMID:19715773

Russom, P., Stodder, D., & Halper, F. (2014). *Real-Time Data, BI and Analytics*. TDWI Best Practices Report. Retrieved June 08, 2018 from https://tdwi.org/research/2014/09/best-practices-report-real-time-data-bi-and-analytics.aspx

Sahoo, Mehfuz, & Rai (2013). Applications of Cloud Computing for Agriculture Sector. *CSI Communications Journal, 37*(8), 10-17.

Samdantsoodol, A., Cang, S., Yu, H., Eardley, A., & Buyantsogt, A. (2017). Predicting the relationships between virtual enterprises and agility in supply chains. *Expert Systems with Applications*, *84*, 58–73. doi:10.1016/j.eswa.2017.04.037

Scanlon, T., Schroeder, W., Snyder, C., & Spool, J. (1998). Websites that work: Designing with your eyes open. In *Proceedings of the SIGCHI on Human Factors in Computing Systems*. Los Angeles, CA: The Association of Computing Machinery.

Schmarzo, B. (2014). *Big Data Understanding How Data Powers Big Business*. New Delhi: Wiley India Private Limited.

Schulz, G. (2012). *Cloud and Virtual Data Storage Net Working, Your Journey to Efficient & Effective Information Services*. New York: Taylor & Francis Group.

Schulz, G. (2012). *Cloud and Virtual Data Storage, Networking*. New York: Taylor & Francis Group.

Schulz, G. (2012). *Cloud and Virtual Storage Networking- Your Journey to Efficient & Effective Information Services*. New York: CRC Press.

Schumacher, A., Erol, S., & Sihn, W. (2016). A maturity model for assessing industry 4.0 readiness and maturity of manufacturing enterprises. *Procedia CIRP*, *52*, 161–166. doi:10.1016/j.procir.2016.07.040

Schumpeter, J. A. (1942). Capitalism, Socialism, and Democracy (2nd ed.). Impact Books.

Schwab, K. (2017). *The fourth industrial revolution*. Crown Business.

SelectHub. (2018), Compare BI Software: Business Intelligence Tools. *SelectHub*. Retrieved July 08, 2018 from https://selecthub.com/business-intelligence-tools/

Semolic & Baisya. (2013). *Globalization and Innovative Business Models*. New Delhi: Ane Books Private Limited.

Semolic & Baisya. (2013). *Globalization and Innovative Models*. New Delhi: Ane Books Private Limited.

Shackel, B. (2009). Usability-context, framework, definition, design and evaluation. *Interacting with Computers, 21*(5), 339–346. doi:10.1016/j.intcom.2009.04.007

Sharada, V. N. (2006). *Environment and Agriculture*. New Delhi: Malhotra Publishing House.

Sharma, J. (2011). *Research Methodology-The Discipline and Its Dimensions*. New Delhi: Deep & Deep Publications Private Limited.

Sharma, R., & Panigrahi, P. (2015). Developing a roadmap for planning and implementation of interoperability capability in e-government. *Transforming Government: People. Process and Policy, 9*(4), 426–447.

Simon, P. (2011). *The age of the platform: How Amazon, Apple, Facebook, and Google have redefined business*. BookBaby.

Şimşit, Z., Günay, S., & Vayvay, Ö. (2014). Theory of Constraints: A Literature Review. *Procedia: Social and Behavioral Sciences, 150*, 930–936. doi:10.1016/j.sbspro.2014.09.104

Sindhuja, P., & Surajith, G. (2009). Impact of the factors influencing website usability on user satisfaction. *The IUP Journal of Management Research, 8*(12), 54–66.

Singh & Kumar. (2014). Big Data Visualization using Cassandra and R. *CSI Communications Journal, 38*(8), 15, 21.

Singh, A., & Wesson, J. (2009). Evaluation Criteria for Assessing the Usability of ERP Systems. In *Proceedings of the 2009 Annual Conference of the South African Institute of Computer Scientists and Information Technologists*. Vaal River, South Africa: The Association of Computing Machinery.

Statista. (2018). *Cloud computing*. Retrieved from https://www.statista.com/study/15293/cloud-computing-statista-dossier/

Strømmen-Bakhtiar, A., & Razavi, A. R. (2011). Should the "CLOUD" be Regulated? An Assessment. *Issues in Informing Science and Information Technology, 8*, 219–230. doi:10.28945/1414

Sunitha, C., VasanthaKokilam, K., & MeenaPreethi, B. (2013). Medical Informatics-Perk up Health Care through Information. *CSI Communications Journal, 37*(9), 7-8.

Tan, J. (2018, February 25). *Cloud Computing Is Crucial To The Future Of Our Societies -- Here's Why*. Retrieved August 13, 2018, from https://www.forbes.com/sites/joytan/2018/02/25/cloud-computing-is-the-foundation-of-tomorrows-intelligent-world/

Tao, F. (2012). FC-PACO-RM: A parallel method for service com-position optimal-selection in cloud manufacturing system. *IEEE Transactions on Industrial Informatics*, doi:10.1109/TII.2012.2232936

Tao, F., Cheng, Y., Zhang, L., & Zhao, D. (2012). Utility modelling, equilibrium, and coordination of resource service transaction in service-oriented manufacturing system. *Proceedings of the Institution of Mechanical Engineers. Part B, Journal of Engineering Manufacture*, 226(6), 1099–1117. doi:10.1177/0954405412438011

Tao, F., Guo, H., Zhang, L., & Cheng, Y. (2012). Modeling of combinable relationship-basedcomposition service network and the theoretical proof of its scale-free characteristics. *Enterprise Information Systems*, 6(4), 373–404. doi:10.1080/17517575.2011.621981

Tao, F., Hu, Y. F., & Zhou, Z. D. (2008). Study on manufacturing grid & its resource service optimal-selection system. *International Journal of Advanced Manufacturing Technology*, 37(9), 1022–1041. doi:10.100700170-007-1033-9

Tao, F., Hu, Y. F., & Zhou, Z. D. (2009). Application and modeling of resource service trust – QoS evaluation in manufacturing grid system. *International Journal of Production Research*, 47(6), 1521–1550. doi:10.1080/00207540701551927

Tao, F., Zhang, L., Venkatesh, V. C., Luo, Y., & Cheng, Y. (2011). Cloud manufacturing: A computing and service oriented manufacturing model. *Proceedings of the Institution of Mechanical Engineers. Part B, Journal of Engineering Manufacture*, 225(10), 1969–1976. doi:10.1177/0954405411405575

Tao, F., Zhao, D., Yefa, H., & Zhou, Z. (2010). Correlation-aware resource service compositionand optimal-selection in manufacturing grid. *European Journal of Operational Research*, 201(1), 129–143. doi:10.1016/j.ejor.2009.02.025

Tapscott, D. (2014). *The digital economy*. McGraw-Hill Education.

Teradata. (2018). *Survey: Companies are Bullish on Cloud Analytics, But need to speed up the pace*. Retrieved June 02, 2018 from https://in.teradata.com/Press-Releases/2018/Survey-Companies-are-Bullish-on-Cloud-Analyt

Thakur, I. S. (2006). *Introduction Environmental Biotechnology*. New Delhi: I.K. International.

Thornton, G. (2015). *Overcome the 5 challenges of cloud BI*. Retrieved May 23, 2018 from https://www.grantthornton.com/-/media/content-page-files/advisory/pdfs/2015/BAS-Cloud-BI.ashx

Tiwari. (2010). *Infrastructure for Sustainable Rural Development*. New Delhi: Regal Publications.

Toosi, A., Calheiros, R., & Buyya, R. (2014). Interconnected cloud computing environments: Challenges, taxonomy, and survey. *ACM Computing Surveys*, *47*(1), 7. doi:10.1145/2593512

Tran, H., Zdun, U., Oberortner, E., Mulo, E., & Dustdar, S. (2012). Compliance in service-oriented architectures: A model-driven and view-based approach. *Information and Software Technology*, *54*(6), 531–552. doi:10.1016/j.infsof.2012.01.001

Tzitzikas, Y., Manolis, N., & Papadakos, P. (2017). Faceted exploration of RDF/S datasets: A survey. *Journal of Intelligent Information Systems*, *48*(2), 329–364. doi:10.100710844-016-0413-8

Veen, J. (2000). *The Art & Science of Web Design*. Indianapolis, IN: New Riders Publishing.

Venkatesh, V. (1985). Determinants of Perceived Ease of Use: Integrating Control, Intrinsic Motivation, and Emotion into the Technology Acceptance Model. *Information Systems Research*, *11*(4), 342–365. doi:10.1287/isre.11.4.342.11872

Verbaan, M., & Silvius, A. (2014). The Impact of IT Management Processes on Enterprise Agility. *Communications of the IIMA*, *12*(1), 7.

Verborgh, R., Harth, A., Maleshkova, M., Stadtmüller, S., Steiner, T., Taheriyan, M., & Van de Walle, R. (2014). Survey of semantic description of REST APIs. In C. Pautasso, E. Wilde, & R. Alarcon (Eds.), *REST: Advanced Research Topics and Practical Applications* (pp. 69–89). New York, NY: Springer. doi:10.1007/978-1-4614-9299-3_5

Vijayrani, S. (2013). Economic Health Records- An Overview. *CSI Communications Journal*, *37*(9), 9-11.

Vysas. (2014). *Business Process Transformation*. New Delhi: Regal Publishers.

Walters, R. (2018). *Business Intelligence vital to employer decision making*. Retrieved May 22, 2018 from https://www.robertwalters.co.uk/hiring/hiring-advice/BI-market-guide-2018.html

Wang, X. V. (2012). *Development of an Interoperable Cloud-based Manufacturing System* (PhD thesis). Mechanical Engineering, University of Auckland.

Wang, H., Gibbins, N., Payne, T., Patelli, A., & Wang, Y. (2015). A survey of semantic web services formalisms. *Concurrency and Computation*, *27*(15), 4053–4072. doi:10.1002/cpe.3481

Want, R., Schilit, B., & Jenson, S. (2015). Enabling the Internet of Things. *IEEE Computer*, *48*(1), 28–35. doi:10.1109/MC.2015.12

Warden, P. (2012). *Big Data Glossary*. Mumbai: Shroff Publishers & Distributors Private Limited.

Weeger, A., Wang, X., & Gewald, H. (2016). IT consumerization: BYOD-program acceptance and its impact on employer attractiveness. *Journal of Computer Information Systems*, *56*(1), 1–10. doi:10.1080/08874417.2015.11645795

What Is Disruptive Technology? (n.d.). In *WhatIs.com*. Retrieved from https://whatis.techtarget. com/definition/disruptive-technology

Wu, D., Thames, J. L., Rosen, D. W., & Shaefer, D. (2012). Towards a cloud-based design and manufacturing paradigm: looking backward, looking forward. *ASME 2012 International Design Engineering Technical Conferences & Computers and Information in Engineering Conference (IDETC 2012) IDETC/CIE.*

Wu, D., Greer, M. J., Rosen, D. W., & Schaefer, D. (2013). Cloud Manufacturing: Drivers, Current Status, and Future Trends. *Proceedings of the ASME 2013 International Manufacturing Science and Engineering Conference (MSEC13), Paper Number: MSEC2013-1106, Madison, Wisconsin, U.S.* 10.1115/MSEC2013-1106

Wu, D., Schaefer, D., & Rosen, D. W. (2013). Cloud-Based Design and Manufacturing Systems: A Social Network Analysis. *International Conference on Engineering Design (ICED13)*, Seoul, Korea.

Xu, X. (2012). From cloud computing to cloud manufacturing. *Robotics and Computer-integrated Manufacturing*, *28*(1), 75–86. doi:10.1016/j.rcim.2011.07.002

Yadekar, Y., Shehab, E., & Mehnen, J. (2013). Challenges of Cloud Technology in Manufacturing Environment. *Proceedings of the 11th International Conference on Manufacturing Research*, 177-182.

Yang, H., Ma, K., Deng, C., Liao, H., Yan, J., & Zhang, J. (2013). Towards conformance testing of choreography based on scenario. In *Proceedings of the International Symposium on Theoretical Aspects of Software Engineering* (pp. 59-62). Piscataway, NJ: IEEE Computer Society Press. 10.1109/TASE.2013.23

Zanero, S. (2017). Cyber-physical systems. *IEEE Computer*, *50*(4), 14–16. doi:10.1109/MC.2017.105

Zhang, L., Luo, Y., Tao, F., Li, B. H., Ren, L., & Zhang, X. (2012). Cloud manufacturing: A new manufacturing paradigm. *Enterprise Information Systems*, 1–21.

Zhang, Z., Wu, C., & Cheung, D. (2013). A survey on cloud interoperability: Taxonomies, standards, and practice. *Performance Evaluation Review*, *40*(4), 13–22. doi:10.1145/2479942.2479945

Zheng, G. J. (2017). *Data Visualization in Business Intelligence* (M. J. Munoz, Ed.). Global Business Intelligence Taylor and Francis.

Zimmermann, O., Tomlinson, M., & Peuser, S. (2012). *Perspectives on Web Services: Applying SOAP, WSDL and UDDI to Real-World Projects*. New York, NY: Springer Science & Business Media.

Related References

To continue our tradition of advancing information science and technology research, we have compiled a list of recommended IGI Global readings. These references will provide additional information and guidance to further enrich your knowledge and assist you with your own research and future publications.

Aasi, P., Rusu, L., & Vieru, D. (2017). The Role of Culture in IT Governance Five Focus Areas: A Literature Review. *International Journal of IT/Business Alignment and Governance, 8*(2), 42-61. doi:10.4018/IJITBAG.2017070103

Abdrabo, A. A. (2018). Egypt's Knowledge-Based Development: Opportunities, Challenges, and Future Possibilities. In A. Alraouf (Ed.), *Knowledge-Based Urban Development in the Middle East* (pp. 80–101). Hershey, PA: IGI Global. doi:10.4018/978-1-5225-3734-2.ch005

Abu Doush, I., & Alhami, I. (2018). Evaluating the Accessibility of Computer Laboratories, Libraries, and Websites in Jordanian Universities and Colleges. *International Journal of Information Systems and Social Change, 9*(2), 44–60. doi:10.4018/IJISSC.2018040104

Adeboye, A. (2016). Perceived Use and Acceptance of Cloud Enterprise Resource Planning (ERP) Implementation in the Manufacturing Industries. *International Journal of Strategic Information Technology and Applications, 7*(3), 24–40. doi:10.4018/IJSITA.2016070102

Adegbore, A. M., Quadri, M. O., & Oyewo, O. R. (2018). A Theoretical Approach to the Adoption of Electronic Resource Management Systems (ERMS) in Nigerian University Libraries. In A. Tella & T. Kwanya (Eds.), *Handbook of Research on Managing Intellectual Property in Digital Libraries* (pp. 292–311). Hershey, PA: IGI Global. doi:10.4018/978-1-5225-3093-0.ch015

Adhikari, M., & Roy, D. (2016). Green Computing. In G. Deka, G. Siddesh, K. Srinivasa, & L. Patnaik (Eds.), *Emerging Research Surrounding Power Consumption and Performance Issues in Utility Computing* (pp. 84–108). Hershey, PA: IGI Global. doi:10.4018/978-1-4666-8853-7.ch005

Afolabi, O. A. (2018). Myths and Challenges of Building an Effective Digital Library in Developing Nations: An African Perspective. In A. Tella & T. Kwanya (Eds.), *Handbook of Research on Managing Intellectual Property in Digital Libraries* (pp. 51–79). Hershey, PA: IGI Global. doi:10.4018/978-1-5225-3093-0.ch004

Agarwal, R., Singh, A., & Sen, S. (2016). Role of Molecular Docking in Computer-Aided Drug Design and Development. In S. Dastmalchi, M. Hamzeh-Mivehroud, & B. Sokouti (Eds.), *Applied Case Studies and Solutions in Molecular Docking-Based Drug Design* (pp. 1–28). Hershey, PA: IGI Global. doi:10.4018/978-1-5225-0362-0.ch001

Ali, O., & Soar, J. (2016). Technology Innovation Adoption Theories. In L. Al-Hakim, X. Wu, A. Koronios, & Y. Shou (Eds.), *Handbook of Research on Driving Competitive Advantage through Sustainable, Lean, and Disruptive Innovation* (pp. 1–38). Hershey, PA: IGI Global. doi:10.4018/978-1-5225-0135-0.ch001

Alsharo, M. (2017). Attitudes Towards Cloud Computing Adoption in Emerging Economies. *International Journal of Cloud Applications and Computing, 7*(3), 44–58. doi:10.4018/IJCAC.2017070102

Amer, T. S., & Johnson, T. L. (2016). Information Technology Progress Indicators: Temporal Expectancy, User Preference, and the Perception of Process Duration. *International Journal of Technology and Human Interaction, 12*(4), 1–14. doi:10.4018/IJTHI.2016100101

Amer, T. S., & Johnson, T. L. (2017). Information Technology Progress Indicators: Research Employing Psychological Frameworks. In A. Mesquita (Ed.), *Research Paradigms and Contemporary Perspectives on Human-Technology Interaction* (pp. 168–186). Hershey, PA: IGI Global. doi:10.4018/978-1-5225-1868-6.ch008

Anchugam, C. V., & Thangadurai, K. (2016). Introduction to Network Security. In D. G., M. Singh, & M. Jayanthi (Eds.), Network Security Attacks and Countermeasures (pp. 1-48). Hershey, PA: IGI Global. doi:10.4018/978-1-4666-8761-5.ch001

Anchugam, C. V., & Thangadurai, K. (2016). Classification of Network Attacks and Countermeasures of Different Attacks. In D. G., M. Singh, & M. Jayanthi (Eds.), Network Security Attacks and Countermeasures (pp. 115-156). Hershey, PA: IGI Global. doi:10.4018/978-1-4666-8761-5.ch004

Anohah, E. (2016). Pedagogy and Design of Online Learning Environment in Computer Science Education for High Schools. *International Journal of Online Pedagogy and Course Design*, 6(3), 39–51. doi:10.4018/IJOPCD.2016070104

Anohah, E. (2017). Paradigm and Architecture of Computing Augmented Learning Management System for Computer Science Education. *International Journal of Online Pedagogy and Course Design*, 7(2), 60–70. doi:10.4018/IJOPCD.2017040105

Anohah, E., & Suhonen, J. (2017). Trends of Mobile Learning in Computing Education from 2006 to 2014: A Systematic Review of Research Publications. *International Journal of Mobile and Blended Learning*, 9(1), 16–33. doi:10.4018/IJMBL.2017010102

Assis-Hassid, S., Heart, T., Reychav, I., & Pliskin, J. S. (2016). Modelling Factors Affecting Patient-Doctor-Computer Communication in Primary Care. *International Journal of Reliable and Quality E-Healthcare*, 5(1), 1–17. doi:10.4018/IJRQEH.2016010101

Bailey, E. K. (2017). Applying Learning Theories to Computer Technology Supported Instruction. In M. Grassetti & S. Brookby (Eds.), *Advancing Next-Generation Teacher Education through Digital Tools and Applications* (pp. 61–81). Hershey, PA: IGI Global. doi:10.4018/978-1-5225-0965-3.ch004

Balasubramanian, K. (2016). Attacks on Online Banking and Commerce. In K. Balasubramanian, K. Mala, & M. Rajakani (Eds.), *Cryptographic Solutions for Secure Online Banking and Commerce* (pp. 1–19). Hershey, PA: IGI Global. doi:10.4018/978-1-5225-0273-9.ch001

Baldwin, S., Opoku-Agyemang, K., & Roy, D. (2016). Games People Play: A Trilateral Collaboration Researching Computer Gaming across Cultures. In K. Valentine & L. Jensen (Eds.), *Examining the Evolution of Gaming and Its Impact on Social, Cultural, and Political Perspectives* (pp. 364–376). Hershey, PA: IGI Global. doi:10.4018/978-1-5225-0261-6.ch017

Banerjee, S., Sing, T. Y., Chowdhury, A. R., & Anwar, H. (2018). Let's Go Green: Towards a Taxonomy of Green Computing Enablers for Business Sustainability. In M. Khosrow-Pour (Ed.), *Green Computing Strategies for Competitive Advantage and Business Sustainability* (pp. 89–109). Hershey, PA: IGI Global. doi:10.4018/978-1-5225-5017-4.ch005

Basham, R. (2018). Information Science and Technology in Crisis Response and Management. In M. Khosrow-Pour, D.B.A. (Ed.), Encyclopedia of Information Science and Technology, Fourth Edition (pp. 1407-1418). Hershey, PA: IGI Global. doi:10.4018/978-1-5225-2255-3.ch121

Batyashe, T., & Iyamu, T. (2018). Architectural Framework for the Implementation of Information Technology Governance in Organisations. In M. Khosrow-Pour, D.B.A. (Ed.), Encyclopedia of Information Science and Technology, Fourth Edition (pp. 810-819). Hershey, PA: IGI Global. doi:10.4018/978-1-5225-2255-3.ch070

Bekleyen, N., & Çelik, S. (2017). Attitudes of Adult EFL Learners towards Preparing for a Language Test via CALL. In D. Tafazoli & M. Romero (Eds.), *Multiculturalism and Technology-Enhanced Language Learning* (pp. 214–229). Hershey, PA: IGI Global. doi:10.4018/978-1-5225-1882-2.ch013

Bennett, A., Eglash, R., Lachney, M., & Babbitt, W. (2016). Design Agency: Diversifying Computer Science at the Intersections of Creativity and Culture. In M. Raisinghani (Ed.), *Revolutionizing Education through Web-Based Instruction* (pp. 35–56). Hershey, PA: IGI Global. doi:10.4018/978-1-4666-9932-8.ch003

Bergeron, F., Croteau, A., Uwizeyemungu, S., & Raymond, L. (2017). A Framework for Research on Information Technology Governance in SMEs. In S. De Haes & W. Van Grembergen (Eds.), *Strategic IT Governance and Alignment in Business Settings* (pp. 53–81). Hershey, PA: IGI Global. doi:10.4018/978-1-5225-0861-8.ch003

Bhatt, G. D., Wang, Z., & Rodger, J. A. (2017). Information Systems Capabilities and Their Effects on Competitive Advantages: A Study of Chinese Companies. *Information Resources Management Journal, 30*(3), 41–57. doi:10.4018/IRMJ.2017070103

Bogdanoski, M., Stoilkovski, M., & Risteski, A. (2016). Novel First Responder Digital Forensics Tool as a Support to Law Enforcement. In M. Hadji-Janev & M. Bogdanoski (Eds.), *Handbook of Research on Civil Society and National Security in the Era of Cyber Warfare* (pp. 352–376). Hershey, PA: IGI Global. doi:10.4018/978-1-4666-8793-6.ch016

Boontarig, W., Papasratorn, B., & Chutimaskul, W. (2016). The Unified Model for Acceptance and Use of Health Information on Online Social Networks: Evidence from Thailand. *International Journal of E-Health and Medical Communications, 7*(1), 31–47. doi:10.4018/IJEHMC.2016010102

Brown, S., & Yuan, X. (2016). Techniques for Retaining Computer Science Students at Historical Black Colleges and Universities. In C. Prince & R. Ford (Eds.), *Setting a New Agenda for Student Engagement and Retention in Historically Black Colleges and Universities* (pp. 251–268). Hershey, PA: IGI Global. doi:10.4018/978-1-5225-0308-8.ch014

Burcoff, A., & Shamir, L. (2017). Computer Analysis of Pablo Picasso's Artistic Style. *International Journal of Art, Culture and Design Technologies, 6*(1), 1–18. doi:10.4018/IJACDT.2017010101

Byker, E. J. (2017). I Play I Learn: Introducing Technological Play Theory. In C. Martin & D. Polly (Eds.), *Handbook of Research on Teacher Education and Professional Development* (pp. 297–306). Hershey, PA: IGI Global. doi:10.4018/978-1-5225-1067-3.ch016

Calongne, C. M., Stricker, A. G., Truman, B., & Arenas, F. J. (2017). Cognitive Apprenticeship and Computer Science Education in Cyberspace: Reimagining the Past. In A. Stricker, C. Calongne, B. Truman, & F. Arenas (Eds.), *Integrating an Awareness of Selfhood and Society into Virtual Learning* (pp. 180–197). Hershey, PA: IGI Global. doi:10.4018/978-1-5225-2182-2.ch013

Carlton, E. L., Holsinger, J. W. Jr, & Anunobi, N. (2016). Physician Engagement with Health Information Technology: Implications for Practice and Professionalism. *International Journal of Computers in Clinical Practice*, 1(2), 51–73. doi:10.4018/IJCCP.2016070103

Carneiro, A. D. (2017). Defending Information Networks in Cyberspace: Some Notes on Security Needs. In M. Dawson, D. Kisku, P. Gupta, J. Sing, & W. Li (Eds.), Developing Next-Generation Countermeasures for Homeland Security Threat Prevention (pp. 354-375). Hershey, PA: IGI Global. doi:10.4018/978-1-5225-0703-1.ch016

Cavalcanti, J. C. (2016). The New "ABC" of ICTs (Analytics + Big Data + Cloud Computing): A Complex Trade-Off between IT and CT Costs. In J. Martins & A. Molnar (Eds.), *Handbook of Research on Innovations in Information Retrieval, Analysis, and Management* (pp. 152–186). Hershey, PA: IGI Global. doi:10.4018/978-1-4666-8833-9.ch006

Chase, J. P., & Yan, Z. (2017). Affect in Statistics Cognition. In *Assessing and Measuring Statistics Cognition in Higher Education Online Environments: Emerging Research and Opportunities* (pp. 144–187). Hershey, PA: IGI Global. doi:10.4018/978-1-5225-2420-5.ch005

Chen, C. (2016). Effective Learning Strategies for the 21st Century: Implications for the E-Learning. In M. Anderson & C. Gavan (Eds.), *Developing Effective Educational Experiences through Learning Analytics* (pp. 143–169). Hershey, PA: IGI Global. doi:10.4018/978-1-4666-9983-0.ch006

Chen, E. T. (2016). Examining the Influence of Information Technology on Modern Health Care. In P. Manolitzas, E. Grigoroudis, N. Matsatsinis, & D. Yannacopoulos (Eds.), *Effective Methods for Modern Healthcare Service Quality and Evaluation* (pp. 110–136). Hershey, PA: IGI Global. doi:10.4018/978-1-4666-9961-8.ch006

Cimermanova, I. (2017). Computer-Assisted Learning in Slovakia. In D. Tafazoli & M. Romero (Eds.), *Multiculturalism and Technology-Enhanced Language Learning* (pp. 252–270). Hershey, PA: IGI Global. doi:10.4018/978-1-5225-1882-2.ch015

Cipolla-Ficarra, F. V., & Cipolla-Ficarra, M. (2018). Computer Animation for Ingenious Revival. In F. Cipolla-Ficarra, M. Ficarra, M. Cipolla-Ficarra, A. Quiroga, J. Alma, & J. Carré (Eds.), *Technology-Enhanced Human Interaction in Modern Society* (pp. 159–181). Hershey, PA: IGI Global. doi:10.4018/978-1-5225-3437-2. ch008

Cockrell, S., Damron, T. S., Melton, A. M., & Smith, A. D. (2018). Offshoring IT. In M. Khosrow-Pour, D.B.A. (Ed.), Encyclopedia of Information Science and Technology, Fourth Edition (pp. 5476-5489). Hershey, PA: IGI Global. doi:10.4018/978-1-5225-2255-3.ch476

Coffey, J. W. (2018). Logic and Proof in Computer Science: Categories and Limits of Proof Techniques. In J. Horne (Ed.), *Philosophical Perceptions on Logic and Order* (pp. 218–240). Hershey, PA: IGI Global. doi:10.4018/978-1-5225-2443-4.ch007

Dale, M. (2017). Re-Thinking the Challenges of Enterprise Architecture Implementation. In M. Tavana (Ed.), *Enterprise Information Systems and the Digitalization of Business Functions* (pp. 205–221). Hershey, PA: IGI Global. doi:10.4018/978-1-5225-2382-6.ch009

Das, A., Dasgupta, R., & Bagchi, A. (2016). Overview of Cellular Computing-Basic Principles and Applications. In J. Mandal, S. Mukhopadhyay, & T. Pal (Eds.), *Handbook of Research on Natural Computing for Optimization Problems* (pp. 637–662). Hershey, PA: IGI Global. doi:10.4018/978-1-5225-0058-2.ch026

De Maere, K., De Haes, S., & von Kutzschenbach, M. (2017). CIO Perspectives on Organizational Learning within the Context of IT Governance. *International Journal of IT/Business Alignment and Governance, 8*(1), 32-47. doi:10.4018/IJITBAG.2017010103

Demir, K., Çaka, C., Yaman, N. D., İslamoğlu, H., & Kuzu, A. (2018). Examining the Current Definitions of Computational Thinking. In H. Ozcinar, G. Wong, & H. Ozturk (Eds.), *Teaching Computational Thinking in Primary Education* (pp. 36–64). Hershey, PA: IGI Global. doi:10.4018/978-1-5225-3200-2.ch003

Deng, X., Hung, Y., & Lin, C. D. (2017). Design and Analysis of Computer Experiments. In S. Saha, A. Mandal, A. Narasimhamurthy, S. V, & S. Sangam (Eds.), Handbook of Research on Applied Cybernetics and Systems Science (pp. 264-279). Hershey, PA: IGI Global. doi:10.4018/978-1-5225-2498-4.ch013

Denner, J., Martinez, J., & Thiry, H. (2017). Strategies for Engaging Hispanic/ Latino Youth in the US in Computer Science. In Y. Rankin & J. Thomas (Eds.), *Moving Students of Color from Consumers to Producers of Technology* (pp. 24–48). Hershey, PA: IGI Global. doi:10.4018/978-1-5225-2005-4.ch002

Devi, A. (2017). Cyber Crime and Cyber Security: A Quick Glance. In R. Kumar, P. Pattnaik, & P. Pandey (Eds.), *Detecting and Mitigating Robotic Cyber Security Risks* (pp. 160–171). Hershey, PA: IGI Global. doi:10.4018/978-1-5225-2154-9.ch011

Dores, A. R., Barbosa, F., Guerreiro, S., Almeida, I., & Carvalho, I. P. (2016). Computer-Based Neuropsychological Rehabilitation: Virtual Reality and Serious Games. In M. Cruz-Cunha, I. Miranda, R. Martinho, & R. Rijo (Eds.), *Encyclopedia of E-Health and Telemedicine* (pp. 473–485). Hershey, PA: IGI Global. doi:10.4018/978-1-4666-9978-6.ch037

Doshi, N., & Schaefer, G. (2016). Computer-Aided Analysis of Nailfold Capillaroscopy Images. In D. Fotiadis (Ed.), *Handbook of Research on Trends in the Diagnosis and Treatment of Chronic Conditions* (pp. 146–158). Hershey, PA: IGI Global. doi:10.4018/978-1-4666-8828-5.ch007

Doyle, D. J., & Fahy, P. J. (2018). Interactivity in Distance Education and Computer-Aided Learning, With Medical Education Examples. In M. Khosrow-Pour, D.B.A. (Ed.), Encyclopedia of Information Science and Technology, Fourth Edition (pp. 5829-5840). Hershey, PA: IGI Global. doi:10.4018/978-1-5225-2255-3.ch507

Elias, N. I., & Walker, T. W. (2017). Factors that Contribute to Continued Use of E-Training among Healthcare Professionals. In F. Topor (Ed.), *Handbook of Research on Individualism and Identity in the Globalized Digital Age* (pp. 403–429). Hershey, PA: IGI Global. doi:10.4018/978-1-5225-0522-8.ch018

Eloy, S., Dias, M. S., Lopes, P. F., & Vilar, E. (2016). Digital Technologies in Architecture and Engineering: Exploring an Engaged Interaction within Curricula. In D. Fonseca & E. Redondo (Eds.), *Handbook of Research on Applied E-Learning in Engineering and Architecture Education* (pp. 368–402). Hershey, PA: IGI Global. doi:10.4018/978-1-4666-8803-2.ch017

Estrela, V. V., Magalhães, H. A., & Saotome, O. (2016). Total Variation Applications in Computer Vision. In N. Kamila (Ed.), *Handbook of Research on Emerging Perspectives in Intelligent Pattern Recognition, Analysis, and Image Processing* (pp. 41–64). Hershey, PA: IGI Global. doi:10.4018/978-1-4666-8654-0.ch002

Filipovic, N., Radovic, M., Nikolic, D. D., Saveljic, I., Milosevic, Z., Exarchos, T. P., ... Parodi, O. (2016). Computer Predictive Model for Plaque Formation and Progression in the Artery. In D. Fotiadis (Ed.), *Handbook of Research on Trends in the Diagnosis and Treatment of Chronic Conditions* (pp. 279–300). Hershey, PA: IGI Global. doi:10.4018/978-1-4666-8828-5.ch013

Fisher, R. L. (2018). Computer-Assisted Indian Matrimonial Services. In M. Khosrow-Pour, D.B.A. (Ed.), Encyclopedia of Information Science and Technology, Fourth Edition (pp. 4136-4145). Hershey, PA: IGI Global. doi:10.4018/978-1-5225-2255-3.ch358

Fleenor, H. G., & Hodhod, R. (2016). Assessment of Learning and Technology: Computer Science Education. In V. Wang (Ed.), *Handbook of Research on Learning Outcomes and Opportunities in the Digital Age* (pp. 51–78). Hershey, PA: IGI Global. doi:10.4018/978-1-4666-9577-1.ch003

García-Valcárcel, A., & Mena, J. (2016). Information Technology as a Way To Support Collaborative Learning: What In-Service Teachers Think, Know and Do. *Journal of Information Technology Research*, *9*(1), 1–17. doi:10.4018/JITR.2016010101

Gardner-McCune, C., & Jimenez, Y. (2017). Historical App Developers: Integrating CS into K-12 through Cross-Disciplinary Projects. In Y. Rankin & J. Thomas (Eds.), *Moving Students of Color from Consumers to Producers of Technology* (pp. 85–112). Hershey, PA: IGI Global. doi:10.4018/978-1-5225-2005-4.ch005

Garvey, G. P. (2016). Exploring Perception, Cognition, and Neural Pathways of Stereo Vision and the Split–Brain Human Computer Interface. In A. Ursyn (Ed.), *Knowledge Visualization and Visual Literacy in Science Education* (pp. 28–76). Hershey, PA: IGI Global. doi:10.4018/978-1-5225-0480-1.ch002

Ghafele, R., & Gibert, B. (2018). Open Growth: The Economic Impact of Open Source Software in the USA. In M. Khosrow-Pour (Ed.), *Optimizing Contemporary Application and Processes in Open Source Software* (pp. 164–197). Hershey, PA: IGI Global. doi:10.4018/978-1-5225-5314-4.ch007

Ghobakhloo, M., & Azar, A. (2018). Information Technology Resources, the Organizational Capability of Lean-Agile Manufacturing, and Business Performance. *Information Resources Management Journal*, *31*(2), 47–74. doi:10.4018/IRMJ.2018040103

Gianni, M., & Gotzamani, K. (2016). Integrated Management Systems and Information Management Systems: Common Threads. In P. Papajorgji, F. Pinet, A. Guimarães, & J. Papathanasiou (Eds.), *Automated Enterprise Systems for Maximizing Business Performance* (pp. 195–214). Hershey, PA: IGI Global. doi:10.4018/978-1-4666-8841-4.ch011

Gikandi, J. W. (2017). Computer-Supported Collaborative Learning and Assessment: A Strategy for Developing Online Learning Communities in Continuing Education. In J. Keengwe & G. Onchwari (Eds.), *Handbook of Research on Learner-Centered Pedagogy in Teacher Education and Professional Development* (pp. 309–333). Hershey, PA: IGI Global. doi:10.4018/978-1-5225-0892-2.ch017

Gokhale, A. A., & Machina, K. F. (2017). Development of a Scale to Measure Attitudes toward Information Technology. In L. Tomei (Ed.), *Exploring the New Era of Technology-Infused Education* (pp. 49–64). Hershey, PA: IGI Global. doi:10.4018/978-1-5225-1709-2.ch004

Grace, A., O'Donoghue, J., Mahony, C., Heffernan, T., Molony, D., & Carroll, T. (2016). Computerized Decision Support Systems for Multimorbidity Care: An Urgent Call for Research and Development. In M. Cruz-Cunha, I. Miranda, R. Martinho, & R. Rijo (Eds.), *Encyclopedia of E-Health and Telemedicine* (pp. 486–494). Hershey, PA: IGI Global. doi:10.4018/978-1-4666-9978-6.ch038

Gupta, A., & Singh, O. (2016). Computer Aided Modeling and Finite Element Analysis of Human Elbow. *International Journal of Biomedical and Clinical Engineering*, *5*(1), 31–38. doi:10.4018/IJBCE.2016010104

H., S. K. (2016). Classification of Cybercrimes and Punishments under the Information Technology Act, 2000. In S. Geetha, & A. Phamila (Eds.), *Combating Security Breaches and Criminal Activity in the Digital Sphere* (pp. 57-66). Hershey, PA: IGI Global. doi:10.4018/978-1-5225-0193-0.ch004

Hafeez-Baig, A., Gururajan, R., & Wickramasinghe, N. (2017). Readiness as a Novel Construct of Readiness Acceptance Model (RAM) for the Wireless Handheld Technology. In N. Wickramasinghe (Ed.), *Handbook of Research on Healthcare Administration and Management* (pp. 578–595). Hershey, PA: IGI Global. doi:10.4018/978-1-5225-0920-2.ch035

Hanafizadeh, P., Ghandchi, S., & Asgarimehr, M. (2017). Impact of Information Technology on Lifestyle: A Literature Review and Classification. *International Journal of Virtual Communities and Social Networking*, *9*(2), 1–23. doi:10.4018/IJVCSN.2017040101

Harlow, D. B., Dwyer, H., Hansen, A. K., Hill, C., Iveland, A., Leak, A. E., & Franklin, D. M. (2016). Computer Programming in Elementary and Middle School: Connections across Content. In M. Urban & D. Falvo (Eds.), *Improving K-12 STEM Education Outcomes through Technological Integration* (pp. 337–361). Hershey, PA: IGI Global. doi:10.4018/978-1-4666-9616-7.ch015

Haseski, H. İ., Ilic, U., & Tuğtekin, U. (2018). Computational Thinking in Educational Digital Games: An Assessment Tool Proposal. In H. Ozcinar, G. Wong, & H. Ozturk (Eds.), *Teaching Computational Thinking in Primary Education* (pp. 256–287). Hershey, PA: IGI Global. doi:10.4018/978-1-5225-3200-2.ch013

Hee, W. J., Jalleh, G., Lai, H., & Lin, C. (2017). E-Commerce and IT Projects: Evaluation and Management Issues in Australian and Taiwanese Hospitals. *International Journal of Public Health Management and Ethics*, 2(1), 69–90. doi:10.4018/IJPHME.2017010104

Hernandez, A. A. (2017). Green Information Technology Usage: Awareness and Practices of Philippine IT Professionals. *International Journal of Enterprise Information Systems*, 13(4), 90–103. doi:10.4018/IJEIS.2017100106

Hernandez, A. A., & Ona, S. E. (2016). Green IT Adoption: Lessons from the Philippines Business Process Outsourcing Industry. *International Journal of Social Ecology and Sustainable Development*, 7(1), 1–34. doi:10.4018/IJSESD.2016010101

Hernandez, M. A., Marin, E. C., Garcia-Rodriguez, J., Azorin-Lopez, J., & Cazorla, M. (2017). Automatic Learning Improves Human-Robot Interaction in Productive Environments: A Review. *International Journal of Computer Vision and Image Processing*, 7(3), 65–75. doi:10.4018/IJCVIP.2017070106

Horne-Popp, L. M., Tessone, E. B., & Welker, J. (2018). If You Build It, They Will Come: Creating a Library Statistics Dashboard for Decision-Making. In L. Costello & M. Powers (Eds.), *Developing In-House Digital Tools in Library Spaces* (pp. 177–203). Hershey, PA: IGI Global. doi:10.4018/978-1-5225-2676-6.ch009

Hossan, C. G., & Ryan, J. C. (2016). Factors Affecting e-Government Technology Adoption Behaviour in a Voluntary Environment. *International Journal of Electronic Government Research*, 12(1), 24–49. doi:10.4018/IJEGR.2016010102

Hu, H., Hu, P. J., & Al-Gahtani, S. S. (2017). User Acceptance of Computer Technology at Work in Arabian Culture: A Model Comparison Approach. In M. Khosrow-Pour (Ed.), *Handbook of Research on Technology Adoption, Social Policy, and Global Integration* (pp. 205–228). Hershey, PA: IGI Global. doi:10.4018/978-1-5225-2668-1.ch011

Huie, C. P. (2016). Perceptions of Business Intelligence Professionals about Factors Related to Business Intelligence input in Decision Making. *International Journal of Business Analytics, 3*(3), 1–24. doi:10.4018/IJBAN.2016070101

Hung, S., Huang, W., Yen, D. C., Chang, S., & Lu, C. (2016). Effect of Information Service Competence and Contextual Factors on the Effectiveness of Strategic Information Systems Planning in Hospitals. *Journal of Global Information Management, 24*(1), 14–36. doi:10.4018/JGIM.2016010102

Ifinedo, P. (2017). Using an Extended Theory of Planned Behavior to Study Nurses' Adoption of Healthcare Information Systems in Nova Scotia. *International Journal of Technology Diffusion, 8*(1), 1–17. doi:10.4018/IJTD.2017010101

Ilie, V., & Sneha, S. (2018). A Three Country Study for Understanding Physicians' Engagement With Electronic Information Resources Pre and Post System Implementation. *Journal of Global Information Management, 26*(2), 48–73. doi:10.4018/JGIM.2018040103

Inoue-Smith, Y. (2017). Perceived Ease in Using Technology Predicts Teacher Candidates' Preferences for Online Resources. *International Journal of Online Pedagogy and Course Design, 7*(3), 17–28. doi:10.4018/IJOPCD.2017070102

Islam, A. A. (2016). Development and Validation of the Technology Adoption and Gratification (TAG) Model in Higher Education: A Cross-Cultural Study Between Malaysia and China. *International Journal of Technology and Human Interaction, 12*(3), 78–105. doi:10.4018/IJTHI.2016070106

Islam, A. Y. (2017). Technology Satisfaction in an Academic Context: Moderating Effect of Gender. In A. Mesquita (Ed.), *Research Paradigms and Contemporary Perspectives on Human-Technology Interaction* (pp. 187–211). Hershey, PA: IGI Global. doi:10.4018/978-1-5225-1868-6.ch009

Jamil, G. L., & Jamil, C. C. (2017). Information and Knowledge Management Perspective Contributions for Fashion Studies: Observing Logistics and Supply Chain Management Processes. In G. Jamil, A. Soares, & C. Pessoa (Eds.), *Handbook of Research on Information Management for Effective Logistics and Supply Chains* (pp. 199–221). Hershey, PA: IGI Global. doi:10.4018/978-1-5225-0973-8.ch011

Jamil, G. L., Jamil, L. C., Vieira, A. A., & Xavier, A. J. (2016). Challenges in Modelling Healthcare Services: A Study Case of Information Architecture Perspectives. In G. Jamil, J. Poças Rascão, F. Ribeiro, & A. Malheiro da Silva (Eds.), *Handbook of Research on Information Architecture and Management in Modern Organizations* (pp. 1–23). Hershey, PA: IGI Global. doi:10.4018/978-1-4666-8637-3.ch001

Janakova, M. (2018). Big Data and Simulations for the Solution of Controversies in Small Businesses. In M. Khosrow-Pour, D.B.A. (Ed.), Encyclopedia of Information Science and Technology, Fourth Edition (pp. 6907-6915). Hershey, PA: IGI Global. doi:10.4018/978-1-5225-2255-3.ch598

Jha, D. G. (2016). Preparing for Information Technology Driven Changes. In S. Tiwari & L. Nafees (Eds.), *Innovative Management Education Pedagogies for Preparing Next-Generation Leaders* (pp. 258–274). Hershey, PA: IGI Global. doi:10.4018/978-1-4666-9691-4.ch015

Jhawar, A., & Garg, S. K. (2018). Logistics Improvement by Investment in Information Technology Using System Dynamics. In A. Azar & S. Vaidyanathan (Eds.), *Advances in System Dynamics and Control* (pp. 528–567). Hershey, PA: IGI Global. doi:10.4018/978-1-5225-4077-9.ch017

Kalelioğlu, F., Gülbahar, Y., & Doğan, D. (2018). Teaching How to Think Like a Programmer: Emerging Insights. In H. Ozcinar, G. Wong, & H. Ozturk (Eds.), *Teaching Computational Thinking in Primary Education* (pp. 18–35). Hershey, PA: IGI Global. doi:10.4018/978-1-5225-3200-2.ch002

Kamberi, S. (2017). A Girls-Only Online Virtual World Environment and its Implications for Game-Based Learning. In A. Stricker, C. Calongne, B. Truman, & F. Arenas (Eds.), *Integrating an Awareness of Selfhood and Society into Virtual Learning* (pp. 74–95). Hershey, PA: IGI Global. doi:10.4018/978-1-5225-2182-2.ch006

Kamel, S., & Rizk, N. (2017). ICT Strategy Development: From Design to Implementation – Case of Egypt. In C. Howard & K. Hargiss (Eds.), *Strategic Information Systems and Technologies in Modern Organizations* (pp. 239–257). Hershey, PA: IGI Global. doi:10.4018/978-1-5225-1680-4.ch010

Kamel, S. H. (2018). The Potential Role of the Software Industry in Supporting Economic Development. In M. Khosrow-Pour, D.B.A. (Ed.), Encyclopedia of Information Science and Technology, Fourth Edition (pp. 7259-7269). Hershey, PA: IGI Global. doi:10.4018/978-1-5225-2255-3.ch631

Karon, R. (2016). Utilisation of Health Information Systems for Service Delivery in the Namibian Environment. In T. Iyamu & A. Tatnall (Eds.), *Maximizing Healthcare Delivery and Management through Technology Integration* (pp. 169–183). Hershey, PA: IGI Global. doi:10.4018/978-1-4666-9446-0.ch011

Kawata, S. (2018). Computer-Assisted Parallel Program Generation. In M. Khosrow-Pour, D.B.A. (Ed.), Encyclopedia of Information Science and Technology, Fourth Edition (pp. 4583-4593). Hershey, PA: IGI Global. doi:10.4018/978-1-5225-2255-3.ch398

Khanam, S., Siddiqui, J., & Talib, F. (2016). A DEMATEL Approach for Prioritizing the TQM Enablers and IT Resources in the Indian ICT Industry. *International Journal of Applied Management Sciences and Engineering, 3*(1), 11–29. doi:10.4018/IJAMSE.2016010102

Khari, M., Shrivastava, G., Gupta, S., & Gupta, R. (2017). Role of Cyber Security in Today's Scenario. In R. Kumar, P. Pattnaik, & P. Pandey (Eds.), *Detecting and Mitigating Robotic Cyber Security Risks* (pp. 177–191). Hershey, PA: IGI Global. doi:10.4018/978-1-5225-2154-9.ch013

Khouja, M., Rodriguez, I. B., Ben Halima, Y., & Moalla, S. (2018). IT Governance in Higher Education Institutions: A Systematic Literature Review. *International Journal of Human Capital and Information Technology Professionals, 9*(2), 52–67. doi:10.4018/IJHCITP.2018040104

Kim, S., Chang, M., Choi, N., Park, J., & Kim, H. (2016). The Direct and Indirect Effects of Computer Uses on Student Success in Math. *International Journal of Cyber Behavior, Psychology and Learning, 6*(3), 48–64. doi:10.4018/IJCBPL.2016070104

Kiourt, C., Pavlidis, G., Koutsoudis, A., & Kalles, D. (2017). Realistic Simulation of Cultural Heritage. *International Journal of Computational Methods in Heritage Science, 1*(1), 10–40. doi:10.4018/IJCMHS.2017010102

Korikov, A., & Krivtsov, O. (2016). System of People-Computer: On the Way of Creation of Human-Oriented Interface. In V. Mkrttchian, A. Bershadsky, A. Bozhday, M. Kataev, & S. Kataev (Eds.), *Handbook of Research on Estimation and Control Techniques in E-Learning Systems* (pp. 458–470). Hershey, PA: IGI Global. doi:10.4018/978-1-4666-9489-7.ch032

Köse, U. (2017). An Augmented-Reality-Based Intelligent Mobile Application for Open Computer Education. In G. Kurubacak & H. Altinpulluk (Eds.), *Mobile Technologies and Augmented Reality in Open Education* (pp. 154–174). Hershey, PA: IGI Global. doi:10.4018/978-1-5225-2110-5.ch008

Lahmiri, S. (2018). Information Technology Outsourcing Risk Factors and Provider Selection. In M. Gupta, R. Sharman, J. Walp, & P. Mulgund (Eds.), *Information Technology Risk Management and Compliance in Modern Organizations* (pp. 214–228). Hershey, PA: IGI Global. doi:10.4018/978-1-5225-2604-9.ch008

Landriscina, F. (2017). Computer-Supported Imagination: The Interplay Between Computer and Mental Simulation in Understanding Scientific Concepts. In I. Levin & D. Tsybulsky (Eds.), *Digital Tools and Solutions for Inquiry-Based STEM Learning* (pp. 33–60). Hershey, PA: IGI Global. doi:10.4018/978-1-5225-2525-7.ch002

Lau, S. K., Winley, G. K., Leung, N. K., Tsang, N., & Lau, S. Y. (2016). An Exploratory Study of Expectation in IT Skills in a Developing Nation: Vietnam. *Journal of Global Information Management, 24*(1), 1–13. doi:10.4018/JGIM.2016010101

Lavranos, C., Kostagiolas, P., & Papadatos, J. (2016). Information Retrieval Technologies and the "Realities" of Music Information Seeking. In I. Deliyannis, P. Kostagiolas, & C. Banou (Eds.), *Experimental Multimedia Systems for Interactivity and Strategic Innovation* (pp. 102–121). Hershey, PA: IGI Global. doi:10.4018/978-1-4666-8659-5.ch005

Lee, W. W. (2018). Ethical Computing Continues From Problem to Solution. In M. Khosrow-Pour, D.B.A. (Ed.), Encyclopedia of Information Science and Technology, Fourth Edition (pp. 4884-4897). Hershey, PA: IGI Global. doi:10.4018/978-1-5225-2255-3.ch423

Lehto, M. (2016). Cyber Security Education and Research in the Finland's Universities and Universities of Applied Sciences. *International Journal of Cyber Warfare & Terrorism, 6*(2), 15–31. doi:10.4018/IJCWT.2016040102

Lin, C., Jalleh, G., & Huang, Y. (2016). Evaluating and Managing Electronic Commerce and Outsourcing Projects in Hospitals. In A. Dwivedi (Ed.), *Reshaping Medical Practice and Care with Health Information Systems* (pp. 132–172). Hershey, PA: IGI Global. doi:10.4018/978-1-4666-9870-3.ch005

Lin, S., Chen, S., & Chuang, S. (2017). Perceived Innovation and Quick Response Codes in an Online-to-Offline E-Commerce Service Model. *International Journal of E-Adoption, 9*(2), 1–16. doi:10.4018/IJEA.2017070101

Liu, M., Wang, Y., Xu, W., & Liu, L. (2017). Automated Scoring of Chinese Engineering Students' English Essays. *International Journal of Distance Education Technologies, 15*(1), 52–68. doi:10.4018/IJDET.2017010104

Luciano, E. M., Wiedenhöft, G. C., Macadar, M. A., & Pinheiro dos Santos, F. (2016). Information Technology Governance Adoption: Understanding its Expectations Through the Lens of Organizational Citizenship. *International Journal of IT/Business Alignment and Governance, 7*(2), 22-32. doi:10.4018/IJITBAG.2016070102

Mabe, L. K., & Oladele, O. I. (2017). Application of Information Communication Technologies for Agricultural Development through Extension Services: A Review. In T. Tossy (Ed.), *Information Technology Integration for Socio-Economic Development* (pp. 52–101). Hershey, PA: IGI Global. doi:10.4018/978-1-5225-0539-6.ch003

Manogaran, G., Thota, C., & Lopez, D. (2018). Human-Computer Interaction With Big Data Analytics. In D. Lopez & M. Durai (Eds.), *HCI Challenges and Privacy Preservation in Big Data Security* (pp. 1–22). Hershey, PA: IGI Global. doi:10.4018/978-1-5225-2863-0.ch001

Margolis, J., Goode, J., & Flapan, J. (2017). A Critical Crossroads for Computer Science for All: "Identifying Talent" or "Building Talent," and What Difference Does It Make? In Y. Rankin & J. Thomas (Eds.), *Moving Students of Color from Consumers to Producers of Technology* (pp. 1–23). Hershey, PA: IGI Global. doi:10.4018/978-1-5225-2005-4.ch001

Mbale, J. (2018). Computer Centres Resource Cloud Elasticity-Scalability (CRECES): Copperbelt University Case Study. In S. Aljawarneh & M. Malhotra (Eds.), *Critical Research on Scalability and Security Issues in Virtual Cloud Environments* (pp. 48–70). Hershey, PA: IGI Global. doi:10.4018/978-1-5225-3029-9.ch003

McKee, J. (2018). The Right Information: The Key to Effective Business Planning. In *Business Architectures for Risk Assessment and Strategic Planning: Emerging Research and Opportunities* (pp. 38–52). Hershey, PA: IGI Global. doi:10.4018/978-1-5225-3392-4.ch003

Mensah, I. K., & Mi, J. (2018). Determinants of Intention to Use Local E-Government Services in Ghana: The Perspective of Local Government Workers. *International Journal of Technology Diffusion*, 9(2), 41–60. doi:10.4018/IJTD.2018040103

Mohamed, J. H. (2018). Scientograph-Based Visualization of Computer Forensics Research Literature. In J. Jeyasekar & P. Saravanan (Eds.), *Innovations in Measuring and Evaluating Scientific Information* (pp. 148–162). Hershey, PA: IGI Global. doi:10.4018/978-1-5225-3457-0.ch010

Moore, R. L., & Johnson, N. (2017). Earning a Seat at the Table: How IT Departments Can Partner in Organizational Change and Innovation. *International Journal of Knowledge-Based Organizations*, 7(2), 1–12. doi:10.4018/IJKBO.2017040101

Mtebe, J. S., & Kissaka, M. M. (2016). Enhancing the Quality of Computer Science Education with MOOCs in Sub-Saharan Africa. In J. Keengwe & G. Onchwari (Eds.), *Handbook of Research on Active Learning and the Flipped Classroom Model in the Digital Age* (pp. 366–377). Hershey, PA: IGI Global. doi:10.4018/978-1-4666-9680-8.ch019

Mukul, M. K., & Bhattaharyya, S. (2017). Brain-Machine Interface: Human-Computer Interaction. In E. Noughabi, B. Raahemi, A. Albadvi, & B. Far (Eds.), *Handbook of Research on Data Science for Effective Healthcare Practice and Administration* (pp. 417–443). Hershey, PA: IGI Global. doi:10.4018/978-1-5225-2515-8.ch018

Na, L. (2017). Library and Information Science Education and Graduate Programs in Academic Libraries. In L. Ruan, Q. Zhu, & Y. Ye (Eds.), *Academic Library Development and Administration in China* (pp. 218–229). Hershey, PA: IGI Global. doi:10.4018/978-1-5225-0550-1.ch013

Nabavi, A., Taghavi-Fard, M. T., Hanafizadeh, P., & Taghva, M. R. (2016). Information Technology Continuance Intention: A Systematic Literature Review. *International Journal of E-Business Research*, *12*(1), 58–95. doi:10.4018/IJEBR.2016010104

Nath, R., & Murthy, V. N. (2018). What Accounts for the Differences in Internet Diffusion Rates Around the World? In M. Khosrow-Pour, D.B.A. (Ed.), Encyclopedia of Information Science and Technology, Fourth Edition (pp. 8095-8104). Hershey, PA: IGI Global. doi:10.4018/978-1-5225-2255-3.ch705

Nedelko, Z., & Potocan, V. (2018). The Role of Emerging Information Technologies for Supporting Supply Chain Management. In M. Khosrow-Pour, D.B.A. (Ed.), Encyclopedia of Information Science and Technology, Fourth Edition (pp. 5559-5569). Hershey, PA: IGI Global. doi:10.4018/978-1-5225-2255-3.ch483

Ngafeeson, M. N. (2018). User Resistance to Health Information Technology. In M. Khosrow-Pour, D.B.A. (Ed.), Encyclopedia of Information Science and Technology, Fourth Edition (pp. 3816-3825). Hershey, PA: IGI Global. doi:10.4018/978-1-5225-2255-3.ch331

Nozari, H., Najafi, S. E., Jafari-Eskandari, M., & Aliahmadi, A. (2016). Providing a Model for Virtual Project Management with an Emphasis on IT Projects. In C. Graham (Ed.), *Strategic Management and Leadership for Systems Development in Virtual Spaces* (pp. 43–63). Hershey, PA: IGI Global. doi:10.4018/978-1-4666-9688-4.ch003

Nurdin, N., Stockdale, R., & Scheepers, H. (2016). Influence of Organizational Factors in the Sustainability of E-Government: A Case Study of Local E-Government in Indonesia. In I. Sodhi (Ed.), *Trends, Prospects, and Challenges in Asian E-Governance* (pp. 281–323). Hershey, PA: IGI Global. doi:10.4018/978-1-4666-9536-8.ch014

Odagiri, K. (2017). Introduction of Individual Technology to Constitute the Current Internet. In *Strategic Policy-Based Network Management in Contemporary Organizations* (pp. 20–96). Hershey, PA: IGI Global. doi:10.4018/978-1-68318-003-6.ch003

Okike, E. U. (2018). Computer Science and Prison Education. In I. Biao (Ed.), *Strategic Learning Ideologies in Prison Education Programs* (pp. 246–264). Hershey, PA: IGI Global. doi:10.4018/978-1-5225-2909-5.ch012

Olelewe, C. J., & Nwafor, I. P. (2017). Level of Computer Appreciation Skills Acquired for Sustainable Development by Secondary School Students in Nsukka LGA of Enugu State, Nigeria. In C. Ayo & V. Mbarika (Eds.), *Sustainable ICT Adoption and Integration for Socio-Economic Development* (pp. 214–233). Hershey, PA: IGI Global. doi:10.4018/978-1-5225-2565-3.ch010

Oliveira, M., Maçada, A. C., Curado, C., & Nodari, F. (2017). Infrastructure Profiles and Knowledge Sharing. *International Journal of Technology and Human Interaction*, *13*(3), 1–12. doi:10.4018/IJTHI.2017070101

Otarkhani, A., Shokouhyar, S., & Pour, S. S. (2017). Analyzing the Impact of Governance of Enterprise IT on Hospital Performance: Tehran's (Iran) Hospitals – A Case Study. *International Journal of Healthcare Information Systems and Informatics*, *12*(3), 1–20. doi:10.4018/IJHISI.2017070101

Otunla, A. O., & Amuda, C. O. (2018). Nigerian Undergraduate Students' Computer Competencies and Use of Information Technology Tools and Resources for Study Skills and Habits' Enhancement. In M. Khosrow-Pour, D.B.A. (Ed.), Encyclopedia of Information Science and Technology, Fourth Edition (pp. 2303-2313). Hershey, PA: IGI Global. doi:10.4018/978-1-5225-2255-3.ch200

Özçınar, H. (2018). A Brief Discussion on Incentives and Barriers to Computational Thinking Education. In H. Ozcinar, G. Wong, & H. Ozturk (Eds.), *Teaching Computational Thinking in Primary Education* (pp. 1–17). Hershey, PA: IGI Global. doi:10.4018/978-1-5225-3200-2.ch001

Pandey, J. M., Garg, S., Mishra, P., & Mishra, B. P. (2017). Computer Based Psychological Interventions: Subject to the Efficacy of Psychological Services. *International Journal of Computers in Clinical Practice, 2*(1), 25–33. doi:10.4018/IJCCP.2017010102

Parry, V. K., & Lind, M. L. (2016). Alignment of Business Strategy and Information Technology Considering Information Technology Governance, Project Portfolio Control, and Risk Management. *International Journal of Information Technology Project Management, 7*(4), 21–37. doi:10.4018/IJITPM.2016100102

Patro, C. (2017). Impulsion of Information Technology on Human Resource Practices. In P. Ordóñez de Pablos (Ed.), *Managerial Strategies and Solutions for Business Success in Asia* (pp. 231–254). Hershey, PA: IGI Global. doi:10.4018/978-1-5225-1886-0.ch013

Patro, C. S., & Raghunath, K. M. (2017). Information Technology Paraphernalia for Supply Chain Management Decisions. In M. Tavana (Ed.), *Enterprise Information Systems and the Digitalization of Business Functions* (pp. 294–320). Hershey, PA: IGI Global. doi:10.4018/978-1-5225-2382-6.ch014

Paul, P. K. (2016). Cloud Computing: An Agent of Promoting Interdisciplinary Sciences, Especially Information Science and I-Schools – Emerging Techno-Educational Scenario. In L. Chao (Ed.), *Handbook of Research on Cloud-Based STEM Education for Improved Learning Outcomes* (pp. 247–258). Hershey, PA: IGI Global. doi:10.4018/978-1-4666-9924-3.ch016

Paul, P. K. (2018). The Context of IST for Solid Information Retrieval and Infrastructure Building: Study of Developing Country. *International Journal of Information Retrieval Research, 8*(1), 86–100. doi:10.4018/IJIRR.2018010106

Paul, P. K., & Chatterjee, D. (2018). iSchools Promoting "Information Science and Technology" (IST) Domain Towards Community, Business, and Society With Contemporary Worldwide Trend and Emerging Potentialities in India. In M. Khosrow-Pour, D.B.A. (Ed.), Encyclopedia of Information Science and Technology, Fourth Edition (pp. 4723-4735). Hershey, PA: IGI Global. doi:10.4018/978-1-5225-2255-3.ch410

Pessoa, C. R., & Marques, M. E. (2017). Information Technology and Communication Management in Supply Chain Management. In G. Jamil, A. Soares, & C. Pessoa (Eds.), *Handbook of Research on Information Management for Effective Logistics and Supply Chains* (pp. 23–33). Hershey, PA: IGI Global. doi:10.4018/978-1-5225-0973-8.ch002

Pineda, R. G. (2016). Where the Interaction Is Not: Reflections on the Philosophy of Human-Computer Interaction. *International Journal of Art, Culture and Design Technologies*, 5(1), 1–12. doi:10.4018/IJACDT.2016010101

Pineda, R. G. (2018). Remediating Interaction: Towards a Philosophy of Human-Computer Relationship. In M. Khosrow-Pour (Ed.), *Enhancing Art, Culture, and Design With Technological Integration* (pp. 75–98). Hershey, PA: IGI Global. doi:10.4018/978-1-5225-5023-5.ch004

Poikela, P., & Vuojärvi, H. (2016). Learning ICT-Mediated Communication through Computer-Based Simulations. In M. Cruz-Cunha, I. Miranda, R. Martinho, & R. Rijo (Eds.), *Encyclopedia of E-Health and Telemedicine* (pp. 674–687). Hershey, PA: IGI Global. doi:10.4018/978-1-4666-9978-6.ch052

Qian, Y. (2017). Computer Simulation in Higher Education: Affordances, Opportunities, and Outcomes. In P. Vu, S. Fredrickson, & C. Moore (Eds.), *Handbook of Research on Innovative Pedagogies and Technologies for Online Learning in Higher Education* (pp. 236–262). Hershey, PA: IGI Global. doi:10.4018/978-1-5225-1851-8.ch011

Radant, O., Colomo-Palacios, R., & Stantchev, V. (2016). Factors for the Management of Scarce Human Resources and Highly Skilled Employees in IT-Departments: A Systematic Review. *Journal of Information Technology Research*, 9(1), 65–82. doi:10.4018/JITR.2016010105

Rahman, N. (2016). Toward Achieving Environmental Sustainability in the Computer Industry. *International Journal of Green Computing*, 7(1), 37–54. doi:10.4018/IJGC.2016010103

Rahman, N. (2017). Lessons from a Successful Data Warehousing Project Management. *International Journal of Information Technology Project Management*, 8(4), 30–45. doi:10.4018/IJITPM.2017100103

Rahman, N. (2018). Environmental Sustainability in the Computer Industry for Competitive Advantage. In M. Khosrow-Pour (Ed.), *Green Computing Strategies for Competitive Advantage and Business Sustainability* (pp. 110–130). Hershey, PA: IGI Global. doi:10.4018/978-1-5225-5017-4.ch006

Rajh, A., & Pavetic, T. (2017). Computer Generated Description as the Required Digital Competence in Archival Profession. *International Journal of Digital Literacy and Digital Competence*, 8(1), 36–49. doi:10.4018/IJDLDC.2017010103

Raman, A., & Goyal, D. P. (2017). Extending IMPLEMENT Framework for Enterprise Information Systems Implementation to Information System Innovation. In M. Tavana (Ed.), *Enterprise Information Systems and the Digitalization of Business Functions* (pp. 137–177). Hershey, PA: IGI Global. doi:10.4018/978-1-5225-2382-6.ch007

Rao, Y. S., Rauta, A. K., Saini, H., & Panda, T. C. (2017). Mathematical Model for Cyber Attack in Computer Network. *International Journal of Business Data Communications and Networking*, *13*(1), 58–65. doi:10.4018/IJBDCN.2017010105

Rapaport, W. J. (2018). Syntactic Semantics and the Proper Treatment of Computationalism. In M. Danesi (Ed.), *Empirical Research on Semiotics and Visual Rhetoric* (pp. 128–176). Hershey, PA: IGI Global. doi:10.4018/978-1-5225-5622-0.ch007

Raut, R., Priyadarshinee, P., & Jha, M. (2017). Understanding the Mediation Effect of Cloud Computing Adoption in Indian Organization: Integrating TAM-TOE- Risk Model. *International Journal of Service Science, Management, Engineering, and Technology*, *8*(3), 40–59. doi:10.4018/IJSSMET.2017070103

Regan, E. A., & Wang, J. (2016). Realizing the Value of EHR Systems Critical Success Factors. *International Journal of Healthcare Information Systems and Informatics*, *11*(3), 1–18. doi:10.4018/IJHISI.2016070101

Rezaie, S., Mirabedini, S. J., & Abtahi, A. (2018). Designing a Model for Implementation of Business Intelligence in the Banking Industry. *International Journal of Enterprise Information Systems*, *14*(1), 77–103. doi:10.4018/IJEIS.2018010105

Rezende, D. A. (2016). Digital City Projects: Information and Public Services Offered by Chicago (USA) and Curitiba (Brazil). *International Journal of Knowledge Society Research*, *7*(3), 16–30. doi:10.4018/IJKSR.2016070102

Rezende, D. A. (2018). Strategic Digital City Projects: Innovative Information and Public Services Offered by Chicago (USA) and Curitiba (Brazil). In M. Lytras, L. Daniela, & A. Visvizi (Eds.), *Enhancing Knowledge Discovery and Innovation in the Digital Era* (pp. 204–223). Hershey, PA: IGI Global. doi:10.4018/978-1-5225-4191-2.ch012

Riabov, V. V. (2016). Teaching Online Computer-Science Courses in LMS and Cloud Environment. *International Journal of Quality Assurance in Engineering and Technology Education*, *5*(4), 12–41. doi:10.4018/IJQAETE.2016100102

Related References

Ricordel, V., Wang, J., Da Silva, M. P., & Le Callet, P. (2016). 2D and 3D Visual Attention for Computer Vision: Concepts, Measurement, and Modeling. In R. Pal (Ed.), *Innovative Research in Attention Modeling and Computer Vision Applications* (pp. 1–44). Hershey, PA: IGI Global. doi:10.4018/978-1-4666-8723-3.ch001

Rodriguez, A., Rico-Diaz, A. J., Rabuñal, J. R., & Gestal, M. (2017). Fish Tracking with Computer Vision Techniques: An Application to Vertical Slot Fishways. In M. S., & V. V. (Eds.), Multi-Core Computer Vision and Image Processing for Intelligent Applications (pp. 74-104). Hershey, PA: IGI Global. doi:10.4018/978-1-5225-0889-2.ch003

Romero, J. A. (2018). Sustainable Advantages of Business Value of Information Technology. In M. Khosrow-Pour, D.B.A. (Ed.), Encyclopedia of Information Science and Technology, Fourth Edition (pp. 923-929). Hershey, PA: IGI Global. doi:10.4018/978-1-5225-2255-3.ch079

Romero, J. A. (2018). The Always-On Business Model and Competitive Advantage. In N. Bajgoric (Ed.), *Always-On Enterprise Information Systems for Modern Organizations* (pp. 23–40). Hershey, PA: IGI Global. doi:10.4018/978-1-5225-3704-5.ch002

Rosen, Y. (2018). Computer Agent Technologies in Collaborative Learning and Assessment. In M. Khosrow-Pour, D.B.A. (Ed.), Encyclopedia of Information Science and Technology, Fourth Edition (pp. 2402-2410). Hershey, PA: IGI Global. doi:10.4018/978-1-5225-2255-3.ch209

Rosen, Y., & Mosharraf, M. (2016). Computer Agent Technologies in Collaborative Assessments. In Y. Rosen, S. Ferrara, & M. Mosharraf (Eds.), *Handbook of Research on Technology Tools for Real-World Skill Development* (pp. 319–343). Hershey, PA: IGI Global. doi:10.4018/978-1-4666-9441-5.ch012

Roy, D. (2018). Success Factors of Adoption of Mobile Applications in Rural India: Effect of Service Characteristics on Conceptual Model. In M. Khosrow-Pour (Ed.), *Green Computing Strategies for Competitive Advantage and Business Sustainability* (pp. 211–238). Hershey, PA: IGI Global. doi:10.4018/978-1-5225-5017-4.ch010

Ruffin, T. R. (2016). Health Information Technology and Change. In V. Wang (Ed.), *Handbook of Research on Advancing Health Education through Technology* (pp. 259–285). Hershey, PA: IGI Global. doi:10.4018/978-1-4666-9494-1.ch012

Ruffin, T. R. (2016). Health Information Technology and Quality Management. *International Journal of Information Communication Technologies and Human Development*, 8(4), 56–72. doi:10.4018/IJICTHD.2016100105

Ruffin, T. R., & Hawkins, D. P. (2018). Trends in Health Care Information Technology and Informatics. In M. Khosrow-Pour, D.B.A. (Ed.), Encyclopedia of Information Science and Technology, Fourth Edition (pp. 3805-3815). Hershey, PA: IGI Global. doi:10.4018/978-1-5225-2255-3.ch330

Safari, M. R., & Jiang, Q. (2018). The Theory and Practice of IT Governance Maturity and Strategies Alignment: Evidence From Banking Industry. *Journal of Global Information Management, 26*(2), 127–146. doi:10.4018/JGIM.2018040106

Sahin, H. B., & Anagun, S. S. (2018). Educational Computer Games in Math Teaching: A Learning Culture. In E. Toprak & E. Kumtepe (Eds.), *Supporting Multiculturalism in Open and Distance Learning Spaces* (pp. 249–280). Hershey, PA: IGI Global. doi:10.4018/978-1-5225-3076-3.ch013

Sanna, A., & Valpreda, F. (2017). An Assessment of the Impact of a Collaborative Didactic Approach and Students' Background in Teaching Computer Animation. *International Journal of Information and Communication Technology Education, 13*(4), 1–16. doi:10.4018/IJICTE.2017100101

Savita, K., Dominic, P., & Ramayah, T. (2016). The Drivers, Practices and Outcomes of Green Supply Chain Management: Insights from ISO14001 Manufacturing Firms in Malaysia. *International Journal of Information Systems and Supply Chain Management, 9*(2), 35–60. doi:10.4018/IJISSCM.2016040103

Scott, A., Martin, A., & McAlear, F. (2017). Enhancing Participation in Computer Science among Girls of Color: An Examination of a Preparatory AP Computer Science Intervention. In Y. Rankin & J. Thomas (Eds.), *Moving Students of Color from Consumers to Producers of Technology* (pp. 62–84). Hershey, PA: IGI Global. doi:10.4018/978-1-5225-2005-4.ch004

Shahsavandi, E., Mayah, G., & Rahbari, H. (2016). Impact of E-Government on Transparency and Corruption in Iran. In I. Sodhi (Ed.), *Trends, Prospects, and Challenges in Asian E-Governance* (pp. 75–94). Hershey, PA: IGI Global. doi:10.4018/978-1-4666-9536-8.ch004

Siddoo, V., & Wongsai, N. (2017). Factors Influencing the Adoption of ISO/IEC 29110 in Thai Government Projects: A Case Study. *International Journal of Information Technologies and Systems Approach, 10*(1), 22–44. doi:10.4018/IJITSA.2017010102

Sidorkina, I., & Rybakov, A. (2016). Computer-Aided Design as Carrier of Set Development Changes System in E-Course Engineering. In V. Mkrttchian, A. Bershadsky, A. Bozhday, M. Kataev, & S. Kataev (Eds.), *Handbook of Research on Estimation and Control Techniques in E-Learning Systems* (pp. 500–515). Hershey, PA: IGI Global. doi:10.4018/978-1-4666-9489-7.ch035

Sidorkina, I., & Rybakov, A. (2016). Creating Model of E-Course: As an Object of Computer-Aided Design. In V. Mkrttchian, A. Bershadsky, A. Bozhday, M. Kataev, & S. Kataev (Eds.), *Handbook of Research on Estimation and Control Techniques in E-Learning Systems* (pp. 286–297). Hershey, PA: IGI Global. doi:10.4018/978-1-4666-9489-7.ch019

Simões, A. (2017). Using Game Frameworks to Teach Computer Programming. In R. Alexandre Peixoto de Queirós & M. Pinto (Eds.), *Gamification-Based E-Learning Strategies for Computer Programming Education* (pp. 221–236). Hershey, PA: IGI Global. doi:10.4018/978-1-5225-1034-5.ch010

Sllame, A. M. (2017). Integrating LAB Work With Classes in Computer Network Courses. In H. Alphin Jr, R. Chan, & J. Lavine (Eds.), *The Future of Accessibility in International Higher Education* (pp. 253–275). Hershey, PA: IGI Global. doi:10.4018/978-1-5225-2560-8.ch015

Smirnov, A., Ponomarev, A., Shilov, N., Kashevnik, A., & Teslya, N. (2018). Ontology-Based Human-Computer Cloud for Decision Support: Architecture and Applications in Tourism. *International Journal of Embedded and Real-Time Communication Systems*, *9*(1), 1–19. doi:10.4018/IJERTCS.2018010101

Smith-Ditizio, A. A., & Smith, A. D. (2018). Computer Fraud Challenges and Its Legal Implications. In M. Khosrow-Pour, D.B.A. (Ed.), Encyclopedia of Information Science and Technology, Fourth Edition (pp. 4837-4848). Hershey, PA: IGI Global. doi:10.4018/978-1-5225-2255-3.ch419

Sohani, S. S. (2016). Job Shadowing in Information Technology Projects: A Source of Competitive Advantage. *International Journal of Information Technology Project Management*, *7*(1), 47–57. doi:10.4018/IJITPM.2016010104

Sosnin, P. (2018). Figuratively Semantic Support of Human-Computer Interactions. In *Experience-Based Human-Computer Interactions: Emerging Research and Opportunities* (pp. 244–272). Hershey, PA: IGI Global. doi:10.4018/978-1-5225-2987-3.ch008

Spinelli, R., & Benevolo, C. (2016). From Healthcare Services to E-Health Applications: A Delivery System-Based Taxonomy. In A. Dwivedi (Ed.), *Reshaping Medical Practice and Care with Health Information Systems* (pp. 205–245). Hershey, PA: IGI Global. doi:10.4018/978-1-4666-9870-3.ch007

Srinivasan, S. (2016). Overview of Clinical Trial and Pharmacovigilance Process and Areas of Application of Computer System. In P. Chakraborty & A. Nagal (Eds.), *Software Innovations in Clinical Drug Development and Safety* (pp. 1–13). Hershey, PA: IGI Global. doi:10.4018/978-1-4666-8726-4.ch001

Srisawasdi, N. (2016). Motivating Inquiry-Based Learning Through a Combination of Physical and Virtual Computer-Based Laboratory Experiments in High School Science. In M. Urban & D. Falvo (Eds.), *Improving K-12 STEM Education Outcomes through Technological Integration* (pp. 108–134). Hershey, PA: IGI Global. doi:10.4018/978-1-4666-9616-7.ch006

Stavridi, S. V., & Hamada, D. R. (2016). Children and Youth Librarians: Competencies Required in Technology-Based Environment. In J. Yap, M. Perez, M. Ayson, & G. Entico (Eds.), *Special Library Administration, Standardization and Technological Integration* (pp. 25–50). Hershey, PA: IGI Global. doi:10.4018/978-1-4666-9542-9.ch002

Sung, W., Ahn, J., Kai, S. M., Choi, A., & Black, J. B. (2016). Incorporating Touch-Based Tablets into Classroom Activities: Fostering Children's Computational Thinking through iPad Integrated Instruction. In D. Mentor (Ed.), *Handbook of Research on Mobile Learning in Contemporary Classrooms* (pp. 378–406). Hershey, PA: IGI Global. doi:10.4018/978-1-5225-0251-7.ch019

Syväjärvi, A., Leinonen, J., Kivivirta, V., & Kesti, M. (2017). The Latitude of Information Management in Local Government: Views of Local Government Managers. *International Journal of Electronic Government Research*, *13*(1), 69–85. doi:10.4018/IJEGR.2017010105

Tanque, M., & Foxwell, H. J. (2018). Big Data and Cloud Computing: A Review of Supply Chain Capabilities and Challenges. In A. Prasad (Ed.), *Exploring the Convergence of Big Data and the Internet of Things* (pp. 1–28). Hershey, PA: IGI Global. doi:10.4018/978-1-5225-2947-7.ch001

Teixeira, A., Gomes, A., & Orvalho, J. G. (2017). Auditory Feedback in a Computer Game for Blind People. In T. Issa, P. Kommers, T. Issa, P. Isaías, & T. Issa (Eds.), *Smart Technology Applications in Business Environments* (pp. 134–158). Hershey, PA: IGI Global. doi:10.4018/978-1-5225-2492-2.ch007

Thompson, N., McGill, T., & Murray, D. (2018). Affect-Sensitive Computer Systems. In M. Khosrow-Pour, D.B.A. (Ed.), Encyclopedia of Information Science and Technology, Fourth Edition (pp. 4124-4135). Hershey, PA: IGI Global. doi:10.4018/978-1-5225-2255-3.ch357

Trad, A., & Kalpić, D. (2016). The E-Business Transformation Framework for E-Commerce Control and Monitoring Pattern. In I. Lee (Ed.), *Encyclopedia of E-Commerce Development, Implementation, and Management* (pp. 754–777). Hershey, PA: IGI Global. doi:10.4018/978-1-4666-9787-4.ch053

Triberti, S., Brivio, E., & Galimberti, C. (2018). On Social Presence: Theories, Methodologies, and Guidelines for the Innovative Contexts of Computer-Mediated Learning. In M. Marmon (Ed.), *Enhancing Social Presence in Online Learning Environments* (pp. 20–41). Hershey, PA: IGI Global. doi:10.4018/978-1-5225-3229-3.ch002

Tripathy, B. K. T. R., S., & Mohanty, R. K. (2018). Memetic Algorithms and Their Applications in Computer Science. In S. Dash, B. Tripathy, & A. Rahman (Eds.), Handbook of Research on Modeling, Analysis, and Application of Nature-Inspired Metaheuristic Algorithms (pp. 73-93). Hershey, PA: IGI Global. doi:10.4018/978-1-5225-2857-9.ch004

Turulja, L., & Bajgoric, N. (2017). Human Resource Management IT and Global Economy Perspective: Global Human Resource Information Systems. In M. Khosrow-Pour (Ed.), *Handbook of Research on Technology Adoption, Social Policy, and Global Integration* (pp. 377–394). Hershey, PA: IGI Global. doi:10.4018/978-1-5225-2668-1.ch018

Unwin, D. W., Sanzogni, L., & Sandhu, K. (2017). Developing and Measuring the Business Case for Health Information Technology. In K. Moahi, K. Bwalya, & P. Sebina (Eds.), *Health Information Systems and the Advancement of Medical Practice in Developing Countries* (pp. 262–290). Hershey, PA: IGI Global. doi:10.4018/978-1-5225-2262-1.ch015

Vadhanam, B. R. S., M., Sugumaran, V., V., V., & Ramalingam, V. V. (2017). Computer Vision Based Classification on Commercial Videos. In M. S., & V. V. (Eds.), Multi-Core Computer Vision and Image Processing for Intelligent Applications (pp. 105-135). Hershey, PA: IGI Global. doi:10.4018/978-1-5225-0889-2.ch004

Valverde, R., Torres, B., & Motaghi, H. (2018). A Quantum NeuroIS Data Analytics Architecture for the Usability Evaluation of Learning Management Systems. In S. Bhattacharyya (Ed.), *Quantum-Inspired Intelligent Systems for Multimedia Data Analysis* (pp. 277–299). Hershey, PA: IGI Global. doi:10.4018/978-1-5225-5219-2.ch009

Vassilis, E. (2018). Learning and Teaching Methodology: "1:1 Educational Computing. In K. Koutsopoulos, K. Doukas, & Y. Kotsanis (Eds.), *Handbook of Research on Educational Design and Cloud Computing in Modern Classroom Settings* (pp. 122–155). Hershey, PA: IGI Global. doi:10.4018/978-1-5225-3053-4.ch007

Wadhwani, A. K., Wadhwani, S., & Singh, T. (2016). Computer Aided Diagnosis System for Breast Cancer Detection. In Y. Morsi, A. Shukla, & C. Rathore (Eds.), *Optimizing Assistive Technologies for Aging Populations* (pp. 378–395). Hershey, PA: IGI Global. doi:10.4018/978-1-4666-9530-6.ch015

Wang, L., Wu, Y., & Hu, C. (2016). English Teachers' Practice and Perspectives on Using Educational Computer Games in EIL Context. *International Journal of Technology and Human Interaction, 12*(3), 33–46. doi:10.4018/IJTHI.2016070103

Watfa, M. K., Majeed, H., & Salahuddin, T. (2016). Computer Based E-Healthcare Clinical Systems: A Comprehensive Survey. *International Journal of Privacy and Health Information Management, 4*(1), 50–69. doi:10.4018/IJPHIM.2016010104

Weeger, A., & Haase, U. (2016). Taking up Three Challenges to Business-IT Alignment Research by the Use of Activity Theory. *International Journal of IT/Business Alignment and Governance, 7*(2), 1-21. doi:10.4018/IJITBAG.2016070101

Wexler, B. E. (2017). Computer-Presented and Physical Brain-Training Exercises for School Children: Improving Executive Functions and Learning. In B. Dubbels (Ed.), *Transforming Gaming and Computer Simulation Technologies across Industries* (pp. 206–224). Hershey, PA: IGI Global. doi:10.4018/978-1-5225-1817-4.ch012

Williams, D. M., Gani, M. O., Addo, I. D., Majumder, A. J., Tamma, C. P., Wang, M., ... Chu, C. (2016). Challenges in Developing Applications for Aging Populations. In Y. Morsi, A. Shukla, & C. Rathore (Eds.), *Optimizing Assistive Technologies for Aging Populations* (pp. 1–21). Hershey, PA: IGI Global. doi:10.4018/978-1-4666-9530-6.ch001

Wimble, M., Singh, H., & Phillips, B. (2018). Understanding Cross-Level Interactions of Firm-Level Information Technology and Industry Environment: A Multilevel Model of Business Value. *Information Resources Management Journal, 31*(1), 1–20. doi:10.4018/IRMJ.2018010101

Wimmer, H., Powell, L., Kilgus, L., & Force, C. (2017). Improving Course Assessment via Web-based Homework. *International Journal of Online Pedagogy and Course Design, 7*(2), 1–19. doi:10.4018/IJOPCD.2017040101

Wong, Y. L., & Siu, K. W. (2018). Assessing Computer-Aided Design Skills. In M. Khosrow-Pour, D.B.A. (Ed.), Encyclopedia of Information Science and Technology, Fourth Edition (pp. 7382-7391). Hershey, PA: IGI Global. doi:10.4018/978-1-5225-2255-3.ch642

Wongsurawat, W., & Shrestha, V. (2018). Information Technology, Globalization, and Local Conditions: Implications for Entrepreneurs in Southeast Asia. In P. Ordóñez de Pablos (Ed.), *Management Strategies and Technology Fluidity in the Asian Business Sector* (pp. 163–176). Hershey, PA: IGI Global. doi:10.4018/978-1-5225-4056-4.ch010

Yang, Y., Zhu, X., Jin, C., & Li, J.J. (2018). Reforming Classroom Education Through a QQ Group: A Pilot Experiment at a Primary School in Shanghai. In H. Spires (Ed.), *Digital Transformation and Innovation in Chinese Education* (pp. 211–231). Hershey, PA: IGI Global. doi:10.4018/978-1-5225-2924-8.ch012

Yilmaz, R., Sezgin, A., Kurnaz, S., & Arslan, Y. Z. (2018). Object-Oriented Programming in Computer Science. In M. Khosrow-Pour, D.B.A. (Ed.), Encyclopedia of Information Science and Technology, Fourth Edition (pp. 7470-7480). Hershey, PA: IGI Global. doi:10.4018/978-1-5225-2255-3.ch650

Yu, L. (2018). From Teaching Software Engineering Locally and Globally to Devising an Internationalized Computer Science Curriculum. In S. Dikli, B. Etheridge, & R. Rawls (Eds.), *Curriculum Internationalization and the Future of Education* (pp. 293–320). Hershey, PA: IGI Global. doi:10.4018/978-1-5225-2791-6.ch016

Yuhua, F. (2018). Computer Information Library Clusters. In M. Khosrow-Pour, D.B.A. (Ed.), Encyclopedia of Information Science and Technology, Fourth Edition (pp. 4399-4403). Hershey, PA: IGI Global. doi:10.4018/978-1-5225-2255-3.ch382

Zare, M. A., Taghavi Fard, M. T., & Hanafizadeh, P. (2016). The Assessment of Outsourcing IT Services using DEA Technique: A Study of Application Outsourcing in Research Centers. *International Journal of Operations Research and Information Systems*, 7(1), 45–57. doi:10.4018/IJORIS.2016010104

Zhao, J., Wang, Q., Guo, J., Gao, L., & Yang, F. (2016). An Overview on Passive Image Forensics Technology for Automatic Computer Forgery. *International Journal of Digital Crime and Forensics*, 8(4), 14–25. doi:10.4018/IJDCF.2016100102

Zimeras, S. (2016). Computer Virus Models and Analysis in M-Health IT Systems: Computer Virus Models. In A. Moumtzoglou (Ed.), *M-Health Innovations for Patient-Centered Care* (pp. 284–297). Hershey, PA: IGI Global. doi:10.4018/978-1-4666-9861-1.ch014

Zlatanovska, K. (2016). Hacking and Hacktivism as an Information Communication System Threat. In M. Hadji-Janev & M. Bogdanoski (Eds.), *Handbook of Research on Civil Society and National Security in the Era of Cyber Warfare* (pp. 68–101). Hershey, PA: IGI Global. doi:10.4018/978-1-4666-8793-6.ch004

About the Contributors

N. Raghavendra Rao has a doctorate in the area of Finance. He has a rare distinction of having experience in the combined areas of Information Technology and Business applications. His rich experience in the Industry is matched with a parallel academic experience in Management & IT in Business Schools. He has over two decades of experience in the development of application software related to manufacturing, healthcare and hospitality sectors, financial institutions and business enterprises. He contributes chapters for research reference books. He presents papers related to Information Technology and Management at National and International conferences. He contributes articles on Information Technology in mainstream newspapers and journals. His area of research interest is Mobile Computing, Virtual Technology, and Commerce in Space, Ubiquitous Commerce, Cloud Computing, e-governance, Knowledge Management, and Social Media for Business Applications. He is the author of the book titled "Effective Open Innovation in Modern Business-Emerging Research and Opportunities" (2018) published by IGI Global USA. This book comes under the category of "Research Insights". He is the editor for the three research reference books published by IGI Global USA. The books are 1-Social Media listening and Monitoring for Business Applications (2016), 2- Enterprise Strategies in the Era of Cloud Computing (2015), (3) Virtual Technologies for Business and Industrial Applications: Innovative and Synergistic Approaches (2010).

***

José Delgado is an Associate Professor at the Computer Science and Engineering Department of the Instituto Superior Técnico (University of Lisbon), in Lisbon, Portugal, where he earned the Ph.D. degree in 1988. He lectures courses in the areas of Computer Architecture, Information Technology and Service Engineering. He has performed several management roles in his faculty, namely Director of the Taguspark campus, near Lisbon, and Coordinator of the B.Sc. and M.Sc. in

Computer Science and Engineering at that campus. He has been the coordinator of and researcher in several international research projects. As an author, his publications include one book, 20 book chapters and more than 50 papers in international refereed conferences and journals.

K. Hariharanath, MBA, PhD, has 15+ years of experience in IT product design, development and implementation. He has experience in IT products ranging from enterprise suite of products to e-commerce products. His doctoral work is in Business Process Management. His doctoral thesis is on 'Enterprise Application Integration' as a tool for integrating IT infrastructure in companies. This will help companies realize their business objectives with the effective deployment of Information Technology. All along his career, he has been at the center of teaching either on a visiting professor basis or on full time basis at ENPC Paris (International Business School set up in collaboration with IIS Infotech Limited at Cochin, Kerala), ICFAI Business School, Hyderabad and SSN School of Management, Chennai. His teaching interests are strategic management and IT Business Strategy. His consulting area focus is working with e-commerce start-ups in building sustainable business models.

Sudarsan Jayasingh is working as an Assistant Professor in SSN School of Management, Chennai. He has nearly 20 years of teaching and research experience. Prior to joining SSN School of Management, he worked as a faculty member in Swinburne University of Technology (Malaysia Campus), KDU College (Malaysia) and Vels University. Dr. Sudarsan's teaching interests currently include brand management, consumer behaviour and marketing research. His research interests are in the area of consumer behaviour, digital marketing and social media marketing.

Venkatesh R. is a Professor of Marketing in VIT Business School Chennai. He has over 30 years of work experience (13 in Industry and 18 in Academics). Having completed his PhD in IIT Madras, he has guided five scholars in their research work in VIT Chennai. Three more scholars are doing their research now.

Sudarsanam S. K. is a Professor in VIT Business School Chennai with more than 22 years of teaching and industry experience. His research areas include Fuzzy systems, project management, predictive analytics, knowledge management, and smart farming.

R. Todd Stephens is a Senior Technical Architect for Strategy and Architecture (Evolving Technologies) for the AT&T Corporation. Todd has worked in the telecommunications business since 1999 (AT&T, Bellsouth, and Cingular) and have been responsible for setting the corporate strategy and architecture for the development and implementation of Enterprise Knowledge Stores, Enterprise Metadata, Collaborative Applications, Wireless Technologies, Collaboration Technology and Social Software. Todd holds degrees in Mathematics and Computer Science from Columbus State University, an MBA degree from Georgia State University, and a Ph.D. in Information Systems from Nova Southeastern University. Additionally, Todd has been awarded 21 U.S. patents in the field of Technology and authored/co-authored books on Web-enabled applications, open source, social media, collaboration, and career development.

Abbas Strømmen-Bakhtiar is the associate professor in strategy and digital economy at the Graduate Business School in Nord University. He has degrees in Aerospace Engineering Technology, ICT, Manufacturing and Business Management. He has published articles in various journals including IEEE, Issues in Informing Science and Information Technology, Journal of Information Technology Education, Society and Economy, International Journal of Innovation in Sharing Economy, and others. His research interests include digital economy, Sharing Economy, Cloud Computing, Technology Management and Strategic Management.

Umasankar V. has 30 years of Industrial Experience in reputed industries like L & T, Rane and TVS Group Companies and worked as General Manager, Operations. He has received PhD in the field of Metal Matrix Composites and as Head, Materials and Manufacturing Group in VIT, Chennai published several papers in International Journals and also got funding from Government agencies for carrying out research useful for Space research, Science and Technology as well Nuclear research. He has more than 10 years of teaching experience in the field of Manufacturing, Quality and Integrated Manufacturing for undergraduate and post graduate students.

Index

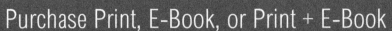
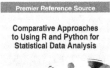
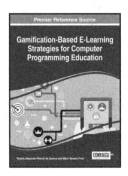

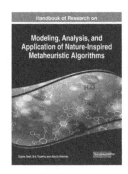

Ensure Quality Research is Introduced to the Academic Community

Become an IGI Global Reviewer for Authored Book Projects

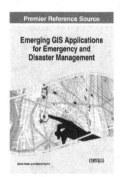
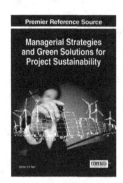

The overall success of an authored book project is dependent on quality and timely reviews.

In this competitive age of scholarly publishing, constructive and timely feedback significantly expedites the turnaround time of manuscripts from submission to acceptance, allowing the publication and discovery of forward-thinking research at a much more expeditious rate. Several IGI Global authored book projects are currently seeking highly qualified experts in the field to fill vacancies on their respective editorial review boards:

Applications may be sent to:
development@igi-global.com

Applicants must have a doctorate (or an equivalent degree) as well as publishing and reviewing experience. Reviewers are asked to write reviews in a timely, collegial, and constructive manner. All reviewers will begin their role on an ad-hoc basis for a period of one year, and upon successful completion of this term can be considered for full editorial review board status, with the potential for a subsequent promotion to Associate Editor.

If you have a colleague that may be interested in this opportunity, we encourage you to share this information with them.

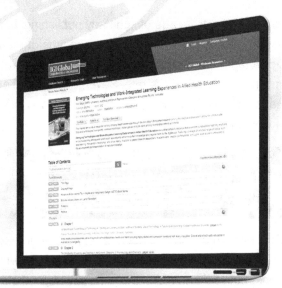

Printed in the United States
By Bookmasters